Transpacific Evangelicalism
in the Twentieth Century

Transpacific Evangelicalism
in the Twentieth Century

Revival and Evangelism
in America and Korea

William T. Purinton

OMS · ONE MISSION SOCIETY

By God's grace, One Mission Society unites, inspires, and equips Christians to make disciples of Jesus Christ, multiplying dynamic communities of believers around the world.

One Mission Society is an evangelical, interdenominational faith mission that multiplies disciples, churches, missionary movements, and leaders around the world.

One Mission Society
PO Box A
Greenwood, IN 46142
317.888.3333
www.onemissionsociety.org
http://oms.media
Cover design by Jonathan Lewis

Transpacific Evangelicalism in the Twentieth Century – William T. Purinton.
© 2020 by William T. Purinton
Published by One Mission Society

All rights reserved. No part of this publication may be reproduced, stored in a retrieval system, or transmitted in any form or by any means—for example, electronic, photocopy, and recording—without the prior written permission of the publisher. The only exception is brief quotations in printed reviews.

Scripture quotations labeled NIV are from the Holy Bible, New International Version®. NIV®. Copyright© 1973, 1978, 2011 by Biblica, Inc.™ Used by permission of Zondervan. All rights reserved worldwide. www.zondervan.com

Scripture quotations labeled KJV are from the King James Version of the Bible.

Printed in the United States of America

10 9 8 7 6 5 4 3 2 1

Paperback ISBN: 978-1-62245-682-6

eBook ISBN: 978-1-62245-683-3

Library of Congress Cataloging-in-Publication Data
Purinton, William T.
    p. cm.
    Includes bibliographical references and index.
    1. Evangelicalism—United States—History. 2 Korea—Church History. I. Title

Contents

Preface ix

Acknowledgements xiii

Ch. 1: Introduction 1

Ch. 2: Weighing Words 19

Ch. 3: Tracking Time 43

Ch. 4: Endings and Beginnings: The Late Nineteenth Century 55

Ch. 5: Global Revivals in the New Century 91

Ch. 6: Independence and the Three Selves 117

Ch. 7: Battle Lines and Cold Wars 167

Ch. 8: Charisma and Evangelism 205

Ch. 9: Worshiping God and Making Megachurches 223

Ch. 10: Conclusion: Being Evangelical, Doing Gospel, and Going Global 241

About the Author 251

Select Bibliography 253

*To
my wife,
Kumok Lee Purinton,
grateful for the shared journey
of faith, hope, and love*

In this textbook, attention will be paid to the various crises that shaped and defined evangelicalism: biblical authority, the fundamentals, missionary movements, Pentecostalism, the challenge of the ecumenical movement, the formation of the National Association of Evangelicals, the World Evangelical Alliance, Calvinist and Arminian identities, the innovative ministry methods of parachurch organizations, and the rise of megachurches.

Preface

Evangelicalism, like any other religious movement, is hard to handle, simply because it will not stand still. There is a spiritual dynamic inherent in all theological movements through the church's two millennia of history. At times, the movements have become traditions, at other times they wither and die, but for the most part they grow and spread like evangelicalism's history through the twentieth century. This textbook is prepared to introduce a movement that, again, might not stop completely for our careful study, but we can take a series of pictures that will together tell the stories. First, let me tell my story.

I was born and grew up in a city that was next to a state line, so there were two cities with the same name: Kansas City. I have lived eighteen years of my adult life on a peninsula that is divided by an international boundary that has been guarded by two opposing military forces, although the line is called ironically the "demilitarized zone." Because borders can divide one into two, it is common that people would be confused over which side is which. They have the same name, but are separate geographically or politically, or even in this study, culturally. So people would ask me, "Which one?" when I told them I was from Kansas City. My answer was always, "Both." Although borders seem to be at times natural geographical formations, more often than not they are merely lines drawn on maps or in our minds to sort out places and people, putting them in the right position.

In this book, I will begin to talk about the borders that define *evangelical*, along with *revival* and *evangelism*. We might see these words as easily defined, but when you look carefully at the historical record and consider the shifting theological and missiological understandings, we will rather find it a complicated task just to say who we are and what we do.

This becomes even more difficult when we look at both sides of the Pacific and consider the changes involved in nationality and culture. While we will spend some time at the start to define and begin to understand these terms, the majority of this book will be committed to seeing how these words are contextualized through the long twentieth century, "fleshed out," you could say, decade by decade from the 1880s to the 1990s.[1]

While borders do divide and separate, and at times those lines are drawn by God himself as a means of showing what belongs to him alone, there is also a call to cross the lines that we ourselves have constructed as divisive, contrary to God's call to unite. In the end, my hope is that we will turn toward the ongoing task of challenging all humanly constructed boundaries with the eternal truth of Holy Scripture and crossing them for the sake of the gospel. You can read from the narrative of Holy Scripture that the gospel does indeed reverse the curse of division and separation. Being cast out of the garden as divine judgment for eating the fruit of the forbidden tree in Genesis 3, we read later an announcement that the curse has ceased, and

---

[1] While the twentieth century officially began on January 1, 1901, we will follow an academic view that sees a century at times longer than one hundred years and, at times, shorter than the standard chronology. For a longer century, see Edward Ross Dickinson, *The World in the Long Twentieth Century: An Interpretive History* (Oakland: University of California Press, 2018). For our long twentieth century, we will begin in the year 1880.

the tree of life stands, "bearing twelve crops of fruit, yielding its fruit every month. And the leaves of the tree are for the healing of the nations" (Revelation 22:2 NIV).

We have, however, in theological and historical studies, become all too comfortable with boundaries/borders. It is convenient to attach a label to someone, whether it is cultural or religious. When we can label someone, we can position him or her to our right or left, or above us or below us. But in the middle of all the labeling and positioning, we open the New Testament and read these startling words: "For ye are all the children of God by faith in Christ Jesus. For as many of you as have been baptized into Christ have put on Christ. There is neither Jew nor Greek, there is neither bond nor free, there is neither male nor female: for ye are all one in Christ Jesus" (Galatians 3:26-28 KJV). There is a new label and position that cancels all the lesser ones; it is "in Christ." In this book, I want to introduce some of those borders that designate areas of separate historical and theological identities, but which in the case of missions and revivals are more easily crossed; not that our identity is marred or confused but that it becomes more authentically and broadly evangelical. It is only within evangelicalism, according to my argument, that one is able to position a variety of theological confessions, thus making the evangelical "brand," you might say, more ecumenical than Wesleyan or Holiness, other names that have been applied to One Mission Society within its more than a century of global ministry and through the nations that it has touched with the healing message of God's grace and holiness.

Acknowledgements

I owe a debt I can never repay to numerous individuals who both guided and assisted me through the writing of this textbook. First, I must mention the generous research year funded by Seoul Theological University's president and board of trustees. This allowed me release from teaching and administrative responsibilities during the 2016 academic year, along with the necessary funding to make my research journey to Wheaton, Illinois, and the Billy Graham Center Archives and Wheaton's Special Collections, treasures in the truest sense of the word. Thanks to Bob Shuster, Keith Call, and Gregory Morrison for their assistance during my time at Wheaton. Behind the scenes were my mentors at Trinity Evangelical Divinity School who not only taught but also modeled evangelical scholarship; for Dr. Douglas Sweeney and Dr. John Woodbridge, I am truly grateful. Looking far back to the very beginning in 2005 were two academic conferences that helped me to see the possibility of both transpacific and global evangelicalism. Thanks to Dr. Park Myung Soo for his invitation to read a paper at the international meeting of the Wesleyan Theological Society in 2005 at Seoul Theological University, and for Dr. Edith Blumhofer's invitation to the Changing Face of American Evangelicalism conference, sponsored graciously by the Institute for the Study of American Evangelicals (Wheaton, Illinois), and funded generously by the Henry Luce Foundation.

During the past six years, the Wesleyan-Holiness Summer Study Program (WHSSP) was parented by the Institute for the Study of Modern Christianity, Seoul Theological University, Korea Evangelical Holiness Church, and One Mission Society. For those committed to theological education and spiritual formation within the Wesleyan-Holiness family, I would like to mention Dr. William Vermillion, Dr. Myung Soo Park, Dr. Changhoon Park, and Dr. Susan Truitt. As field director in Korea, Dr. Truitt went the extra distance and supported the publication of this textbook. For our WHSSP team, I want to say thank-you again and again.

While this book has a publication date of 2020, the work began long ago, even before I arrived in Korea in 2002. More recent presentations at academic societies/conferences and the writing of articles related to Korean and US evangelicalism have been utilized in various forms in the writing of this textbook. In addition, my lecture materials from the six times I have taught evangelicalism have proven helpful in putting all the pieces together in the research and writing of this book. I am grateful for all my students who have heard this material before and have asked more questions than I was always able to answer.

Special thanks to Susan Loobie for the editing that made the manuscript into a book—not an easy task, but one done with grace and wisdom. For the folks in Greenwood who put their hearts and hands to work on making this into a textbook, I express a sense of sincere gratitude.

As with any book publication project, the author takes full responsibility for all the shortcomings and omissions that happened along the way. Truly, all the assistance from the many others mentioned above has made this work more than it could ever have been envisioned from this one writer.

Finally, I must express my thanks to my wife and partner in life, love, and ministry: Kumok Lee. She kept me going with words of grace and whispers of peace when I was disappointed and felt defeated. I offer my thanks and dedicate this book to my wife, my dearest friend.

William T. Purinton
Seoul, South Korea
Feast day of St. Bede the Venerable (25 May 2019)

1

Introduction

Evangelical is one of those words you can see in many places and in a variety of expressions. You do not have to look far to see the names of churches/denominations with "evangelical" somewhere in their official title. All the members of One Mission Society will recognize their sisters and brothers from both the Evangelical Church of India, the Faith Evangelical Church of the Philippines, and the Korea Evangelical Holiness Church. Looking a little farther, you can see the St. Thomas Evangelical Church of India, the Evangelical Church of North America, the Evangelical Free Church of America, the Evangelical Lutheran Church in America, and the Evangelical Presbyterian Church, to name only a handful.

When you further consider all the books written on the subject of evangelicalism, you realize this popular word has been discussed at length for decades, but we desire to continue the conversation with some focus and hopefully a little clarity. This book does not pretend to be the final word; I am not foolish enough to assume that a single textbook, and a shorter one at that, can cover everything on a subject, whether even concisely, much less comprehensively. That is why we have libraries for the journey and joy of learning. This textbook is designed for the Wesleyan-Holiness Summer Study Program that began in 2013. It is a program of study tailored for both One Mission Society and the Korea Evangelical Holiness Church and all our global partners. Because of that special need, this textbook has two special focuses: transpacific (Korea and the US) and evangelicalism (revival and evangelism).

During the past century, the title "fundamentalist" became one that was so negatively caricatured that no one wanted to be called by that name. A shift was made, especially after the end of World War II, to instead adopt the name "evangelical," although it was first termed "neo-fundamentalist" or even "neo-evangelical."[2] Perhaps the simplest and shortest definition of *evangelical* was expressed with the phrase "anyone who likes Billy Graham," which might have been accurate during the 1950s and 1960s, but does not convey the complexity of a simple word's meaning in the twenty-first century.[3] But we will see soon enough that it is not that easy. In this section, we will spend a lot of time asking this question: What is evangelicalism?

The name "evangelical" seemed to be at the peak of its popularity as a term and group identity when *Newsweek* magazine proclaimed 1976 to be the Year of the Evangelical. In the same way that "fundamentalism" was a name people disowned eighty years ago, by the second decade of the twenty-first century, people now are turning away from the name "evangelical," feeling that it is merely one more word for being overly conservative

---

2   Whether the word *evangelical* begins with an uppercase "E" or a lowercase "e" might appear to be a mere grammatical issue or one of style/usage. There is, however, some "shifting sand" between a proper noun and a collective noun, and it is in the very nature of my quest that I prefer to use the lowercase "evangelical/ism." Note that I am attempting to understand a term that has a distinctive history and usage as a theological word, expressive of definite religious communities, however diverse they may be. Although my preference and standard usage will be "evangelical," I will not alter any other author's usage when it is part of a quote.

3   George M. Marsden, *Understanding Fundamentalism and Evangelicalism* (Grand Rapids: Wm. B. Eerdmans, 1991), 6.

and narrow-minded. We have seen books published recently to clarify that people can be evangelical and not conservative in their politics or social views.[4]

One of the more difficult seasons of attempting to define evangelicalism was during the 1980s when the debate arose between George Marsden and Donald Dayton. It appeared that evangelicalism had two antithetical sides: Presbyterian and Pentecostal, and one of the two was given majority status or priority in both describing the historiography of the movement and in identifying the ancestors.[5] Although our text will focus more on the Wesleyan-Holiness (Dayton's Pentecostal) side, it will not exclude or lessen the importance of others in the evangelical community/family. We will visit the Dayton/Marsden debate at length later in this chapter.

Perhaps the initial steps in understanding evangelical identity are through a few dimensions. When we consider evangelical(ism), we need to know how long it is (length = history), how wide it is (spread = evangelism), and how deep it is (depth = spirituality and theology). First, let us briefly consider together its length (history). We will do this extensively in chapter 3: Tracking Time.

When did evangelicalism or the evangelical movement actually begin? Was it in the nineteenth century? In the eighteenth century? Or, can we look back at least five hundred years and see its origin in the Protestant Reformation of the sixteenth century? Or, finally, does evangelicalism extend all the way back to the early church and find its genesis in the New Testament writings? We will look at these options one at a time, from

---

4   Two examples are Roger E. Olson, *How to Be Evangelical Without Being Conservative* (Grand Rapids: Zondervan, 2008) and Steve Wilkens and Don Thorsen, *Everything You Know about Evangelicals Is Wrong (Well, Almost Everything): An Insider's Look at Myths and Realities* (Grand Rapids: Baker, 2010).

5   Douglas A. Sweeney, "The Essential Evangelicalism Dialectic: The Historiography of the Early Neo-Evangelical Movement and the Observer-Participant Dilemma," *Church History*, Vol. 60 (March 1991): 70–84.

shortest history to longest. First, we see the nineteenth-century origins in the writing of Douglas W. Frank. He focused on the historical period in North America from 1850 until 1920.

Frank listed three focuses as characteristics of evangelicalism: (1) Dispensational premillennialism, (2) Victorious Life theology, and (3) Evangelistic Revivalism (focused on Billy Sunday).[6]

Now, to further explore evangelicalism's length, let us go back one hundred years and find the most common source of history for evangelicalism. From originally noting the neglect of Britain in the historiography of evangelicalism, David W. Bebbington goes further than merely describing it; he has written (rewritten) the book that has, more than others, carefully constructed a quadrilateral, with four characteristics that trace the contours of the movement. They are conversionism (the belief that lives need to be changed), activism (the expression of the gospel in effort), biblicism (a particular regard for the Bible), and crucicentrism (a stress on the sacrifice of Christ on the cross).

Note Bebbington's dates are from the 1730s to the 1980s. This means that evangelicalism, according to Bebbington, did not exist before the evangelical awakening (Britain) or the Great Awakening (North America). Bebbington's dates of inclusion are reflected in the recent survey of evangelicalism published by InterVarsity Press. The series is named "A History of Evangelicalism: People, Movements and Ideas in the English-Speaking World," with the general editors David W. Bebbington and Mark A. Noll.

The now-complete five volumes are identified as: Vol. 1—Mark A. Noll, *The Rise of Evangelicalism: The Age of Edwards, Whitefield and the Wesleys* (2003); Vol. 2—John Wolffe, *The Expansion of Evangelicalism: The Age of More, Wilberforce, Chalmers and*

---

[6] Douglas W. Frank, *Less than Conquerors: How Evangelicals Entered the Twentieth Century* (Grand Rapids: Wm. B. Eerdmans, 1986).

Finney (2006); Vol. 3—David W. Bebbington, *The Dominance of Evangelicalism: The Age of Spurgeon and Moody* (2005); Vol. 4—Geoffrey R. Treloar, *The Disruption of Evangelicalism: The Age of Torrey, Mott, McPherson and Hammond* (2017); and Vol. 5—Brian Stanley, *The Global Diffusion of Evangelicalism: The Age of Billy Graham and John Stott* (2013). First, notice the series limitation to the English-speaking world. Our study will include Korea, and to a lesser extent China, India, and Japan. Second, note the start date for evangelicalism is in the 1730s.

As a response to Bebbington's dating the evangelical movement from the 1730s, a group of scholars gathered together as a conference, read papers, and published them as the essays in a volume titled *The Advent of Evangelicalism*.[7] This view sees evangelicalism as existing prior to the Great Awakening in eighteenth-century America, and even reaching back to the sixteenth-century Protestant reformers (Luther, Calvin, Knox) and the Puritans.

But there are other views, both British and North American, that see evangelicalism as a heritage or tradition reaching back beyond the sixteenth century all the way to the first century. Edmund Hamer Broadbent (1861–1945) wrote *The Pilgrim Church* in 1931.[8] As a member of the Plymouth Brethren, he saw a continual history of New Testament churches from the first century to the twentieth. This is similar to the Landmark view of church history, which we will view briefly below. Rather than seeing the Roman Catholic Church as part of Christ's body, for both views there were always underground or hidden churches through the centuries. Some of the groups Broadbent lists in his book include Paulicians, Bogomils, Persians/Nestorians,

---

7   Haykin, Michael A. G., and Kenneth J. Stewart, eds. *The Advent of Evangelicalism: Exploring Historical Continuities* (Nashville: B&H Academic, 2008).
8   E. H. Broadbent, *The Pilgrim Church: Being Some Account of the Continuance through Succeeding Centuries of Churches Practising the Principles Taught and Exemplified in the New Testament* (Reprinted, London: Pickering & Inglis, 1978).

Waldensians, Albigensians, Lollards, and Hussites (until the sixteenth-century Reformation). The Reformation includes Luther, the Anabaptists, Farel and Calvin, as well as William Tyndale. The post-Reformation period includes George Fox, Labadie, the Pietists, Zinzendorf, the Wesleys, William Carey, James Haldane, Robert Haldane, Thomas Campbell, Alexander Campbell, Barton Warren Stone, Walter Scott, Nazarenes (Russia), A. N. Groves, J. N. Darby, George Müller, Robert Chapman, and Charles H. Spurgeon (noting his separation from the Evangelical Alliance and the Baptist Union).

A different view of church history arose in the nineteenth century among Baptists in the US. It was called the Landmark movement. In the view of the Landmarkers, there are no Christians but Baptists, and the Baptists began with John the Baptist. This historiography included a "scarlet thread" of Baptists throughout the centuries of the church, similar to Broadbent's history.

The Trail of Blood (1931) is a booklet by James Milton Carroll. It was based on the lectures he gave on Baptist history. The booklet's full title is *The Trail of Blood: Following the Christians Down through the Centuries or The History of Baptist Churches from the Time of Christ, Their Founder, to the Present Day*. Landmarkism actually was started by James Robinson Graves in the mid-nineteenth century and persists in some Baptist denominations in North America, called "Landmark Baptists" by outsiders. It also continues under the surface in the religious thought and practice of some more conservative Baptists, including some in the Southern Baptist Convention (SBC). It becomes noticeable when a Baptist church requests or, you could say, requires rebaptism for church membership or ministry.

As a quick summary, we can say there are four "schools" in tracking time for evangelicalism. We will consider them one at a time with the longest period first, leading up to our own view of evangelicalism as a twentieth-century revival movement. The first school, with the longest period of history, sees evangelicalism in the twenty-first century as an extension of the first-century church, which has demonstrated its faithfulness to Christ's message of salvation by grace alone through faith alone and based upon Scripture alone. Studying the two millennia of Christian history reveals that some of the centuries, from an evangelical perspective, were predominately "dark" with unbelief and superstition, thus the common usage of "Dark Ages" to discuss the seventh through twelfth centuries. The second school begins evangelicalism with the sixteenth century and the Protestant Reformation and focuses on the development of "solas" that distinguish Protestant belief from Catholic dogma. The earlier list of three solas from the Augsburg Confession (1530) continued with the rise and expansion of Lutheranism. As a means of viewing the context of the Protestant Reformation and the birth of evangelicalism, *Sola Scriptura*, *Sola fide*, and *Sola gratis* ("only Scripture," "only faith," and "only grace") can act as lenses through which we can see the contours and identity of a young theological movement. The third and more commonly accepted time period sees evangelicalism's rise in the eighteenth century. The focus, in this case, provides a more steadied gaze at the ministries of Jonathan Edwards, George Whitefield, and John and Charles Wesley.

The next dimension of evangelicalism is width. The geographical spread of the church to all nations is part of the plan Christ gave his disciples, known simply as the Great Commission. We can see from two of the five texts in the New Testament that the spread was to all nations. First, we can read the text from Luke:

> He said to them, "This is what I told you while I was still with you: Everything must be fulfilled

that is written about me in the Law of Moses, the Prophets and the Psalms." Then he opened their minds so they could understand the Scriptures. He told them, "This is what is written: The Messiah will suffer and rise from the dead on the third day, and repentance for the forgiveness of sins will be preached in his name to all nations, beginning at Jerusalem. You are witnesses of these things. I am going to send you what my Father has promised; but stay in the city until you have been clothed with power from on high." (Luke 24:44–49, NIV)

As we study evangelicalism, it is helpful to note in this text that understanding the Scriptures is a primary task given prior to the actual act of "sending," commonly called "missions."

Now, we can hear the second part of Luke's writings, the Great Commission from Acts. "But you will receive power when the Holy Spirit comes on you; and you will be my witnesses in Jerusalem, and in all Judea and Samaria, and to the ends of the earth" (Acts 1:8 NIV). "To all nations" and "to the ends of the earth" both portray the task of evangelization as needing completion or fulfillment. When evangelical missionaries began to spread from North America and Europe to the nations of the world, evangelicalism itself as "gospel people" globalized. But, like every religious movement, it had to become contextualized, or planted in the soil, to truly prosper and reproduce faithfully in another culture.

As the nations were reached and the church began to spread geographically, missiologists were studying mass movements, people movements, and church-growth trends from as early as the 1930s.[9] The statistics were analyzed by David B.

---

[9] The Church Growth School arose from the research and writings of Donald A. McGavran (1897–1990), especially from the publication of his *The Bridges of God: A Study in the Strategy of Missions* (New York: Friendship Press, 1955).

Barrett (1927–2011) and incorporated into his *World Christian Encyclopedia*.[10] For the general public, the global shift from north to south was not realized until 2002, with the publication of Philip Jenkins's *The Next Christendom: The Coming of Global Christianity*.[11] This movement was initially considered a matter of the West sending Christian missionaries to the "rest." But the new expression has become "The gospel from everywhere to everyone" or "To all nations from all nations."[12]

The final dimension of evangelicalism is depth. Since evangelicalism's history is not as long as that of other Christian traditions (Catholic, Lutheran, Orthodox, Reformed), it might appear from some views as shallow. You need deep roots for tall growth. Such deep roots of evangelicalism come from both spirituality and theology. Evangelical spirituality includes prayer, sermons, reading the Bible, devotional texts, the sacraments, fasting, and music.[13] As we view spirituality, we note the distinctive forms of spiritual expression among evangelicals in both North America and East Asia. We can consider the following categories: prayer, devotional texts, preaching, hymns/gospel music, and the sacraments.

J. Waskom Pickett's earlier *Christian Mass Movements in India: A Study with Recommendations* (Lucknow: Lucknow Publishing House, 1933) was influential in developing McGavran's passion and strategy for church growth. Alan R. Tippett's *People Movements in Southern Polynesia: Studies in the Dynamics of Church-Planting and Growth in Tahiti, New Zealand, Tonga, and Samoa* (Chicago: Moody Press, 1971) and Frederick E. Stock's *People Movements in the Punjab* (Pasadena, CA: Wm. Carey Library, 1975) are two early case studies.

10   *World Christian Encyclopedia: A Comparative Survey of Churches and Religions in the Modern World, A.D. 1900–2000* (New York: Oxford University Press, 1982). An updated and expanded second edition was released in 2001.

11   Philip Jenkins, *The Next Christendom: The Coming of Global Christianity* (New York: Oxford University Press, 2002).

12   Samuel Escobar, *The New Global Mission: The Gospel from Everywhere to Everyone* (Downers Grove, IL: InterVarsity Press, 2003) and Carlos F. Cardoza-Orlandi and Justo L. González, *To All Nations from All Nations: A History of the Christian Missionary Movement* (Nashville: Abingdon Press, 2013).

13   For further reading on evangelical spirituality, see James M. Gordon, *Evangelical Spirituality* (London: SPCK, 1991) and Ian Randall, *What a Friend We Have in Jesus: The Evangelical Tradition*, Traditions of Christian Spirituality (Maryknoll, NY: Orbis Books, 2005).

Prayer, from the time of the eighteenth-century evangelical revivals in both Britain and America, became more extempore and personal, rather than simply existing as a prayer text read from a book. By the nineteenth century, large groups of people in evangelism and revival meetings would bow their heads and close their eyes, not dependent upon reading a prayer from a book, but trusting in the guidance of the Holy Spirit who would help believers to pray in the Spirit. "In the same way, the Spirit helps us in our weakness. We do not know what we ought to pray for, but the Spirit himself intercedes for us through wordless groans" (Romans 8:26 NIV). Later, we will look at the prayer forms that emerged from the Great Pyeongyang Revival in 1907, the "Sinner's Prayer" as it arose from public revival and evangelism meetings in the twentieth century, and the charismatic prayer forms, especially those identified with a distinctive prayer language.[14]

Devotional texts surfaced from the twentieth century as best sellers, leading the religious book publishing market. Oswald Chambers's *My Utmost for His Highest* and Lettie B. Cowman's *Streams in the Desert* are two of the more popular among an ever-expanding religious genre. The daily devotional was a shorthand response to the idea of a daily quiet time, where traditionally one hour would be spent each morning in prayer and reading the Bible. The daily devotional made it possible for people to have spiritual guidance from a shortened text and a reduced time commitment, with only a few minutes required to receive spiritual nourishment. One could say that the daily quiet time of one hour turned into a quick-time spirituality.

Through the two millennia of Christianity, sermons or homilies have always been a significant part of Sunday worship services, as well as other times of Christian gatherings,

---

14 On the "Sinner's Prayer," see "The Evangelical Jesus Prayer: It's not Perfect, but the Sinner's Prayer is a Work of Genius," *Christianity Today*, Vol. 56, No. 8 (September 2012): 73.

INTRODUCTION

whether worship or revival meetings. In evangelical preaching, the location and the message were changing in the eighteenth century, as exemplified by George Whitefield's field preaching and his proclamation of the need for the new birth. Whitefield preached "urgently, immediately and as the great question for every hearer *right now*."[15] The real distinctive for evangelical preaching is that the text becomes primary as a guide for the construction and delivery of a sermon. Biblical exposition is alongside biblical exegesis, as both provide spiritual nourishment.

The church had the Psalter and other religious lyrics as it gathered together in worship, expressing musically its praise. With the advent of evangelicalism in the eighteenth century came the acceptance of hymns in worship, written and composed by contemporary Christians and not the writers of the biblical books. In the earlier eighteenth century of evangelicalism, we see the names of Isaac Watts (1674–1748), Charles Wesley (1707–1788), John Newton (1725–1807), and William Cowper (1731–1800).

The Protestant emphasis upon two sacraments only (baptism and the Lord's Supper) prevails within evangelicalism, with only a few churches adding foot washing as a third sacrament.[16] With the North American emphasis upon believer's baptism, baptism by immersion for adults or at least school-age children became the new model of conversion to Christ and addition to the church.

Evangelical spirituality prioritizes religious experience, especially that all-important initial experience of the "new birth"

---

15 Mark A. Noll, *The Rise of Evangelicalism: The Age of Edwards, Whitefield and the Wesleys*, Vol. 1, A History of Evangelicalism: People, Movements and Ideas in the English-Speaking World (Downers Grove, IL: InterVarsity Press, 2003), 88.

16 Two churches that continue to practice foot washing as an additional sacrament are the Church of the Brethren (Anabaptist) and the General Association of Baptists. John 13:14–15 is the text used to support the ongoing practice of foot washing as a sacrament. "Now that I, your Lord and Teacher, have washed your feet, you also should wash one another's feet. I have set you an example that you should do as I have done for you" (NIV).

(religious conversion) or simply being "born again." While adjustments were made between Protestantism and evangelicalism, it can be said that "[at] its worst, this new evangelicalism neglected, caricatured and distorted the inherited traditions of Reformation Protestantism." On the best side, however, "evangelicalism provided needed revitalization to English-speaking Protestant Christianity."[17]

We need to consider again the broader lines that mark the division between evangelical and non-evangelical. With the world population being approximately seven billion persons, there are at least half a billion evangelicals, roughly 7.14 percent of the world's population. As Douglas Sweeney notes, David B. Barrett (1927–2011) had counted 570 million as Pentecostals and charismatics, with other evangelicals at 242 million.[18] It should be noted again that the greater majority of evangelicals are either Pentecostal or charismatic. This should prevent the tendency to either exclude or marginalize those who practice speaking in tongues, even as a prayer language. Statistics are significant, but the number of global evangelicals, again, is determined by how a person defines *evangelical*. Let us consider in more depth a number of basic academic definitions.

At the simplest level, we have the text called the Great Commission (Matthew 28:18–20). From that text, among a total of five Great Commission texts, our identity is tied with the gospel. We are gospel people, people of "good news."[19]

Timothy George, founding dean of Beeson Divinity School,

---

17 Noll, *The Rise of Evangelicalism*, 292.
18 Douglas A. Sweeney, *The American Evangelical Story: A History of the Movement* (Grand Rapids: Baker Academic, 2005), 9. More recent statistical records published by David Barrett's associates list a total of 349,499,000 global evangelicals. See the "Status of Global Christianity, 2018, in the Context of 1900–2050," http://www.gordonconwell.edu/ockenga/research/documents/StatusofGlobalChristianity2018.pdf. Accessed 13 August 2018.
19 While Matthew 28:18–20 is the most familiar and often called definitively the "Great Commission," there are four other texts in the New Testament. They are Mark 16:14–18, Luke 24:46–48, John 20:19–23, and Acts 1:6–11.

wrote, "Evangelicals are a worldwide family of Bible-believing Christians committed to sharing with everyone everywhere the transforming good news of new life in Jesus Christ, an utterly free gift that comes through faith alone in the crucified and risen Savior."[20]

In addition to Bebbington's helpful quadrilateral of evangelicalism, Alister McGrath has listed six controlling convictions. They are: the authority of Scripture, the majesty of Jesus Christ, the lordship of the Holy Spirit, the need for personal conversion, the priority of evangelism, and the importance of the Christian community.[21] We can add a few more definitions or analogies to our growing list on evangelicalism. One is Timothy Smith's "evangelical mosaic." Still another is Randall Balmer's "patchwork quilt." The idea of these is that diversity in both color and confession can add beauty to an artwork (mosaic or quilt).

Dr. Timothy Smith (1924–1997) was a Nazarene who became the first evangelical historian to gain tenure and teach on the faculty of a major research university in the US (Johns Hopkins University in Baltimore, Maryland). Smith received his BA and MA from the University of Virginia, and later earned his PhD at Harvard. Smith liked to view evangelicalism as a mosaic, meaning that each beautiful piece maintains its distinct identity and shape, as all the pieces fit together to create an exquisite composition. He later would adopt the term *kaleidoscope* to describe the evangelical community, indicating that the colors are more dynamic and not static or set within a permanent frame.[22]

---

20 Sweeney, *The American Evangelical Story*, 17–18.
21 Alister E. McGrath, *Evangelicalism and the Future of Christianity* (Downers Grove, IL: InterVarsity Press, 1995), 55–56.
22 Timothy L. Smith, "The Evangelical Kaleidoscope and the Call to Christian Unity," *Christian Scholar's Review*, Vol. 15 (1986): 125–140. For further biographical information and historiographical views on Smith, see Floyd T. Cunningham's "Common Ground: The Perspectives of Timothy L. Smith on

Randall Balmer (1954–), currently a professor at Dartmouth College, prefers the analogy of a patchwork quilt to describe American evangelicalism, since it is "folk art rather than fine art" and "requires the work of many hands, each of which contributes its own 'signature' to the project. Its beauty, moreover, lies precisely in its variegated texture and even, sometimes, in the absence of an overall pattern. Unlike a mosaic, it is also quintessentially American."[23]

In *The Variety of American Evangelicalism*, edited by Donald W. Dayton and Robert K. Johnston, we can see distinctly that there is a growing level of diversity and complexity within the various expressions of evangelicalism. In this collection of chapters by members of the representative denominations from the larger evangelical family, we see how some are not too comfortable being called evangelical, rather than presenting their own confessional identities which were forged through the past and even in the turbulent 1920s and 1930s, when many of the more conservative believers departed or were thrown out of the more liberal/progressive denominations in America. While denominations divided into even more denominations (churches/fellowships), the colleges, universities, and seminaries remained with the liberal/progressive side. Some faith traditions feel that *evangelical* should not be worn as a label at all or believe that being evangelical would detract simply from their own unique confessional and historical family roots. Included among the groups that question whether or not they should belong to evangelicalism are various expressions of Anabaptists, the Stone-Campbell Tradition, some Pentecostals, and the

---

American Religious History," *Fides et Historia*, Vol. 44, No. 2 (Summer 2012): 21–55.

23 Randall Balmer, *Mine Eyes Have Seen the Glory: A Journey into the Evangelical Subculture in America*, 5th ed. (New York: Oxford University Press, 2014): 353–354.

more liturgical churches, including Anglicans, Episcopalians, and Lutherans.

While we have Donald Dayton involved in our discussion, revisiting the debate between George Marsden and Donald Dayton which has contributed toward the ongoing discussion of who is evangelical and what makes for evangelicalism in America would be helpful.

Originally, the historiography was established by the publication of Bernard Ramm's *The Evangelical Heritage: A Study in Historical Theology*.[24] Ramm began with the early centuries of the church's history and divided the tradition into two sides, indicating which one of the two was aligned theologically with evangelicalism. First, chronologically, evangelical theology "belongs to the Christian West." Next it "belongs to Reformation Theology." Next, the tradition can be traced through scholastic orthodoxy and placed in comparison with Christian liberalism, neo-orthodoxy, and offering a final reaffirmation of evangelicalism's identity and future.

Ramm's *The Evangelical Heritage* was initially published in 1973, which predates the time when Marsden and Dayton would initiate their debate over the identity and heritage of evangelicalism. Dayton's reply to Ramm was in the form of a similarly titled volume: *Discovering an Evangelical Heritage* (Grand Rapids: Baker Academic, 1976). Included in this volume are chapters related to Jonathan Blanchard, Charles Finney, Theodore Weld, Lane Theological Seminary and Oberlin College, the Tappans, Wesleyan Methodists, Christian feminism, and ministry to the poor. All chapters point toward a socially aware and active evangelicalism in the nineteenth century, rather than one solely committed to doctrinal purity and social separation.[25]

---

24 Bernard Ramm, *The Evangelical Heritage: A Study in Historical Theology*, foreword by Kevin Vanhoozer (Grand Rapids: Baker Books, 2000).
25 A second edition, published also by Baker Academic, was released in 2014 with a new introduction by Douglas M. Strong of Seattle Pacific University. The first edition was translated into Korean by Dawk-Mahn Bae in 2003.

Originally, the book chapters appeared in the *Post American* (later titled *Sojourners*), part of the ministry of the Sojourners Community in Washington, DC, and first under the editorial leadership of Jim Wallis (1948–). It was committed to making a statement on social justice by evangelicals.

In 1988, the Marsden/Dayton debate began at the annual meeting of the American Academy of Religion. The previous year saw the publication of George M. Marsden's (1939–) *Reforming Fundamentalism: Fuller Seminary and the New Evangelicalism* (Grand Rapids: Wm. B. Eerdmans, 1987). Since the Methodist, Holiness, and Pentecostal relations within evangelicalism had been marginalized from the narrative of Fuller's history, Dayton suggested that Marsden was telling only the Presbyterian story while the Pentecostal one remained untold. Marsden's Presbyterian model of evangelical history focused on the top (the elites), and Donald W. Dayton's (1942–) Pentecostal model of evangelical history focused on the bottom or the underside (the common folk).

The two-sided division of evangelicalism during the second half of the twentieth century causes more than a slight delay toward seeking and finding the goal of Christian unity, and it provides an overall pattern that reflects "an intentional move from toleration to cooperation to accommodation with liberalism," according to Sweeney. He further views the history of neo-evangelicalism (after 1945) as having a choice between becoming a separate but equal "exclusive fellowship" or of exhibiting "historic evangelical piety" within the larger family of American spirituality. Sweeney concludes his article by pointing out the path chosen as being the latter of the two. If that remains true in the twenty-first century, which I believe it does, we can see further drifting from fundamentalism toward Protestant liberalism, with the evangelical brand and its rhetoric still remaining the same. Losing confessional credibility or

INTRODUCTION

authenticity, however, should cause some concern, and it certainly has. David F. Wells (1939–) has written a series of five books on the drifting away from God's absolute truth toward a postmodern plurality where diversity and personal opinion rule.[26] Through Sweeney's survey of American evangelicalism, we further see the many attempts to define and describe evangelicalism. In that work, he lists two representatives from the conservative side of the Reformed tradition as scholars who view the evangelical label as misleading or unnecessary for theological identity and vitality.[27] The first is Dr. Michael Horton (1964–), currently on faculty at Westminster Seminary California. Horton himself converted to Calvinism (Reformed tradition) during his college years at Biola and has been involved at the highest levels with the Alliance of Confessing Evangelicals (1994–). Horton's concern, as discussed by Roger Olson, is to show that evangelicalism was formed in 1520 by Martin Luther as an identity that holds to strict Reformation principles which, in his view, would exclude anyone who is Wesleyan or Arminian.[28]

The other voice of dissent is the conservative Reformed historian Darryl G. Hart (1956–). In his *Deconstructing Evangelicalism: Conservative Protestantism in the Age of Billy Graham*, he expresses the view that "relinquish[ing]" the use of *evangelical* in academic discourse would assist in the writing

---

26 David F. Wells, *No Place for Truth: Or, Whatever Happened to Evangelical Theology* (Grand Rapids: Wm. B. Eerdmans, 1993); *God in the Wasteland: The Reality of Truth in a World of Fading Dreams* (Grand Rapids: Wm. B. Eerdmans, 1994); *Losing Our Virtue: Why the Church Must Recover Its Moral Vision* (Grand Rapids: Wm. B. Eerdmans, 1998); *Above All Earthly Pow'rs: Christ in a Postmodern World* (Grand Rapids: Wm. B. Eerdmans, 2004); *The Courage to be Protestant: Truth-lovers, Marketers and Emergents in the Postmodern World* (Grand Rapids: Wm. B. Eerdmans, 2008). Another book in the same category of decrying the shift from evangelicalism's authentic confessional positions is G. K. Beale's *The Erosion of Inerrancy in Evangelicalism: Responding to New Challenges to Biblical Authority* (Wheaton, IL: Crossway, 2008).
27 Sweeney, *The American Evangelical Story*, 23.
28 Roger E. Olson, "Arminianism is Evangelical Theology," *Wesleyan Theological Journal*, Vol. 46, No. 2 (Fall 2011): 7–8.

of "better scholarship on American religion."[29] In his study of J. Gresham Machen, Hart lists four distinct groups within American Protestantism in the 1940s. One of the four is evangelicalism, but Hart's preference would no doubt be with another group: the confessionalists.[30]

After introducing a variety of views in his survey of American evangelicalism, Douglas Sweeney offers his own definition: "Evangelicals comprise a movement that is rooted in classical Christian orthodoxy, shaped by a largely Protestant understanding of the gospel, and distinguished from other such movements by an eighteenth-century twist."[31] In this definition there are three movements that contribute to evangelicalism: Christian orthodoxy (indicating the early ecumenical creeds and confessions of the church), the Protestant Reformation (focusing on the sixteenth century as a turning again toward orthodoxy—reaffirming what Christians believed for centuries but were distracted from by medieval Catholicism), and evangelical awakening (meaning the seventeenth-century Great Awakening in North America associated with both Jonathan Edwards and George Whitefield, as well as that of Britain with Wesley and others during the same time period).

As we continue focusing on definitions of *evangelicalism*, it might prove helpful to see four views next to one another, as they will present together an entire spectrum. This discussion will begin our next chapter, looking at different definitions of *revival*, *evangelism*, and *mission*. As we complete this next chapter on "Weighing Words," we will move on to "Tracking Time" as a chronological overview of the long twentieth century, from 1880 to 2000.

---

29 D. G. Hart, *Deconstructing Evangelicalism: Conservative Protestantism in the Age of Billy Graham* (Grand Rapids: Baker Academic, 2004), 32.
30 D. G. Hart, *Defending the Faith: J. Gresham Machen and the Crisis of Conservative Protestantism in Modern America* (Phillipsburg, NJ: P&R Publishing, 1994), 169. The title of this book itself makes a connection between Machen and "conservative Protestantism" and not fundamentalism nor evangelicalism.
31 Sweeney, *The American Evangelical Story*, 23–24.

2

Weighing Words

In postmodernism, much ink has been spilled over words and what they mean or do not mean.[32] Long before anyone created the "postmodern" era, there was a simple Victorian-era children's book that transformed a character named Humpty Dumpty into a postmodern philosopher of language. In a conversation between Alice and Humpty Dumpty, it becomes clear that semantics has become the servant of the speaker.

"When I use a word," Humpty Dumpty said in rather a scornful tone, "it means just what I choose it to mean—neither more nor less." "The question is," said Alice, "whether you CAN make words mean so many different things.... That's a great deal to make one word mean," Alice said in a thoughtful tone. "When I make a word do a lot of work like that," said Humpty Dumpty, "I always pay it extra."[33]

The absence of a singular or fixed meaning in language then becomes a problem that has flowed into the writing of

---

32 For a survey of contemporary hermeneutics and its challenges to evangelical theology, see Kevin J. Vanhoozer, *Is There a Meaning in This Text?: The Bible, The Reader, and the Morality of Literary Knowledge* (Grand Rapids: Zondervan, 1998).

33 Lewis Carroll, *Through the Looking-Glass: And What Alice Found There* (New York: A. L. Burt, 1897), 123-124. The book was originally published in 1871.

both history and theology. Since words are now used with a multiplicity of meanings, writers head in opposite directions while still claiming allegiance to the same word. The name of a religious identity like "evangelical" now carries multiple meanings, with corresponding definitions being so divergent that they appear to describe not one but many words.

For the non-specialist in the academic study of religions, "evangelical" has become a catch-all for people who take their faith seriously, a use which stretches the word beyond its historical context. Within the past thirty years, we have witnessed such a variety of usages for the term *evangelical* that Donald Dayton has called for a moratorium of that word to avoid even further confusion.[34] Dayton has persistently argued against the views of both Bernard Ramm and George Marsden in claiming that Ramm and Marsden have drawn lines too closely both historically and theologically around the single word *evangelical*.[35] While we do not have the time and space in this book to describe all the struggles over understanding the true meaning of the following terms: *Fundamentalist, Reformed, Pentecostal, Wesleyan-Holiness, Anglican,* and even *Baptist,* all of these confessional families have hotly debated their own identities in order to determine who is in and who is out. Theological terms have also become the territory of lively discussion and intense debate. What does it mean to believe in inerrancy? What is dispensationalism? Are they modernists, liberals, or progressives? We could continue this discussion for many pages, but our concern is more specifically with the identity of the Wesleyan-Holiness and Pentecostal families of churches as we focus on radical holiness.

---

34 Donald W. Dayton, "Some Doubts about the Usefulness of the Category 'Evangelical,'" in *The Variety of American Evangelicalism*, eds. Donald W. Dayton and Robert K. Johnston (Downers Grove, IL: InterVarsity Press, 1991), 251.

35 See Kenneth J. Collins, *The Evangelical Moment: The Promise of an American Religion* (Grand Rapids: Baker Academic, 2005), 64–70.

First, think for a moment of your family. How do you count the individual members of your own family? Part of the counting depends on culture, the other part on personality. As we consider this anecdote as a model for viewing the breadth or diversity of evangelicalism, it should assist us in viewing others as either being with us or not, as either inside or outside the evangelical community.

The first part of this chapter contains an extended summary and review of *Four Views on the Spectrum of Evangelicalism*.[36] This volume joins the ever-expanding genre of multiple (usually four or five) views of a selected theological or ministry topic being discussed in a single book. Including four or five views surpasses the two sides of a standard debate in both breadth and complexity.

Now, let us introduce the four views and their advocates. Yes, it is a spectrum, so we will follow the order of the book, from more conservative to more liberal, from exclusive to inclusive. Here are the four views in the order we will discuss them: fundamentalism, confessional evangelicalism, generic evangelicalism, and postconservative evangelicalism.

While many who discuss the range and diversity of evangelicalism in North America would exclude fundamentalists, it is helpful to know the real distinctions between and within both evangelicalism and fundamentalism. In some ways, as clarified by J. I. Packer's early work *"Fundamentalism" and the Word of God*, there is little difference between views of the Bible held by fundamentalists and by those evangelicals who hold to full inerrancy of the autographs (original manuscripts), as all full members of the Evangelical Theological Society (ETS, 1949–) affirm in their annual membership.[37] Also noteworthy is the

---

[36] Kevin T. Bauder et al., *Four Views on the Spectrum of Evangelicalism* (Grand Rapids: Zondervan, 2011).

[37] J. I. Packer, *"Fundamentalism" and the Word of God* (Grand Rapids: Wm. B. Eerdmans, 1958).

actual diversity within global fundamentalism, that neither those on the far right nor those on the far left are uniform in their understanding and expression of the complexity of theological issues involved in living and witnessing in the twenty-first century. As part of evangelicalism's intellectual integrity to at least hear the voices of others and then move on toward understanding them, it behooves us to be willing to study—at length—the views of others, even when they refer to us in less than familial terms. With that said, we will begin looking at a fundamentalist's view of evangelicalism.

Our representative fundamentalist is Dr. Kevin T. Bauder. He was born in Midland, Michigan, began his academic studies at Faith Baptist Bible College (Ankeny, Iowa), and attended seminary at Denver Baptist Bible College and Seminary. Bauder continued beyond the MDiv and MTh degrees with a DMin from Trinity Evangelical Divinity School in Deerfield, Illinois (1991), and a PhD in Systematic and Historical Theology from Dallas Theological Seminary (2001). After joining the faculty at Central Baptist Theological Seminary of Minneapolis (1998), he later served as its president (2003–2011), and since 2011, he has served as research professor of systematic theology.

Bauder's chapter in *Four Views on the Spectrum of Evangelicalism* begins with an explanation—or personal testimony, as he terms it—of what fundamentalism is. At the heart of fundamentalism, according to Bauder, is a definition of Christian fellowship in both minimal and maximal terms. The minimal level helps to "differentiat[e] Christians from other people."[38] What constitutes the gospel, as the basis of Christian identity and fellowship, is more narrowly defined by Bauder than by the other three authors of the *Spectrum* book. It is within his view of "maximal Christian fellowship" that Bauder expresses what has been the standard practice of fundamentalists: "secondary"

---

38   Bauder et al., *Four Views on the Spectrum of Evangelicalism*, 21.

or "second-degree" separation.[39] Second-degree separation is simply termed to "separate from Christian leaders who will not separate from apostates."[40] Someone, then, who might be considered orthodox will be disfellowshipped on the basis of whom they have fellowship with.

This was historically the case when Billy Graham began to work alongside and in cooperation with ecumenical Christians, first with Protestant liberals, then later with Roman Catholics and Orthodox churches. In 1957, Graham was opposed by fundamentalist leaders like Bob Jones, Carl McIntire, and John R. Rice when his New York crusade was sponsored by the Protestant Council of New York, some members of which were "theologically liberal and who denied some of the most important elements of the biblical message."[41]

After Dr. Bauder spends a lot of time (pages) talking about fundamentalism, he finally tells us why evangelicalism is unique. In his view, two areas differentiate evangelicalism from fundamentalism. They are: (1) rethinking or redefining the gospel and (2) extending Christian recognition and fellowship to others (non-evangelicals). In the first area, Bauder lists "newer theologies" such as open theism and the new perspective on Paul, "downplaying the centrality of personal guilt, penal substitution, and personal forgiveness" as examples of rethinking and redefining the gospel.[42] My own understanding is that many evangelicals themselves would take issue with both open theism and the new perspective, including Dr. Mohler, the next theologian to be discussed. Open theism, more so than the new perspective, was considered such an aberration to American evangelicalism that it brought a vote regarding

---

39   Ibid., 37.
40   Ibid., 40.
41   Billy Graham, *Just As I Am: The Autobiography of Billy Graham* (San Francisco: HarperSanFrancisco, 1997), 302.
42   Bauder et al., *Four Views on the Spectrum of Evangelicalism*, 48.

membership to the Evangelical Theological Society in 2001, with the ETS rejecting open theism's heterodox view of divine foreknowledge. Thus, Bauder was unable to take issue with the majority of evangelicals but could only do so with a small group on the theological margins. On his view of the second difference (extending Christian fellowship), Bauder more accurately states that "some evangelicals have formally recognized Roman Catholics as Christians." Later, as we view the 1990s, we will see the divisive reaction to the joint ecumenical document *Evangelicals and Catholics Together* (1994).

The second position in our spectrum is called *confessional evangelicalism*. The representative of this position is Dr. Mohler, who makes this view easily understandable, as his position is truly an embodied one. Richard Albert Mohler Jr. was born in Lakeland, Florida, in 1959. During and after his studies at Southern Baptist Theological Seminary in Louisville, Kentucky (MDiv and PhD), he worked for the seminary in several administrative positions, including assistant to the president. During this same time period, and even earlier, through faculty hiring and shifts in beliefs, a move had been underway to transition this seminary to a more liberal theological position. In the midst of this challenge to the seminary's identity and future ministry among Southern Baptist churches, Mohler was hired as the ninth president of the Southern Baptist Theological Seminary in 1993. Immediately, the faculty was told they would need to sign the "Baptist Faith and Message" to retain their teaching positions at the seminary.[43] For some Baptists, the need to affirm

---

43 Some claim that Southern Baptist Theological Seminary's requirement for each member of the faculty to sign the "Baptist Faith and Message" was not only anti-Baptist but that it was also infringing on the professor's conscience as well as inhibiting freedom of thought and expression. My requests for more information on the requirement of Southern Baptist Theological Seminary and the other Southern Baptist Convention seminaries to have the faculty sign a statement of belief went unanswered. One helpful website lists three versions (1925, 1963, 2000) of the "Baptist Faith and Message" next to one another for a careful comparison. See http://www.sbc.net/bfm2000/ bfmcomparison.asp. Accessed 30 May 2019.

or sign any creed or confession was opposed to the free-church tradition that had arisen from Anabaptists in the sixteenth century, which was resistant to oaths and military service and was positioned to promote peace and religious tolerance.[44] After those who were opposed to this requirement or could not affirm the "Baptist Faith and Message" departed, new faculty were hired and the seminary continued, even expanding and extending its support base and student representation. In the midst of all this change, one cannot help but see the figure of President Al Mohler.

Mohler provides a clear and concise definition of *evangelical* with the following: "An evangelical is recognized by a passion for the gospel of Jesus Christ, by a deep commitment to biblical truth, by a sense of urgency to see lost persons hear the gospel, and by a commitment to personal holiness and the local church."[45] As with other definitions of *evangelical*, we see a parallel with Bebbington's quadrilateral. Mohler continues his definition by delineating his position from Roman Catholics and Protestant liberals, emphasizing that both of these groups can have an "evangelical spirit" but not be part of evangelicalism. In Mohler's view, it is impossible to be both evangelical and a Protestant liberal or a Roman Catholic. He also, on the same page (69), makes it clear that there is a distinction between evangelicals and fundamentalists. To clarify his point, Mohler provides a history of evangelicalism in the twentieth century, especially the post–World War II era, with

---

44   The historiography of Baptists is contested between three main groups: those who view European Anabaptists as the ancestors, others who view Baptists as arising in the English context from the separatists of the seventeenth century, and those who hold the Landmark position which sees a continuation of tradition from the first century to the twenty-first, as noted already in the *Trail of Blood*. For further reading on the position that affirms a relationship with Anabaptists, see William R. Estep, *The Anabaptist Story: An Introduction to Sixteenth-Century Anabaptism*, 3rd ed. (Grand Rapids: Wm. B. Eerdmans, 1995).

45   Bauder et al., *Four Views on the Spectrum of Evangelicalism*, 69.

the rise of neo-evangelicalism as a new conservative alternative to separatist fundamentalism.

In line with the standard historiography, Mohler provides a link with the major historical dates that made evangelicalism in the twentieth century, especially the founding of *Christianity Today* in 1956. While the narrative continues, one cannot help but notice the prominence of Baptists mentioned in his historical and theological overview of evangelicalism. The basic (working) definition from page 69 is supplemented or modified by a definition of *evangelicalism* on page 75. It says, "Evangelicalism is a movement of confessional believers who are determined by God's grace to conserve this faith in the face of its reduction or corruption, even as they gladly take this gospel to the ends of the earth in order to see the nations exult in the name of Jesus Christ."[46]

Further definition of *evangelical* requires the understanding of both centered and bounded evangelicalism—Mohler's "theological triage," including first-level, second-level, and third-level doctrines. After these doctrinal areas and boundaries have been set, Mohler explains how Southern Baptists are evangelicals too. While this is true regarding what they believe and how they promise to remain faithful to their own statements of doctrine, Southern Baptists are not officially members of the National Association of Evangelicals (NAE). More often than not, the Baptist identity, rather than the evangelical side, is promoted exclusively by the names of prominent religious leaders in America, a list that Mohler provides. Mohler clearly states which evangelical statements he signed and did not sign. The *Manhattan Declaration* is one he signed, and *Evangelicals and Catholics Together* is one he did not sign.

To bring Mohler's contribution to a close, we can mention that he protests the view of "revisionist evangelicalism" as "a

---

46   Bauder et al., *Four Views on the Spectrum of Evangelicalism*, 75.

new form of Protestant Liberalism," and includes Roger Olson with that group. Four cardinal doctrines are listed by Mohler as being essential beliefs for all true evangelicals. They include "the trustworthiness of the Bible, the exclusivity of the gospel, the integrity of theism, and the nature of justification and atonement."[47] Now we move to the third contributor in the spectrum of views on evangelicalism: Dr. John G. Stackhouse Jr.

Dr. Stackhouse is Canadian and has studied and taught on both sides of the border. He received his master's degree from Wheaton College, having studied under Mark Noll, who specializes in Christian history of the US. Later, Stackhouse received a PhD from the University of Chicago, writing a dissertation on Canadian evangelicalism under the supervision of Martin Marty. Stackhouse has taught primarily at two Canadian institutions: Regent College and now at Crandall University (New Brunswick) in the position of Samuel J. Mikolaski Professor of Religious Studies.

The position Stackhouse promotes and defends in his article is termed "generic evangelicalism." After he introduces the basic idea of evangelicalism, he gives us two definitions and his personal testimony, stemming from the evangelical quadrilateral of British historian David Bebbington. According to Stackhouse, these four emphases need a singular addition to become comprehensive and clear. Said addition is "transdenominationalism," which stresses the need to see the cooperative work of evangelicals throughout both centuries and various countries. While his definition does appear adequate on its own, Stackhouse gives a second explanation to ensure comprehension of his views. The second definition simply states that evangelicals are those who, as either individuals or as a group, belong to the "movement known as evangelicalism."[48] Thus, evangelical requires

---
47 Ibid., 89.
48 Ibid., 122.

one to affirm an alliance or membership with others who are part of evangelicalism, but this has three levels or groups. The first group is those who originally came out of the evangelical revivals of the eighteenth century, the second are those who have not departed from this historical list, and the third are those who have later joined by connecting with the original groups. This broader group can include some Anglicans and Dutch Reformed, Mennonites, and the more traditionally evangelical Baptists, Presbyterians, and Methodists.

With five criteria, one would assume that Stackhouse would conclude his definition of *evangelical*, but he adds one more requirement: evangelicals as "orthodox and orthoprax."[49] This, for Stackhouse, would exclude "oneness Pentecostals" and "Word-Faith" people. In evangelical fashion, Dr. Stackhouse gives his personal story of becoming an evangelical, noting that he is a Baptist now but was originally a member of the Plymouth Brethren. Future chapters will provide more details on this, and *Evangelicals and Catholics Together* (ECT) contains a test of sorts as to how conservative an evangelical person is. Stackhouse does affirm ECT while, we should remember, Bauder and Mohler did not. Now we move on to the final of the four positions.

Dr. Roger Olson describes his basic understanding of evangelicalism this way: "Evangelicalism is like the charismatic movement or the new thought movement or the New Age movement in that they are all religious-spiritual networks and coalitions without any membership."[50] He provides a distinction between "centered set" and "bounded set," and, to further clarify evangelicalism, he shows the difference between "movement" and "organization" and between "sociology" and "theology." Remembering that we started viewing the spectrum from the

---

49 Bauder et al., *Four Views on the Spectrum of Evangelicalism*, 124.
50 Ibid., 163.

far right and moved to the left identifies Dr. Olson's position as "postconservative evangelicalism," which places it as the most liberal, or farthest left, of the other three positions.[51]

Roger Eugene Olson was born in Des Moines, Iowa, in 1952. He grew up in the Open Bible Standard churches, a classical Pentecostal denomination that holds to a "finished work" view of Christian holiness. After he completed his undergraduate studies at the denomination's Bible college in Des Moines, he continued his studies at Sioux Falls Seminary in South Dakota. This seminary was originally located in Rochester, New York, and was the German Baptist seminary where Walter Rauschenbusch had studied at the end of the nineteenth century. Following his seminary studies and departure from Pentecostalism, he completed a PhD at Rice University, writing his dissertation on the theology of Wolfhart Pannenberg (1928–2014).[52] After a lengthy time teaching at Bethel Seminary in St. Paul, Minnesota, Olson began serving on the faculty at George W. Truett Theological Seminary (part of Baylor University in Waco, Texas). One of his ongoing points of theological emphasis is affirming his own Arminian identity, not as a Wesleyan but as a Baptist. Being an Arminian Baptist is neither a misnomer nor an oxymoron, but is, rather, a truly historical and theologically valid position for many, including the General Baptists and Free Will Baptists in the US.[53]

Although Baylor has taught religion for many years, the George W. Truett Theological Seminary was not opened until

---

51 Dr. Olson has emphasized clearly the "postconservative" in his book: Roger E. Olson, *How to Be Evangelical Without Being Conservative* (Grand Rapids: Zondervan, 2008).

52 It is interesting to note that Albert Mohler's dissertation at Southern Baptist Seminary was a comparison between evangelical views and those of Karl Barth, while Olson wrote his on Pannenberg. Olson's dissertation title is "Trinity and Eschatology: The Historical Being of God in the Theology of Wolfhart Pannenberg" (PhD diss., Rice University, 1984).

53 See Roger E. Olson, *Arminian Theology: Myths and Realities* (Downers Grove, IL: InterVarsity Press, 2006) and *Against Calvinism* (Grand Rapids: Zondervan, 2011).

1994. Truett is not listed as an official Southern Baptist seminary, but instead identifies with the Cooperative Baptists (a more recent group of progressives who departed from the SBC). Further biographical and personal information on Roger Olson can be found at his blog: "My Evangelical Arminian Theological Musings."[54]

Among the many academic writings of Roger Olson, the two more pertinent to the study of evangelicalism are reference volumes edited by Olson.[55] They, along with Randall Balmer's volume, are the most easily accessible one-stop reference books for those who want to learn more on North American evangelicalism.

Now, let us take a close look at Olson's postconservative evangelicalism. At first reading, many of the standard theological or confessional categories that seem to be easily applied to evangelicals do not appear on Olson's list as essentials. There is a breadth, organizationally and doctrinally, that allows for "both ACCC [American Council of Christian Churches]-type and NAE-type evangelicals," meaning the more conservatives and the "mainline" of evangelicals can indeed coexist, but the two organizations would not have fellowship with one another and would even act as rivals or criticize the other as being either too conservative or too liberal.[56] Like the other representative views within the spectrum, Olson's postconservative evangelicalism holds to the four emphases of Bebbington's evangelical quadrilateral, and, like Stackhouse, Olson adds a fifth element: respect for historic, Christian orthodoxy. Further, on page 178, Olson provides case studies and explanations for his position of affirming "unity" and not "uniformity." He then provides

---

54 See www.patheos.com/blogs/rogereolson/biography-2. Accessed 30 May 2019.
55 See Roger E. Olson, *Pocket History of Evangelical Theology* (Downers Grove, IL: IVP Academic, 2007) and *The Westminster Handbook to Evangelical Theology* (Louisville: Westminster John Knox Press, 2004). Also, see Randall Balmer's *Encyclopedia of Evangelicalism*, revised ed. (Waco, TX: Baylor University Press, 2004).
56 Bauder et al., *Four Views on the Spectrum of Evangelicalism*, 168.

the names of those doctrines widely affirmed by conservative evangelicals which, according to Olson, are "threatening to divide evangelicalism today."[57] Among the doctrines more conservative evangelicals hold and insist on others confessing are inerrancy (full), penal substitution, common ground with Roman Catholics, and open theism. While we might view the positions of Olson and easily label them "liberal," Olson crafts a nuanced and precise theological treatise in the process of critiquing and constructing the evangelical ethos. His section in the book is well written and provides a more than adequate description of what he calls "postconservative evangelicalism."

Now that we have covered all four positions within the spectrum, it is now our turn to reflect upon and recognize the differences among them. As we consider the categories, positions, and definitions, we can also add the context of where we live and minister. Culture is never "free size" or "one size fits all." One of the larger challenges in the writing of this textbook is to make it global, far beyond the title's "transpacific." As you consider the four views within the spectrum, be careful to fit your conclusions within your own cultural context. Give them some "meat," so to speak. Make your reflection incarnate.

Now, we turn to the Bible to hear God speak, since "His divine power has given us everything we need for a godly life through our knowledge of him who called us by his own glory and goodness. Through these he has given us his very great and precious promises, so that through them you may participate in the divine nature, having escaped the corruption in the world caused by evil desires" (2 Peter 1:3–4 NIV). The Bible holds many promises from God to his people. Some collections of Bible verses are even called "Promise Books."[58] From

---

57 Ibid., 182–186.
58 One example is the small book compiled by David Wilkerson, *The Jesus Person Promise Book: Over 800 Promises from the Word of God* (Glendale, CA: Regal, 1972). I can remember buying my own copy at a Christian bookstore in Kansas City and carrying it with me through my time in the US Army.

the basis of these promises or covenantal phrases come key words, some words standing out as more essential than others. We might call these either "foundational" or "fundamental." From the foundation of defining key words, as they are based upon Scripture, comes the ability to build wide and high. Two of the fundamentals of this book are revival and evangelism. In fact, evangelicalism itself, and, in this text specifically, "transpacific" evangelicalism, is an integration of two basic thrusts: revival and evangelism. First, we will begin to define revival.

Perhaps a few words are necessary to explain why revival precedes evangelism. The biblical pattern was set in the Gospels and the book of Acts. Already, we have looked at Luke 24 and the Great Commission text in that Gospel. Let us consider the final words of Christ to his disciples again: "I am going to send you what my Father has promised; but stay in the city until you have been clothed with power from on high" (Luke 24:49 NIV). The Great Commission is a command to go and evangelize. In this passage, the emphasis is upon preaching to all nations, beginning at Jerusalem. Before disciples are sent anywhere to preach, however, the Holy Spirit must arrive with the power for Jesus's people to do evangelism. Acts 1:4 repeats these instructions to stay where you are, just prior to the words of receiving "power" and being "witnesses" in the Great Commission text of Acts 1:8. Let us look carefully at Acts 1:4 (NIV): "On one occasion, while he was eating with them, he gave them this command: 'Do not leave Jerusalem, but wait for the gift my Father promised, which you have heard me speak about.'" The fulfillment of this promise of receiving power happens on the day of Pentecost (Acts 2:1–4), and results in the disciples themselves beginning to preach and going in evangelism to the "ends of the earth." What appears overly simplistic is not profound in human terms, but proves providential. God's plan is for power to precede evangelism; in other words, revival first and evangelism second. If it were the opposite and evangelism commenced upon the Lord issuing his command with his people immediately moving, rather than waiting and receiving the power of the Holy Spirit, evangelism would be nothing more than marketing or propaganda, selling holy merchandise or vain repetition of meaningless words. We should know our Lord's attitude toward both; the former was a whip in hand and the latter was a stern rebuke. Now, we begin with our definitions of *revival*.

First we must understand the distinctive meanings of three words, all related to one another: *renewal, revival,* and *awakening*. Renewal can mean what happens to an individual when spiritual change occurs, or it can cover a larger area within the church's life, such as liturgical renewal or a shift in theology or religious experience. One example in the twentieth-century context is charismatic renewal. *Revival* is the word selected for this study, as it notes a more local and occasional move of the Holy Spirit bringing about conversion in sinners and sanctification among believers. I have avoided using the term *revivalism*, as it denotes an extreme expression of revival that is related to either a personality (evangelist) or methodology (new measures). I want to maintain an emphasis on the divine aspects of revivals rather than view human inspiration or leadership as the key ingredient to any revival.

Further, an awakening is seen as larger than a revival, being more expansive in both geography and time. An example is the Great Awakening, a term used by later historians of religion to describe the interdenominational and intercolonial revivals of religion that peaked around 1740–42 in North America. In addition, an awakening will make changes in the larger society and culture, not merely within churches.

Within the history of evangelicalism, especially as noted from the eighteenth century to the twenty-first century, various definitions of *revival* have emerged. In the eighteenth century, during the Great Awakening in North America, Jonathan Edwards's definition is central.[59] In the nineteenth century, the shift was made from revival to what is now known as revivalism. One person most responsible for this shift was Charles Grandison Finney.

Within the North American context, we can find two quite different definitions of *revival*, one by Jonathan Edwards (1703–1758) and the other by Charles Grandison Finney (1792–1875). It appears from a quick reading that Edwards places the emphasis on divine working while Finney sees it more as a matter of human planning and effort.

One simply could note a more Reformed/Calvinist theology in the view of highlighting the supernatural working of God versus a more Arminian theology in the view of the role of human efforts in praying for and in planning revivals. It is true that many in local churches in the mid-twentieth century interpreted revival as two periods of additional meetings with a guest preacher; thus, people would speak of spring revival and fall revival meetings. But in the first decade of the twentieth century, the period we will focus on in our study, revival became more of a geography, where God was supernaturally and directly working in people's lives, with prayer being the seed of revival that was sown faithfully by God's people as preparation for God's outpouring. In addition to the geography of revival, we will note later some names and biographies of revival evangelists (American and Korean) during the twentieth century. Global revivals also have shared a common feature of being "accompanied by a lowering of racial, gender, and class

---

59 During the Great Awakening there was a diversity of theologies of revival; Jonathan Edwards represents one that is more historically noted. See Robert W. Caldwell III, *Theologies of the American Revivalists: From Whitefield to Finney* (Downers Grove, IL: IVP Academic, 2017).

barriers."⁶⁰ This will be most vividly seen in the Azusa Street Revival in Los Angeles (1906–1915).

Now, let us look back to Edwards in the eighteenth century. In *A Narrative of Surprising Conversions*, Edwards links revival and evangelism in the same order and with equal emphasis as in the book of Acts:

> This remarkable *pouring out of the Spirit of God*, which thus extended from one end to the other of this county, was not confined to it, but many places in Connecticut have partaken in the same mercy. For instance, the first parish in Windsor, under the pastoral care of the Rev. Mr. Marsh, was thus blest about the same time as we in Northampton, while we had *no knowledge* of each other's circumstances. There has been a very great ingathering of souls to *Christ* in that place, . . . there having been *four or five* seasons of the *pouring out of the Spirit* to the *general* awakening of the people there.⁶¹

Edwards further describes how the Holy Spirit is working beyond initial conversion. "And God's people who were formerly converted have now partaken of the same shower of divine blessing—in the *renewing, strengthening, edifying influences;* and the work here has also been plainly the same with that of the other places which have been mentioned, as partaking of the same blessing."⁶² For Edwards, revival has two spiritual aims: to sanctify Christians and to convert the lost. Edwards relied upon his meeting with George Whitefield as inspiration for

---

60 Michael J. McClymond, ed. *Embodying the Spirit: New Perspectives on North American Revivalism* (Baltimore: Johns Hopkins University Press, 2004), 25.
61 Edwards, Jonathan, *Jonathan Edwards: On Revival* (Edinburgh: The Banner of Truth Trust, 1965), 17.
62 Ibid., 53.

a fuller view of revival. It not only sharpened his view of the work of God but also helped Edwards to adjust his preaching and prayer life.

In summary, we can quote Hansen and Woodbridge as they write on Edwards: "Edwards did not support everything he heard about in connection with the revival that became known as the Great Awakening. He contributed a set of criteria for discerning a true work of God that helped us write this book. According to Edwards, a true revival exalts Jesus Christ, provokes Satan, prioritizes the Bible, and inspires love."[63]

After viewing Edwards and the Great Awakening, we make a turn, seemingly an extreme one, and arrive in the nineteenth century, assembled with Rev. Charles Grandison Finney. In his *Lectures on Revivals of Religion*, Finney states clearly that means employed by people, not a miracle sent by God, are what bring about revivals. "A revival is not a miracle, nor dependent on a miracle, in any sense. It is purely philosophical result of the right use of the constituted means--as much as any other effect produced by the application of means."[64]

Regrettably, Charles Grandison Finney has been misunderstood as the exact opposite extreme from the Edwardsean understanding of revival, with Finney's view often interpreted as revival being no more than a human work of emotional excitement. Robert Caldwell places the focus on Finney himself, not on the misunderstandings that have arisen from public opinion.

When we actually peer into his works, however, we find a robust and zealously activist revival theology, one that was forged in the controversy that swelled up around his early revivals. Finney's revival theology was not the one-of-a-kind system that dropped from the sky, but was actually an extension of the

---

63   Hansen, Collin, and John Woodbridge, *A God-Sized Vision: Revival Stories that Stretch and Stir* (Grand Rapids: Zondervan, 2010), 182.
64   Charles G. Finney, *Lectures on Revivals of Religion*, 2nd ed. (New York: Leavitt, Lord, and Company, 1835), 12.

Edwardsean tradition. Finney essentially embraced the scaffolding of Edwardsean theology but rejected one of its central components: its affirmation of moral inability.[65]

In summary, Charles Finney notes the important relationship between revival first and evangelism second, saying, "It is altogether improbable that religion will ever make progress among 'heathen' nations except through the influence of revivals."[66]

Although defining *revival* should be somewhat easier than understanding the term *evangelicalism*, there remains a spectrum of definitions that include everything God and/or the church does to a more limited understanding of an intense, sustained period of spiritual experience by large numbers of people. More recently, in the 1990s, when revival broke out in Toronto with "holy laughter," evangelicals began to ask the question whether or not this was a genuine revival in line with the preceding revivals of the eighteenth to early twentieth centuries.[67]

The discussion showed up in the September 11, 1995, issue of *Christianity Today*. In an article by Richard F. Lovelace (professor of church history at Gordon-Conwell Theological Seminary), we hear again the view of Jonathan Edwards on the revivals of the eighteenth century, later called the Great Awakening. Referring to Jonathan Edwards as an expert witness on revivals, Lovelace notes that the local revival in Edwards's congregation in Northampton, Massachusetts, was not an isolated incident. Rather, it showed itself as a pattern of sacred history, "alternat[ing] between periods of spiritual decline, relentless as the gravity of sin, and eras of grace, in which the

---

[65] Caldwell, *Theologies of the American Revivalists*, 165–166.
[66] Charles Grandison Finney, *Lectures on Revivals of Religion*, ed. William G. McLoughlin (Cambridge: Harvard University Press, 1960), 12.
[67] Two articles that compare the "Toronto Blessing" with the Great Awakening of the eighteenth century were John D. Hannah's "Jonathan Edwards, the Toronto Blessing, and the Spiritual Gifts: Are the Extraordinary Ones Actually the Ordinary Ones?" *Trinity Journal*, Vol. 17, No. 2 (Fall 1996): 167–189, and D. Bruce Hindmarsh's "The 'Toronto Blessing' and the Protestant Evangelical Awakening of the Eighteenth Century Compared," *Crux*, Vol. 31, No. 4 (December 1995): 3–13.

Holy Spirit is poured out on the people of God, enabling them for spiritual warfare that will take ground from the flesh, the world, and the Devil."[68] For Edwards, genuine revival has "five biblical marks." It "exalts Jesus Christ; it attacks the powers of darkness; it exalts the Holy Scriptures; it lifts up sound doctrine; and it promotes love to God and man." [69]

As we see with the definition of *evangelicalism*, which has been divided into two sides (Presbyterian and Pentecostal), the revival theology of the eighteenth and nineteenth centuries in the US can also be viewed as "basically Reformed theology (Calvinism) cast in a pietistic accent."[70]

In the Korean context, two diverse views of revival/revivalism are represented by two different evangelical leaders: Kil Seonju and Lee Yongho.[71] Kirsteen Kim mentions that Ryu Tongshik, a scholar of religion in Korea, views the revival movement as being either "paternal" or "maternal." Kil Seonju represents the paternal and Lee Yongho represents the maternal.[72] Chapter 5 will take a closer look at revivals in the early twentieth century and compare the Great Revival at Pyeongyang (1907) with the Azusa Street Revival (1906) to arrive at a transpacific view of revival.

In summary, while revival is sometimes viewed as a supernatural intervention of God, others see it merely as a planned

---

68   Richard F. Lovelace, "The Surprising Works of God, Jonathan Edwards on revival, then and now," *Christianity Today*, Vol. 39, No. 10 (September 1, 1995): 30.
69   Lovelace, "The Surprising Works of God," 30–31.
70   Caldwell, *Theologies of the American Revivalists*, 19.
71   In order to make it easier and more contextual, I will be using the Korean-designed Revised Romanization of Korean (2000) system for transliterating names and titles in hangeul, rather than the older, and in my opinion cumbersome, McCune-Reischauer romanization (1937) system. There are only a few exceptions: I will be using the Latin letter "K" to represent the initial "ㄱ" in Korean surnames, like Kil rather than Gil and Kim rather than Gim. Also, I will be using "Lee" rather than "Yi" for the common Korean surname "이." Also, I will follow the Korean and Japanese cultural name order, surname first and given name second.
72   Kirsteen Kim, "Holy Spirit Movements in Korean—Paternal or Maternal? Reflections on the Analysis of Ryu Tong-Shik (Yu Tong-Shik)," *Exchange*, Vol. 35, No. 2 (2006): 154.

event that "would render the normal movements of the Spirit in salvation impossible. The call for the evangelist, under those conditions, also reveals the fact that the expectation of the church, to a great extent, is toward the man that is invited, rather than toward the Holy Spirit and His appointed ministry through the church itself."[73]

We are looking at evangelism rather than mission for two simple reasons: mission can be viewed either too narrowly or too broadly to be of any help when we attempt to connect it with revival in God's eternal plan for the redemption of the lost. *Mission* is too narrow when defined as exclusively cross-cultural evangelism. It is too broad when we consider the comments of Stephen Neill, mission historian and bishop, who simply wrote, "If everything is mission, nothing is mission."[74] Part of the reason for the ever-expanding definition of *mission* is the field of missiology, especially among Roman Catholic and ecumenical Protestant scholars. Three terms are now basic to an understanding of missiology or mission studies in the twenty-first century. The three terms are here in order from the broader to the more narrow understandings of mission: *Missio Dei*, *Mission*, and *Missions*.

While this conversation seems to be a matter of defining categories carefully in describing mission, it has resulted in less dependence on the actual ministry of evangelism. In some cases, evangelism is removed completely from mission. For our study, then, it is imperative that we retain evangelism both in word and in practice.

The basic definitions of *evangelism* are initially reliant upon the biblical texts we call "Great Commission" texts. They are Matthew 28:16–20, Mark 16:14–18, Luke 24:46–48, John 20:19–23, and Acts 1:6–11. Evangelical and ecumenical theologians have

---

[73] Lewis Sperry Chafer, *True Evangelism* (New York: Gospel Publishing House, 1911), 19.
[74] Stephen Neill, *Creative Tension* (London: Edinburgh House Press, 1959), 81.

contributed their own understandings of evangelism to construct clear definitions. Evangelical theologian and historian J. I. Packer defines evangelism by saying, "Wherever, and by whatever means, the gospel is communicated with a view to conversion, there you have evangelism."[75] Sri Lankan Methodist D. T. Niles has offered a unique definition of evangelism as "one beggar telling another beggar where he found bread."[76]

Hans Kasdorf (a Mennonite Brethren missiologist) provides a more descriptive definition, which links revival with evangelism: "All believers have the power of the Holy Spirit in their lives and are, therefore, living witnesses to give expression in relationships with others of the divine life within. As believers witness by *telling, being, and doing*—and even by dying for their faith—unbelievers become believers."[77]

Irish Methodist theologian William "Billy" Abraham—in an attempt to provide evangelism a central place in theology—has first noted that evangelism is, in his view, not merely proclamation of the gospel or church growth, but evangelism is simply and mainly "initiation into the kingdom of God."[78]

William Packard, in his *Evangelism in America: From Tents to TV*, defines *evangelism* as "any type of conversionary activity that tries to affect an authentic change in someone from the state of thinking and feeling to another."[79]

Finally, from the annals of the Oriental Missionary Society (now known as One Mission Society, hereinafter abbreviated as OMS) we can hear E. A. Kilbourne (1865–1928) in his *Great Commission*. In his chapter titled "Pentecostal Evangelism,"

---

75 J. I. Packer, *Evangelism & the Sovereignty of God* (Downers Grove, IL: InterVarsity Press, 1961), 57.
76 Clinton M. Marsh, *Evangelism is...* (Louisville, KY: Geneva Press, 1997), 31.
77 Hans Kasdorf, "The Anabaptist Approach to Mission," in *Anabaptism and Mission*, ed. Wilbert R. Shenk (Scottsdale, PA: Herald Press, 1984), 69.
78 William J. Abraham, *The Logic of Evangelism* (Grand Rapids: Wm. B. Eerdmans, 1989), 13.
79 William Packard, *Evangelism in America: From Tents to TV* (New York: Paragon House, 1988), 21.

Kilbourne makes a strong case for the failure of missions at the beginning of the twentieth century (and still in the twenty-first century) as being due primarily to a lack of power in missions. We certainly have the technology, the know-how, and the transportation, and we can get to the ends of the earth in a matter of hours now; but when we arrive, there is no power, no Pentecost.[80] Revival and evangelism go together like bread and wine: the body and blood of our Savior.

---

80 E. A. Kilbourne, "Pentecostal Evangelism," in *Great Commission* (Tokyo: Oriental Missionary Society, 1913), 61–67.

3

Tracking Time

In this chapter we will look at time, its eras and centuries, and even its months and days. I realize that dates are one of the more difficult parts of studying history, and perhaps the one reason many are turned away or, to use the American vernacular, "turned off" by the study of the past, even when it happens to be our own story.

What might assist us in studying the history of evangelicalism in the twentieth century is to see how time stretched over this movement and shaped it within the past century. First, we can look at the bigger picture and see the two millennia of Christian history. Those two thousand years have been divided into the three standard eras labeled "ancient," "medieval," and "modern." The ancient period lasted roughly five hundred years, the medieval one thousand years, and the modern five hundred years. We will not be putting an end date on the modern, for this is not a philosophical debate over modern and postmodern, and some discussion even suggests that postmodern is really modern wearing a new set of clothes.

In addition to seeing the larger picture with the eras outlined, two persons, or actually theologians, stand out as makers of change (turning points) between two eras. First, the figure of Augustine (354–430) hovers over the line between ancient and medieval. Second, Luther (1483–1546) sits astride medieval and modern. However, our attention is focused not on eras alone but on the most recent past century: the twentieth. When we consider the transition between the nineteenth and twentieth centuries, we can say technically that it officially began on January 1, 1901, but the evangelical movement was already in transition prior to that date.[81]

We must go back twenty years to view the religious developments in America and Korea that began the "long twentieth century" of transpacific evangelicalism.[82] Two movements within late nineteenth-century evangelicalism in America birthed transpacific evangelicalism and even, one could say, global Pentecostalism within the larger tent of evangelicalism. On the American side are the two developments of "radical holiness" and "radical evangelicalism." Let me explain these two radicals before we address the start of evangelical missions in Korea.

The last two decades of the nineteenth century saw the rise and spread of renewal movements within the larger nineteenth-century evangelical and Holiness movements. For both forms of radicals (evangelical and Holiness), there was a determination to do mission more urgently in the last hour and to usher in the second coming of Christ. Thus, mission and eschatology

---

81 By following the dates of January 1, 1901, until December 31, 2000, we have a "calendar century," a more fluid way of viewing time by periodization and the viewing of turning points in history. See Jürgen Osterhammel, *The Transformation of the World: A Global History of the Nineteenth Century* (Princeton: Princeton University Press, 2014), 45–58.

82 The idea of "short" or "long" twentieth century comes from economic history rather than literary or religious history. Eric Hobsbawm views the "short" one as 1914–1989, while the "long" one (1870–present) is from Giovanni Arrighi. See Hobsbawm, *The Age of Extremes: A History of the World, 1914–1991* (New York: Vintage, 1996) and Giovanni Arrighi, *The Long Twentieth Century: Money, Power, and the Origins of Our Times*, 2nd ed. (New York: Verso, 2010). As we will see with Kenneth Scott Latourette's "Great Century" ending in 1914, his division of time also would make for a "short twentieth century."

became partners within evangelicalism. A significant part of radical evangelicalism was turning away from established colleges and seminaries toward the newly arising Bible schools, institutes, and colleges. There was an urgency for preparation to do mission in the majority world, and part of that was receiving missionary tongues, in order to bypass language school on the mission field. These two radical forms of Protestantism in North America (both Holiness and evangelical) are viewed as either overlapping or as being separate but focused on more drastic change within their respective faith traditions.

While the Holiness movement in North America can be traced to the 1830s in both New York, with the ministry of the Palmers, and Ohio, with the revivalism of Charles Finney, the organization that represented the Holiness movement was the National Camp Meeting Association for the Promotion of Holiness, first officially meeting in Vineland, New Jersey, (1867) and in Manheim, Pennsylvania (1868).[83] As seen with evangelicalism, movements cannot be easily segmented into denominations or institutions. While the "tame holiness" folk continued to view the National Camp Meeting Association as representing them both theologically and spiritually, the movement had a vibrancy that persisted beyond the bounds of Methodism. Already others (non-Methodists) were experiencing entire sanctification and were taking it back to their own churches. They included Baptists, Congregationalists, Episcopalians, Presbyterians, and Quakers. These non-Methodists had their own creeds and confessions as well as their own church sacraments and polity. The establishing of state-association allowed the Holiness movement to morph into an interdenominational

---

83   Two important studies on the National Holiness Association are Charles Edwin Jones, *Perfectionist Persuasion: The Holiness Movement and American Methodism, 1867–1936*, ATLA Monograph Series, 5 (Metuchen, NJ: Scarecrow, 1974) and Delbert R. Rose, *Vital Holiness: A Theology of Christian Experience: Interpreting the Historic Wesleyan Message*, 3rd ed. (Minneapolis: Bethany Fellowship, 1975).

movement. The actual transition of mainline churches toward the ecumenical movement of the twentieth century was more deliberate and planned, while the Holiness movement seemingly just happened.

While the Holiness movement seemed to be organized solely into the National Holiness Association (NHA), radicals were on the fringe (or margins) and began redefining the experience of sanctification; revivalism became the new standard of spirituality. Here are four areas where "holiness" began to dissent from "straight" holiness: ecclesiology, religious experience, eschatology, and personal ethics or holiness.

First, in the area of ecclesiology were a number of Holiness followers who would never leave the Methodist Church and saw holiness as part of John Wesley's theological message and religious experience. Meanwhile, increasing numbers of people experienced holiness outside the Methodist Church. It seemed, in fact, that true believers in holiness should stem from the mainline (and liberal) Methodist Church. The rising popularity and necessity of state-level holiness brought about various associations as radical holiness continued to outgrow the boundaries of the Methodist Church. Two of the early state associations were Iowa (1879) and Georgia (1883).[84]

The second standard of spirituality at this time was the growing dissatisfaction with the status quo. The "tame" holiness experience was more consistently viewed by radicals as negative and nothing more than a "formal" and "fashionable" religion.[85] Thus, religious experience became an area of radical reform.

"Radical holiness" folk referred to themselves as "radical"

---

84 Charles Edwin Jones, *Perfectionist Persuasion: The Holiness Movement and American Methodism, 1867–1936*, ATLA Monograph Series, 5 (Metuchen, NJ: Scarecrow, 1974), 49–50. Another text that covers the history of the movement is Delbert R. Rose, *Vital Holiness: A Theology of Christian Experience: Interpreting the Historic Wesleyan Message*, 3rd ed. (Minneapolis: Bethany Fellowship, 1975).

85 See B. H. Irwin, "Pyrophobia," *The Way of Faith* (October 28, 1896): 2.

and "true holiness" and, at times, used the term "full gospel." The determination of such groups was to either move toward a higher experience of the Spirit, more commonly referred to as "baptism in the Holy Spirit," or to even go beyond that and experience multiple baptisms, as was the case with Benjamin Hardin Irwin and the Fire-Baptized Holiness Church.

The Bible, according to Irwin, emphasized the unlimited potential of religious experience rather than any structure or limitation to experience.[86] There remained the promise of much more, far beyond a second or third experience of grace. More important than the number, as if some structure or standardization of religious experience existed, was that the experience be "definite." Here is Irwin's testimony:

> He gave me the definite baptism with fire, and I have had it for over four years and it is an abiding experience: and I know where that took place. I was out in Oklahoma in a sod house, about 10 or 11 o'clock. Praise God forever and ever for the real experience of the baptism of fire. And I know where I got the dynamite. I had been reading Benjamin Abbott's Journal, and reading about the slaying power that he and other early Methodists had, and I asked God to give me the dynamite and He gave it to me, and I have it still tonight, and still I am seeking for more. I praise the Lord for these

---

86 One of Irwin's proof texts was Ephesians 3:20: "Now unto him that is able to do exceeding abundantly above all that we ask or think, according to the power that worketh in us" (KJV). His commentary of that verse follows: "I am amazed at its fathomless depths. I am determined to experience all there is in this marvelous promise. It will take me to all eternity to do it; but I am going to keep delving into its measureless depths until I reach the bottom. And when I find any one [sic] who has a richer, better experience than I have, I shall redouble my efforts, and seek the more earnestly, not for his experience, but for one as deep and blessed." B. H. Irwin, "Pyrophobia," *The Way of Faith* (October 28, 1896): 2.

definite epochs in my experience. I praise God that He saves me from limiting the Holy One of Israel, and it makes me feel good when I think that the Spirit has free access to my soul, bless His name forever and ever![87]

Irwin's view of an intensified, radical experience of holiness (red-hot holiness) continues to present a challenge to both Holiness and Pentecostal adherents to a continual, experience-based spirituality. In fact, Irwin and others had already experienced fourth, fifth, and sixth "baptisms." According to Melvin Dieter, Irwin fits within the "experimental primitivism" category of radical holiness.[88] Indeed, the emphasis for Irwin is not ecclesiology or eschatology, but it instead lies on religious experience or experimentation.

A third change from straight to radical holiness was eschatology, involving a belief shift from postmillennial to premillennial.[89] Eschatology was changing not only from "post" to "pre," but also its very position as the last chapter in systematic theologies made way for a primacy on hoping for and preparing for the imminent return of the Lord. The number of books on the second coming at the end of the nineteenth century into the early twentieth century indicates this eschatological shift. As a result of the new emphasis upon eschatology, with the design to proclaim the gospel until the last moment, many within radical holiness abandoned the postmillennial plans and programs for social reform and adopted the premillennial call to urgent evangelism. In the midst of a radical emphasis

---

[87] B. H. Irwin, "Whirlwind," part 1, *The Way of Faith*: 2.
[88] Melvin E. Dieter, "Primitivism in the American Holiness Tradition," *Wesleyan Theological Journal*, Vol. 30, No. 1 (Spring 1995): 78–91.
[89] "Straight holiness people" was used by the side opposed to "radical holiness" as a means of self-identification. See A. L. Byers, *Birth of a Reformation, or The Life and Labors of Daniel S. Warner* (1921 reprint, Guthrie, OK: Faith Publishing, House, 1966), 320.

on world evangelization, the "eleventh hour" became the new cry of a vigilant religion.[90] The sanctioning of premillennial thought in the 1890s was a significant step in the establishment of radical holiness.[91]

The fourth emphasis was upon "lifestyle" or "personal holiness." Radical holiness pushed standards of behavior, how a sanctified saint should dress and act in this corrupt world.[92] As radical holiness people called themselves "true holiness," "full gospel," and "Bible standard," it was clear that they were prepared to look the part.[93] Matters related to attire and adornment ranked as highly as the distinctive doctrine of an instantaneous second work of grace. The wearing of jewelry, neckties for men, and makeup and bobbed hair for women were all prohibited by a religious movement that realized the world was not their home.

These two late nineteenth-century movements (radical evangelicalism and radical holiness) were assisted by the rise and spread of both populism and the more focused Populist party in the Midwest and the South.[94] This is not well documented, since historians of religion tended to assume that conservative believers were distanced from both political offices and even the voting booth, holding a non-political position, and resisting the secular and unholy powers of government with the sword of

---

90 For more on the "eleventh-hour," see F. L. Chapell, *The Eleventh-Hour Laborers: A Series of Articles from "The Watchword"* (South Nyack, NY: Christian Alliance, 1898).

91 William Kostlevy, *Holy Jumpers: Evangelicals and Radicals in Progressive Era America* (New York: Oxford University Press, 2010), 17–36.

92 For a discussion of this important, though much maligned, aspect of radical holiness, see Wallace Thornton, *Radical Righteousness: Personal Ethics and the Development of the Holiness Movement* (Salem, OH: Schmul Publishing, 1998).

93 For the references to "true holiness," see Fannie Birdsall, "True Holiness," *The Pentecost Herald* (March 15, 1896): 5; W. S. Craig, "True Holiness," *The Pentecost Herald* (February 1895): 1; and T. H. Nelson, "True Holiness," *The Pentecost Herald* (October 15, 1898): 2.

94 See Randall J. Stephens, "The Convergence of Populism, Religion, and the Holiness-Pentecostal Movements: A Review of the Historical Literature," *Fides et historia*, Vol. 32, No. 1 (Winter/Spring 2000): 51–64.

the Spirit. This perceived non-political position of evangelicalism (and fundamentalism) or "Christ versus culture," possibly believed until the rise of the Religious Right or Moral Majority in the 1970s, makes it very clear that politics is not separated from evangelicalism (and fundamentalism).[95]

While time itself is divided into millennia and centuries, the writing of national histories is designed to fit with the dynastic patterns or reigns of individual monarchs. Thus, in Korea, the majority of Western history's modern period is covered by the Joseon dynasty (1392–1897) or in China with the Qing dynasty (1644–1912). Beyond the writing of traditional histories that followed the dynastic or monarchial periods of separate kingdoms or nation states, both global and world history became the new approaches in the late twentieth century. Global and world histories greatly influenced the standard periodization of history and adjusted how people consider boundaries (geography), with transnationalism prevailing over older national histories. This remaking of historical periods provided the boundaries.

Before further addressing the differences between world history and global history, it might be helpful to take a quick look at the nineteenth century and how it stands out within two millennia of Christian history. Since we are starting our history twenty years before this, let us look again at the nineteenth century as a whole. In his seven-volume *A History of the Expansion of Christianity*, Kenneth Scott Latourette devotes three volumes to the nineteenth century, termed the "Great Century," and offers the initial dates of 1800–1914 (later 1815–1914).

As Latourette introduces the Great Century in another survey of church history, we begin to understand his view of the nineteenth century's unique destiny as it relates to world evangelism.

---

[95] For a view of the "Moral Majority" from mainline Protestantism, see John L. Kater, *Christians on the Right: The Moral Majority in Perspective* (New York: Seabury, 1982).

The ninety-nine years from 1815 to 1914 formed a distinct period in the history of mankind and of Christianity. They, rather than the conventional 1800 to 1900, were the nineteenth century. Because of a combination of geographic expansion, inner vitality, and the effect upon mankind as a whole, they constituted the greatest century which Christianity had thus far known. This achievement of Christianity was associated with a prodigious burst of creativity in Western European peoples, the traditional Christendom. It was paralleled by movements which seemed to threaten the very existence of the faith and by challenges which called forth all its inner resources.[96]

According to Latourette, mission work prospered by both the relative absence of wars in this century and the presence of Western colonialism and international commerce. Church historians have noted a similar context in the first century to promote the idea that early Christianity benefitted from, or was even made possible by, the advent of Pax Romana and the newly constructed roadways through the Roman empire. This sounds reasonable, but some historians are not taking a close-enough look at the first and nineteenth centuries to discover whether or not those cultural conditions were truly present on a global scale. The general absence of major battles and wars in Europe was true for the nineteenth century, especially after the end of the Napoleonic Wars in 1815, but was not true for China in the middle of the nineteenth century. China experienced the Taiping Rebellion, where up to thirty million lives were lost.[97] And the Dungan Revolt (1862–1877), fought between the Qing dynasty and Chinese Muslims, witnessed the loss of up

---

96 Kenneth Scott Latourette, *A History of Christianity, A.D. 1500–A.D. 1975*, Vol. 2, rev. ed (San Francisco: Harper Collins, 1975; Peabody, MA: Prince Press, 2005), 1063.

97 On the Taiping Rebellion, see Carl S. Kilcourse, *Taiping Theology: The Localization of Christianity in China, 1843-64* (New York: Palgrave Macmillan, 2016) and Jonathan D. Spence, *God's Chinese Son: The Taiping Heavenly Kingdom of Hong Xiuquan* (New York: W.W. Norton, 1996).

to twelve million lives.[98] With around forty-two million lives lost in China, it seems surprising that a scholar who wrote a history of China would not be at least that aware of modern Chinese history.[99]

Aligned with the writings of Kenneth Scott Latourette and his understanding of the Great Century (1815–1914) are Sherwood Eddy's (1871–1963) earlier four "remarkable facts" of world Christianity. They are geographical spread, contextualization (rooted in the people of particular nations), ecumenism, and a world influence beyond Christendom.[100] Another church historian who focused on world evangelization was Bishop Stephen Charles Neill (1900–1984). In his *A History of Christian Missions*, Neill notes the dates for a longer nineteenth century as being from 1789 (French Revolution) until 1914 (outbreak of World War I). Within this longer century, "two great changes made possible the beginning of a new era." The first was psychological, including the ideologies of colonialism and imperialism. The second was scientific and economic, including new forms of power: steam and electricity.[101]

With the nineteenth century identified as the Great Century, due to the expansion of the church through world missions, the twentieth century has received different names to show its unique place in history. The first real media mogul in America, Henry Robinson Luce (1898–1967), was the son of Presbyterian missionaries to China.[102] Owner of *Time, Life, Fortune, Sports Illustrated*, and other media outlets, he labeled the twentieth

---

98 Jonathan Neaman Lipman, *Familiar Strangers: A History of Muslims in Northwest China* (Seattle: University of Washington Press, 1998).
99 Kenneth Scott Latourette, *The Chinese: Their History and Culture* (New York: Macmillan, 1934).
100 Rick Nutt, "G. Sherwood Eddy and the Attitudes of Protestants in the United States toward Global Mission," *Church History*, Vol. 66, No. 3 (September 1997): 518.
101 Stephen Neill, *A History of Christian Missions (The Penguin History of the Church)*, 2nd ed (London: Penguin Books, 1986), 208–209.
102 See Alan Brinkley, *The Publisher: Henry Luce and His American Century* (New York: Alfred A. Knopf, 2010).

century the "American Century."[103] This was due to America's rising role as a global power and later superpower, in rivalry with the USSR, and at the end of the twentieth century as sole superpower (or hyperpower) on planet earth.

More in line with the history of Pentecostalism is Vinson Synan's naming the twentieth century the "Century of the Holy Spirit."[104] After settling on a renewal emphasis for the entire century, Synan describes each of the many diverse movements within the larger Pentecostal/charismatic family.

To assist in comprehending the differences between world history and global history and discerning how it marks the history of evangelicalism, I will introduce a few distinctions in these seemingly similar historical methodologies.

First comes the distinctive view of world history's handling of relationship with civilization. Civilization (whether Western or other) is posited as a handmaid to Christianity or the church. The second distinctive of world history is its contextualization in a multitude of places and times. While global history might address separately one or two contexts, the understanding is that all nations together comprise the record of the one church, a plurality in unity. I will be relying on the methodology of global history, rather than world history, through this textbook, but at times it might prove difficult to assess the distinctive emphases of each.

---

103 Henry R. Luce, "The American Century," *Life* (February 17, 1941): 61–65.
104 Vinson Synan, *The Century of the Holy Spirit: 100 Years of Pentecostal and Charismatic Renewal, 1901-2001* (Nashville: Thomas Nelson, 2001).

4

Endings and Beginnings: The Late Nineteenth Century

From 1880 until 1900, we see both continuity and discontinuity with the earlier evangelicalism of the nineteenth century. First, let us look at what has been termed *radical evangelicalism* combined with the connected religious developments within the end of the nineteenth century.

Four distinctives deserve our attention, in addition to those distinctives we have already discussed in relation to radical holiness. For radical evangelicalism, we can add the Bible School movement, the divine healing movement, the Keswick or Higher Life movement, and the acceleration of global evangelism. Second, we will view the contributions of A. B. Simpson and his fourfold gospel toward the making of evangelical theology. Third, we will visit Chicago and see how D. L. Moody stands as a stalwart representative of nineteenth-century evangelicalism. Finally, we will look at the official beginning of evangelical missions to Korea.

While the term *radical evangelicals* has been used to describe a variety of Christian communities, the writings of Heather

D. Curtis and Gary B. McGee (1945–2008) focus on the late nineteenth-century evangelicals who served as "midwives" of early Pentecostalism in the twentieth century, yet they differ from "radical holiness" in their view of sanctification, holding to the Keswick or Higher Life view rather than the Wesleyan one. For the purposes of this textbook, we will be viewing evangelicals more broadly and inclusive of both Wesleyan and Keswick views of holiness, thus "radical evangelicals" is a preferred term indicating a larger community at the end of the nineteenth century.

The very usage of "radical" to describe any group of Christians can be traced academically to George Hunston Williams (1914–2000), a Unitarian and longtime professor at Harvard, who wrote *The Radical Reformation*. In this work, he studies Anabaptism and provides a new typology and context for understanding why and how Anabaptists were not part of the Protestant Reformation or the Magisterial Reformation (Luther, Zwingli, and Calvin).[105]

An earlier period of American religious history is covered by Stephen A. Marini's *Radical Sects of Revolutionary New England*, where he includes Free Will Baptists, Universalists, and Shakers within the category of radical evangelicals.[106] While the National Association of Free Will Baptists (Arminian view of the atonement) continues in North America as an evangelical body, not many current evangelicals would claim ancestry from either the Universalists or the Shakers.

With a European view and within an earlier period (early nineteenth century) perspective, Timothy Stunt's study of radical evangelicals includes Anthony Norris Groves (1795–1853),

---

105 George Hunston Williams, *The Radical Reformation*, 3rd ed. (Kirksville, MO: Truman State University Press, 2000). The first edition was published in 1962 by Westminster Press (Philadelphia).
106 Stephen A. Marini, *Radical Sects of Revolutionary New England* (Cambridge: Harvard University Press, 1982).

the founder of faith missions; Edward Irving (1792–1834), leader of the Catholic Apostolic Church; John Nelson Darby (1800–1882), leader of the Plymouth Brethren; and Thomas Erskine (1788–1870), a Scottish theologian.[107] The larger picture helps us see how the term *radical evangelicals* can describe a group of more ardent believers in either eschatology (second coming of Christ) or world missions, or of the previously listed four emphases: the Bible School movement, the divine healing movement, the Keswick or Higher Life movement, and the acceleration of global evangelism.

The Bible School movement fits within the larger history of theological education in America more as a renewal movement or even as an alternative to the curriculum and educational forms of traditional seminaries. Briefly reviewing the history of theological education in America shows a reaction to this movement. With nearly four hundred years of history, theological education in America has been challenged greatly in two seemingly contrary directions: orientation and location.

The first is in the area of orientation, with a pair of emphases: theological orthodoxy and cultural diversity. It appears that very few can have both in the fullest measure. But in the American context, both are necessary, and every theological seminary should attempt to find the right mix, meaning a correct understanding of both the Word and the world. For the seminaries on the left side (Protestant liberalism), theological orthodoxy has been too easily abandoned to accommodate every form of ethnic, sexual orientation/gender, and sociopolitical diversity.[108] For those on the right (and also in the center), the desire to maintain theological orthodoxy has meant that lines

---

107 Timothy C. F. Stunt, *From Awakening to Secession: Radical Evangelicals in Switzerland and Britain, 1815–35* (Edinburgh, Scotland: T&T Clark, 2000).

108 Attempts to promote diversity do not reach a level of harmony and happiness for all. Unfortunately, the theological and political conservatives have been excluded from programs of unity in many of the more liberal seminaries. The ideal of tolerance for all is never universal in practice.

are drawn and, at times, walls are built to guard and protect the territory of correct beliefs. But sadly, walls not only guard and protect, they also exclude others (strangers/foreigners/unbelievers).

The second set of emphases are church and academy. It would appear that these two are not really unique to American theological education, but are instead inherent in the very historical rise and development of religious education in medieval Europe, from cathedral schools to universities. But in the American context, with its own history of anti-intellectualism, the resistance to higher education and scholarship has placed theological education in a difficult position between profession and practice.[109] One extreme of this view is that even the words *theology/theological* themselves been rejected by some as sounding too lofty or removed from lived religion.

Another anecdote that might help illustrate the prominence of anti-intellectualism in America is that when people say "seminary," they will sometimes substitute "cemetery," as more than a play on words; it becomes a statement of cultural resistance to highly educated pastors who live in an "ivory tower." Now, with these two sets of emphases, let us give a short history of Protestant theological education in the US.

The history of Protestant theological education in America began with the first few waves of British settlers on the Atlantic coast of Massachusetts. Among the first waves of immigrants were a number of Cambridge-educated Puritan clergy in New England. The history of Anglicanism shows that Oxford tended to be resistant to dissent and supportive of the High Church tradition within the Church of England in the seventeenth

---

109 The still-standard book on anti-intellectualism remains Richard Hofstadter, *Anti-intellectualism in American Life* (New York: Alfred A. Knopf, 1963). Parallel with anti-intellectualism is the rise and growth of American populism as both a political position and a philosophy of life. Populism has gained grounds in the US within the past twenty years, but its real strength was in the 1880s and 1890s.

century. Thus, when those Cambridge-educated clergy decided to join and construct a college, their desire was to continue the esteemed name "Cambridge" on the western side of the Atlantic. Three years after Harvard's founding, when John Harvard, a recently deceased Cambridge graduate and minister, willed both a sizeable amount of money and his entire library (four hundred volumes) to the college, it was renamed Harvard College (1639). Even with the highest ideals at its founding, Harvard experienced a theological downturn when presidents held and led with views at odds with the Puritan fathers. The first turning was toward the more populist Baptists, and, later in the nineteenth century, the new majority of Harvard theology professors were Unitarian or Arminian, bringing the school even further away from its Trinitarian and Reformed roots.

As the population moved west, searching for a new frontier, the educational philosophy seemed based upon the founding of new schools, so the East Coast of the United States began to witness the rise of colleges and universities that soon would rival Harvard. First was Yale (1701), founded with the purpose of educating Congregational clergy. Its high point was when Timothy Dwight (1752–1817) served as its eighth president during years of spiritual revival that would be called the Second Great Awakening (1795–1817). After Yale, Princeton was founded (1746) with the intent of educating Presbyterian ministers. Although these colleges had original purposes of educating clergy or offering theological education, they soon expanded their curricula to include arts, sciences, medicine, law, education, agriculture, and engineering. While none would doubt the elite status of Ivy League universities then or now, for those planning to enter the ministry, an alternate route, the simple apprenticeship model of studying for the ministry under the direction of an experienced and ordained member of the clergy, was viewed as more efficient.

Two cases will help to illustrate this. The first is Jonathan Edwards (1703–1758), called "the last of the Puritans." He began his studies at Yale in 1716 and completed his undergraduate degree, then continued to study for an MA there. However, Edwards's real theological education was not in the halls of Yale but in the study of his grandfather Solomon Stoddard (1643–1729), pastor of the Congregationalist church in Northampton, Massachusetts. Edwards would rise to be called America's greatest philosopher, theologian, and revivalist, undoubtedly a result of both his education at Yale (academy) and Northampton (church). We can see the perfect wedding of the two in Edwards.[110]

The second case of apprenticeship over classical education is Charles G. Finney (1792–1875). Finney never studied at any college, much less an Ivy League one, but first served as an apprentice, studying law. At the age of twenty-nine, he began an apprenticeship for the Presbyterian ministry under the guidance/mentoring of George Washington Gale (1789–1861).[111] Finney questioned some of the teachings contained in the Westminster standards (required for Presbyterian ordination) but was able to affirm that he held to Westminster in relation to its views on the Bible. After a term as a revivalist and pastor, Finney became professor of theology at Oberlin College (Oberlin, Ohio) in 1835. He would continue in that role and later as president at Oberlin. In addition to this, he served as pastor of First Congregational Church in Oberlin for almost forty years, until his death in 1875. If Edwards is a perfect match of both church and academy, then Finney is a perfect

---

110 For a comprehensive study of Edwards, see George M. Marsden, *Jonathan Edwards: A Life* (New Haven: Yale University Press, 2003).
111 Gale himself was a graduate of Union College (1814) and Princeton Theological Seminary (1819).

match of evangelical theology and social reform: the Word and the world, or theological orthodoxy and cultural diversity.[112]

While higher education, most of it within the Christian tradition, began flourishing in America in the seventeenth and eighteenth centuries, the nineteenth century marked the start of freestanding theological seminaries. Some of them were established by denominations, while a few were called "interdenominational" or "nondenominational." The first freestanding (meaning not related to a university) seminary was Andover Theological Seminary (1807).

The Association of Theological Schools (ATS, founded in 1918) is a non-government accrediting agency in North America that includes graduate-level theological seminaries from Protestant, Catholic, and Eastern Orthodox churches, and one Jewish seminary.[113] The list of member seminaries includes the largest one with 3,199 students (Fuller Theological Seminary, Pasadena, California, multidenominational). As I looked through the complete roster of member schools, I noticed that all the larger seminaries (more than one thousand students) are evangelical.

The Bible School movement—as part of radical evangelicalism—arose in the late nineteenth century when American higher education (colleges and universities) became more secularized in their curricula, to include biological evolution and higher criticism of the Bible. As both a reaction to the secularization of colleges and universities and as a means of training persons for ministry in a faster mode, with a more urgent plea for world evangelization, Bible schools began to grow and seemingly multiply from this period into the twentieth century. The first

---

112 For biographical reading on Finney, see Charles E. Hambrick-Stowe, *Charles G. Finney and the Spirit of American Evangelicalism* (Grand Rapids: Wm. B. Eerdmans, 1996) and Keith J. Hardman, *Charles Grandison Finney, 1792–1875* (Grand Rapids: Baker Book House, 1990). Donald W. Dayton's *Rediscovering An Evangelical Heritage: A Tradition and Trajectory of Integrating Piety and Justice*, 2nd ed. (Grand Rapids: Baker Academic, 2014) has a fine chapter titled "Reform in the Life and Thought of Evangelist Charles G. Finney," 61–73.

113 See their website at: https://www.ats.edu/about. Accessed 23 March 2019.

among the Bible schools was Nyack College (1882), founded by A. B. Simpson. Moody Bible Institute (founded in 1886 by D. L. Moody), Johnson Bible College (Knoxville, Tennessee— founded in 1893), and the Free Church Bible Institute and Seminary (founded in 1897 by Evangelical Free Christians) soon followed.[114] Now, more than two hundred Bible colleges exist, and their non-governmental accrediting agency is the Association for Biblical Higher Education (founded in 1947).[115] We now turn to divine healing in American evangelicalism.

A necessary caution is to not confuse "faith healing" with "divine healing." "Faith healing" primarily denotes a process by which a person draws upon his or her own faith, in an autonomous manner, and realizes a physical improvement in health. "Divine healing" indicates that a person places trust in God and either through faith or by the prayer of another, experiences healing. With this definition in mind, Christian Science and Native American spiritualties would be enabled to make claim to faith healing but not to divine healing. The idea of a relationship between the atonement and healing arose in the context of the divine healing movement. A. J. Gordon (1836–1895) and A. B. Simpson (1843–1919) both wrote books that promoted the idea of healing as an aspect of atonement. It might appear surprising, since these two names are identified more with evangelicalism rather than with Pentecostalism.

A. J. Gordon explained the twofold ministry of Christ that affected constantly the souls and the bodies of men. "'Thy sins are forgiven thee,' and 'Be whole of thy plague,' are parallel announcements of the Savior's work which are constantly

---

[114] Virginia Lieson Brereton, *Training God's Army: The American Bible School, 1880-1940* (Bloomington and Indianapolis: Indiana University Press, 1990), 71. A recent study on Moody Bible Institute is Timothy E. W. Gloege, *Guaranteed Pure: The Moody Bible Institute, Business, and the Making of Modern Evangelicalism* (Chapel Hill: University of North Carolina Press, 2015).

[115] Their website can be found at: https://www.abhe.org. Accessed 22 March 2019.

running side by side."[116] Gordon's writing emphasized the many accounts of miracles in the Acts of the Apostles as a continuation of Christ's healing ministry. Throughout his citing of Scripture is an appeal to return to the apostolic practice of divine healing. This theme was often repeated by Pentecostal holiness preachers and writers as well. Gordon goes further when he emphasizes the relationship between healing and the atonement:

> In the atonement of Christ there seems to be a foundation laid for faith in bodily healing.... [W]e have Christ set before us as the sickness-bearer as well as the sin-bearer of His people. In the gospel it is written, "And he cast out [devils] and healed all that were sick: that it might be fulfilled which was spoken by Esaias the prophet saying, Himself took our infirmities and *bare our sicknesses*" (Matthew 8:16b-17). Something more than sympathetic fellowship with our sufferings is evidently referred to here. The yoke of His cross by which He lifted our iniquities took hold also of our diseases; so that it is in some sense true that as God "made him to be sin for us, who knew no sin" (2 Corinthians 5:21), so He made Him to be sick for us, who knew no sickness. He who entered into mysterious sympathy without pain which is the fruit of sin, also put Himself underneath our pain which is the penalty of sin. In other words, the passage seems to teach that Christ endured vicariously our diseases as well as our iniquities.[117]

---

116 A. J. Gordon, "The Ministry of Healing," in *The Three Great Classics on Divine Healing*, ed. Jonathan L. Graff (Camp Hill, PA: Christian Publications, 1992), 132.
117 A. J. Gordon, "The Ministry of Healing," 130.

The purpose of this long quote is to show Gordon's method of argument and to note how this idea was accepted by evangelicals, or at least by radical evangelicals.

The divine healing movement was much broader than the influence of both Gordon and Simpson.[118] It should be noted again that Christian Science and the "positive thinkers," along with the "mind cure" practitioners of the nineteenth century, were commonly misunderstood to be a standard representation of healing in America. This made it more difficult for radical evangelicals and later Pentecostals to be heard when they would preach divine healing as part of the gospel.

As students of the Bible, radical evangelicals could not help but notice the many incidents of healing in the ministry of Jesus Christ. Soon after Jesus's temptation in the wilderness, he called his first disciples and began his ministry. His ministry is described in Matthew 4:23: "Jesus went throughout Galilee, teaching in their synagogues, proclaiming the good news of the kingdom, and healing every disease and sickness among the people" (NIV).

Not only at the inauguration of Christ's ministry but also throughout his years in Judea, Samaria, and Galilee, he healed many people. The ministry of healing continued into the book of Acts and throughout the history of the early church. After the time of Constantine, however, the miracles seemed to disappear. When the Reformers reduced the sacraments to two,

---

118 On the history of divine healing through the centuries, see Ronald A. N. Kydd, *Healing Through the Centuries: Models for Understanding* (Peabody, MA: Hendrickson Publishers, 1998) and Amanda Porterfield, *Healing in the History of Christianity* (Oxford: Oxford University Press, 2005). For a more focused examination of the American side of the movement, see Heather D. Curtis, *Faith in the Great Physician: Suffering and Divine Healing in American Culture, 1860–1900* (Baltimore: The Johns Hopkins University Press, 2007) and Raymond J. Cunningham, "From Holiness to Healing: The Faith Cure in America 1872–1892," *Church History*, Vol. 43 (1974): 499–513. And finally, for a treatment of divine healing within the early Pentecostal movement, see Kimberly Ervin Alexander, *Pentecostal Healing: Models in Theology and Practice* (Dorset, England: Deo Publishing, 2006) and Joseph W. Williams, *Spirit Cure: A History of Pentecostal Healing* (New York: Oxford University Press, 2008).

they lessened the importance of extreme unction or anointing of the sick, and medicine became the church's cure.[119] This is, of course, a misreading of much of the historical record, but it indicates the direction of popular theology among radical evangelicals. The driving principle in this re-reading of history is that there has recently (sometimes for many centuries) been a gross discontinuity with the apostolic pattern, and that the return or renewal of the supernatural would provide even more legitimacy to the early Pentecostals.

With divine healing, the link between the modern church and the early church would not be found in a one-time manifestation of the supernatural but would show in a process of historical and theological influence from nineteenth-century evangelicalism. For those who are less acquainted with the history of evangelicalism, it might seem that divine healing only relates to Pentecostalism, and that the current separation between "cessationists" and "continuationists" (views of the spiritual gifts in operation today) places evangelicals in opposition to Pentecostals.[120] But the experience of evangelicals, especially those we term "radical evangelicals," as represented above by A. B. Simpson and A. J. Gordon, is definitely continuationist, meaning God has not disconnected the power source between

---

[119] Martin Luther's 1520 treatise, *The Babylonian Captivity of the Church*, dealt with the Roman Catholic Church's view of seven sacraments: baptism, Eucharist, confirmation, penance, marriage, ordination, and extreme unction (or anointing of the sick). Luther rejected four of the seven as not having sufficient biblical authority to be true sacraments, holding to only baptism, Eucharist, and penance. In the end, however, Protestantism affirmed only two sacraments: baptism and Eucharist.

[120] Without citing the vast polemical literature that focuses on speaking in tongues as not being a valid spiritual gift for today, we can offer two titles from the twentieth century that express the cessationist view more clearly. They are B. B. Warfield, *Counterfeit Miracles* (New York: Charles Scribner's Sons, 1918) and John F. MacArthur Jr., *Charismatic Chaos* (Grand Rapids: Zondervan, 1992). A study on Jonathan Edwards's own view can be found in "And Prophecy Shall Cease": Jonathan Edwards on the Cessation of the Gift of Prophecy," *Westminster Theological Journal*, Vol. 64 (2002): 163–184. An academic study that allows for a spectrum of views to be heard is Richard B. Gaffin Jr. et al, *Are Miraculous Gifts for Today?: Four Views* (Grand Rapids: Zondervan, 2011).

himself and the church's ministry in the twentieth century. Indeed, as the Spirit blows and no one knows from where, so the expectation for supernatural works and their manifestations were pervasive in the radical evangelical milieu.

Some key biblical texts related to divine healing are Exodus 15:26: "I am the Lord that healeth thee" (KJV) and, for the teaching on healing in atonement, Isaiah 53:5: "With his stripes we are healed" (KJV). In addition, evangelicals reading the entire Bible began to see the anointing with oil (James 5:14), and practiced it in church services of healing, along with the laying on of hands. This is an affirmation and rediscovery of the very sacrament of healing. Next, we have a brief overview of the third feature of radical evangelicalism: Keswick or Higher Life holiness.

For those who claim to be part of the Wesleyan-Holiness tradition and have a historical connection with the founders of OMS, Keswick is the other side, even the wrong side. But, within the history of evangelicalism in the late nineteenth century, the Keswick view became more standard as Wesleyans lost their opportunity to represent themselves as the true position on sanctification. Part of this is due to Methodism's decision to embark on the journey toward ecumenism and de-emphasize entire sanctification as the heart of their faith. It was the Wesleyan-Holiness message that would lead further up the road to Pentecost, but many Methodists chose another path.[121]

Let us look briefly at a letter written in *Electric Messages* that clarifies for its readers the position on holiness held by the Cowmans and Kilbournes. In this letter lies a firm denial by the OMS missionaries, meaning they were not advocating and teaching the Keswick view, but rather advocated the Wesleyan one. The title of the article is "What We Teach at the Central

---

121 Jay Riley Case, *An Unpredictable Gospel: American Evangelicals and World Christianity, 1812–1920* (New York: Oxford University Press, 2012), 209.

Gospel Mission and Bible Training Home: Tokyo Japan." Here is a quote on holiness, important for our study, since this article not only denies Keswick but also affirms the Wesleyan view of entire sanctification:

> We have recently received inquiry from one of God's saints in which is the inquiry preceded by the statement "We believe that the Blood of Jesus cleanseth from all sin and not simply represses or covers up sin. We have heard some say that you were Keswick in your doctrine and so kindly ask you to tell us concerning your views on that subject. I do not know as I make it clear what I mean, but will you tell us what you think entire sanctification does for one. Please write me a little note explaining."
>
> "We are rejoiced to be able to answer this question. We *do not* hold the Keswick doctrine, but rather the John Wesley doctrine, or better still the *Bible* doctrine of heart *purity*, not merely *imputed* but *imparted*. The following statement we trust will help this sister and any others who are unacquainted with our teaching to know us better."[122]

So, what is the Keswick message and why was it perceived as being so pernicious for OMS missionaries in the early twentieth century? The Keswick movement refers firstly to a place in northwestern England, in the Lake District, where a gathering of Christians occurred on an annual basis, more often at times to discuss issues related to the Christian Higher Life. But behind

---

[122] *Electric Messages from Japan: A Monthly Holiness Missionary Journal (Unsectarian)*, C. E. Cowman and E. A. Kilbourne, Publishers, Vol. 2, No. 1 (November 1903): 4.

the scenery of the beautiful Lake District were two books that had a phenomenal influence on evangelicalism. They were W. E. Boardman's *The Higher Christian Life* and Hannah Whitall Smith's *The Christian's Secret of a Happy Life*. Smith, a Quaker, along with her husband, Robert Pearsall, had experienced the "second blessing" and encountered an ongoing "secret of victory." By 1875, the conventions on the Higher Life were attracting masses of people from England, other parts of the United Kingdom, Europe, and America.

At the more popular level, radical evangelicals believed in the continual struggle with sin and in Keswick's teaching of a victorious life over the power of sin. This also contrasted with the language of "eradication" taught by some advocates of Wesleyan entire sanctification. Thus, the comparison was made by Wesleyans that Keswick only suppressed the power of sin in the believer's life while true entire sanctification eradicated (removed the root) the very carnal nature, and, in some writings, "original sin" was even undone.

The differences between the Wesleyan teaching on entire sanctification and the Keswick teaching were not only doctrinal, but emotional as well. The experience of entire sanctification in the Wesleyan mode was rampant with what might be described as emotionalism, with people "praying through" at the altar, weeping, and even running around the sanctuary in a victory march. The Keswick teachings were presented by Anglicans, Baptists, and Presbyterians, making it more ecumenical and inclusive of the larger evangelical family. This view was also taught in a more sustained lecture tone, with less emotionalism and more intellectualism.

The Keswick message was accompanied by premillennial dispensationalism and even Calvinism, again expressing more diversity than Wesleyan-Holiness. As the Keswick message became more popular, it traveled to America with speakers and with the books written by Frederick Brotherton Meyer (1847–1929) and Andrew Murray (1828–1917), stalwart supporters and speakers at Keswick.[123] Now, we move on to view the acceleration of world evangelization in light of Christ's soon return.

Already we have seen the importance of the Bible School movement in the growth and development of radical evangelicalism. In addition to the Bible schools offering an alternative to liberal-leaning theological seminaries, there was a sense in which the shorter duration of study expedited the training of more workers for world evangelization. This new brevity, especially, would place the task of world evangelization on the shoulders of not only the clergy but also the entire church. Two further movements within evangelicalism accelerated world evangelization. The first was the Student Volunteer movement and the second was faith missions. The first will reveal how thin the line was which divided evangelicalism from mainline Protestantism, and the second will emphasize the growing distance between denominational missions and the new alternative offered by faith missions.

The Student Volunteer Movement for Foreign Missions was founded in 1886 and led by Arthur Tappan Pierson (1837–1911). The first group of students who were committed to foreign missions organized at Princeton in 1883. Five of them signed a declaration together that said, "We, the undersigned, declare ourselves willing and desirous, God permitting, to go to the unevangelized portions of the world." The original student leader of this group at Princeton was Robert P. Wilder (1863–1938),

---

[123] On Keswick, it would require a lengthy bibliography to include all the writings of Keswick, but for a short reading, see Douglas W. Frank, *Less Than Conquerors: How Evangelicals Entered the Twentieth Century* (Grand Rapids: Wm. B. Eerdmans, 1986), 113–115, and Andrew C. Russell, "Counteracting Classifications: Keswick Holiness Reconsidered," *Wesleyan Theological Journal*, Vol. 49, No. 2 (2014): 86–121.

son of a missionary to India, whose father, Robert's grandfather, was editor of *The Missionary Review.*

In 1885, a plan was proposed to D. L. Moody to sponsor a collegiate-level gathering of students at Moody's Mount Hermon School (Northfield, Massachusetts) to encourage the students' commitment to world missions. The meetings at Northfield become more official and recognized as the center for students to form mission commitments. John R. Mott (1865-1955) was one of the original "Mount Hermon Hundred" and became the chair of the organization, with Robert E. Speer (1867-1947) serving as traveling secretary.[124]

While students were being mobilized, a new form of mission organization, or society, was coming forward to expedite, as with the Bible School movement, the sending of more missionaries for the now urgent task of world evangelization. These new mission societies would be termed "faith missions."

At the end of the nineteenth century, four types of mission organizations existed: denominational, interdenominational, faith missions, and specialized missions. The primary distinctive setting faith missions apart from the others was that faith-missions missionaries were required to raise their own financial support. There were three reasons for the founding and establishing of faith missions within the larger evangelical network at the turn of the century.

First, the founders of these missions were convinced that the denominational agencies were not reaching the unevangelized areas of the world, especially the inland or interior areas. The words *inland* or *interior* in their names indicate this emphasis.

---

124 For further reading on the Student Volunteer movement, see Michael Parker, *The Kingdom of Character: The Student Volunteer Movement for Foreign Missions, 1886-1926* (Pasadena, CA: William Carey Library Publishers, 2008); Robert P. Wilder, *The Student Volunteer Movement for Foreign Missions; Some Personal Reminiscences of its Origin and Early History* (New York: Student Volunteer Movement, 1935); and for the larger religious context of Protestant missions, see William R. Hutchinson, *Errand to the World: American Protestant Thought and Foreign Missions* (Chicago: University of Chicago Press, 1987).

Second, the missions' founders were concerned that denominational missions agencies had been negatively affected by theological liberalism. And third, the founders observed that denominational agencies often lacked sufficient funds to send out missionaries, at least in adequate numbers. To address this dearth of missionaries, the faith missions asked their missionary candidates to raise their own support.[125]

While the reasons for starting faith missions seem clear, the identity of the actual founder of faith missions remains somewhat less distinct.

A short list of possible founders or visionaries includes J. Hudson Taylor (1832–1905), Anthony Norris Groves (1795–1853), and George Müller (1805–1898). My own view, which is also the majority view, is that the original "faith missionary" was Anthony Norris Groves of the Plymouth Brethren in his mission to Baghdad (present-day Iraq). The faith-missions distinctives are explained in a series of contrasts:

> Groves went to Baghdad for a very simple reason: he believed God had sent him. He was not appointed by a mission board with wealthy directors to guarantee secure communications and a regular salary. He did not command the respect given to a man ordained to the ministry of a prominent church denomination. He did not have a team of experienced colleagues to advise in matters of language and culture. He did not have anyone to offer support in time of sickness or political unrest. He did not even have a Bible in the language spoken by the people around him. But he did have the promises of God (which he believed) and a heart

---
125 Terry, John Mark, and Robert L. Gallagher, *Encountering the History of Missions: From the Early Church to Today* (Grand Rapids: Baker Academic, 2017), 262–263.

taught to love everyone he met (whatever their background), and he had a vision to take those promises and that love personally to missions who knew nothing of it.[126]

While this passage describes Groves's amazing faith (in hagiographical language) and how this new way of doing mission departed from the majority practice in the Great Century, Donald Akenson's writing provides a different perspective of Norris Groves and faith missions:

> "In creating modern faith missions, however, the earliest Brethren were not a link in some undocumentable skein of sackcloth-wearing dissidents, but rather a new phenomenon, a group of privileged members of a First World cohort who gave themselves over to an attempt to redeem various Third World cultures. The faith missions of the early Brethren were paradoxical and contradictory, humble in the sense that the missioners followed St. Paul and put themselves through arduous deprivations, and arrogant in the sense that their goal was to supplant the core beliefs of the indigenous cultures which they targeted."[127]

And, at a later date, George Müller, who was also a member of the Christian Brethren, adapted the faith-missions philosophy to his own ministry of caring for orphans in Bristol. It is common knowledge that George Müller married Groves's sister Mary,

---

126 Robert Bernard Dann, *Father of Faith Missions: The Life and Times of Anthony Norris Groves* (Bath, England: Authentic Paternoster, 2004), 13–14.
127 Donald H. Akenson, *Exporting the Rapture: John Nelson Darby and the Victorian Conquest of North-American Evangelicalism* (New York: Oxford University Press, 2018), Kindle Electronic Edition: Location 1010–1014.

so beyond the connection of religious thought and practice are family ties.[128] The bond between Groves and Müller was so close that when Groves returned from the East Indies, he went to visit Müller and ultimately passed away in Müller's home. Pierson describes the relationship between the two:

> "To [Groves] Mr. Müller owed much through grace at the outset of his labours in 1829. By his example his faith had been stimulated and helped when, with no visible support or connection with any missionary society, Mr. Groves had gone to Bagdad [sic] with wife and children, for the sake of mission work in this far-off field, resigning a lucrative practice of about fifteen hundred pounds a year. The tie between these men was very close and tender and the loss of this brother-in-law gave keen sorrow."[129]

Finally, it was George Müller's ministry that became a model for J. Hudson Taylor to journey forth by faith and found the China Inland Mission.[130] In addition to the model of George Müller's orphanage ministry, financial donations from Mr. and Mrs. W. T. Berger, a wealthy family, arrived as the catalyst for a faith mission that "was to be interdenominational in scope. No public or private requests were to be made for contributions, and the enlisted workers were to receive no stated salary, but the work was to be supported on faith, through prayer."[131] With

---
128 A. T. Pierson, *George Müller of Bristol: His Life of Prayer and Faith* (Grand Rapids: Kregel Publications, 1999), 71.
129 Pierson, *George Müller of Bristol*, 223.
130 Taylor, Howard, and Geraldine Taylor, *Hudson Taylor's Spiritual Secret* (Chicago: Moody Publishers, 2009). A helpful resource that covers the larger China Inland Mission (now called Overseas Missionary Fellowship) and is an academic and not a hagiographical work is Alvyn Austin, *China's Millions: The China Inland Mission and Late Qing Society, 1832–1905* (Studies in the History of Christian Missions) (Grand Rapids: Wm. B. Eerdmans, 2005).
131 Floyd L. Carr, *J. Hudson Taylor: Founder of the China Inland Mission* (New York: Baptist Board of Education, 1926), 5.

the history of faith missions as a background, we will now turn to look at the start of Protestant missions in Korea, with a focus on the arrival of two missionaries: Horace G. Underwood and Henry G. Appenzeller.

The global church began on the day of Pentecost, when people gathered in Jerusalem and heard the good news proclaimed in their own languages. The assembled people were from three continents: Asia, Africa, and Europe. Note that Korea is on the Asian continent and is culturally connected with Asia. Half the planet's population lives in Asia, east of Afghanistan and south of the former USSR. Of the world's four ancient civilizations, only one (Nile/Egypt) was located outside Asia. The three in Asia were Mesopotamia (Iraq), Indus Valley (Pakistan), and Yellow River (China). Within the geographical boundaries of Asia are common cultural traits. These include extended family and kin network, high regard for education, veneration of age, submissive role of women in society, hierarchical structure of society, importance of tradition (history/the past), and group welfare considered above individual interests.

While our focus will be on the start of Protestant (evangelical) missions at the end of the nineteenth century, some scholars of Korean religious history contend for earlier dates to mark the beginning of Christianity in Korea. Kyoung Bae Min cites a Japanese scholar, Professor P. Y. Saeki, as pointing toward Nestorian witness during the Chinese Tang dynasty (AD 618-907) in both Korea and Japan.[132] While the claim of Nestorian mission to Korea lies mainly in the area of scholarly surmising, the Roman Catholic Church historically traces its

---

132 Kyoung Bae Min, *A History of Christian Churches in Korea* (Seoul: Yonsei University Press, 2005), 5-6. There are some relics that have been identified as having come from the historical period of Nestorian mission to East Asia. They were found in Kyeongju, the capital of the United Silla dynasty (AD 661-935), and are now in Soongsil University's Christian Museum (John C. England, *The Hidden History of Christianity in Asia: The Churches of the East before 1500* (Delhi: ISPCK, 2002), 103-104).

own history in Korea to a group of laypersons who studied Jesuit tracts in 1777. A group of Korean scholars, under the instruction of Cheol-sin Kwon, attended a religious retreat at a nearby temple, where they studied together the writings of Confucius and Mencius and, at the same time, were introduced to several Catholic books that had been brought from Beijing. In 1783, the Korean scholars sent Seung-hun Yi to visit the Catholic missionaries in China to learn more about this new Western religion. Yi was baptized by a Chinese priest and, in 1784, brought back books and articles on Catholic doctrine, which were given to the scholars. Along with the books and articles, rosaries and crucifixes were also given.

As a result of their new faith, these Korean scholars abandoned all pagan religious rites and preached the Catholic faith openly, converting people and baptizing them. It would take another eleven years before a Catholic priest would arrive from China to celebrate the first mass on Easter Sunday (April 5, 1795).[133] James Huntley Grayson states that "the first characteristic to note about the Korean church is that from the beginning it was self-evangelized."[134] We will examine this more carefully in the evangelical context in chapter 6. A second characteristic of this newfound Korean church would be suffering, by both persecution and martyrdom. Pope John Paul II (made Saint John Paul in 2014) was the first Roman Catholic pope to visit Korea, in 1984. It is significant, and even symbolic, that a pope from Poland, perhaps the only nation that has suffered more than Korea, would canonize 103 martyrs (including ten French missionary priests) killed during the great persecutions of 1839, 1846, and 1866. In 2014, Pope Francis visited Korea and gave

---

133 Kim, Sebastian C. H., and Kirsteen Kim, *A History of Korean Christianity* (Cambridge: Cambridge University Press, 2015), 28.
134 James Huntley Grayson, "A Quarter-Millennium of Christianity in Korea," in *Christianity in Korea*, eds. Robert E. Buswell Jr. and Timothy S. Lee (Honolulu: University of Hawaii Press, 2006), 9.

124 martyrs from earlier persecutions the "blessed" status.[135] Later in this book (chapters 8 and 10), we will look at two periods that are marked by intense suffering (1930s and 1950s). The nineteenth century was a time of renewed commitment to foreign missions in both Europe and North America, and during the last few decades of this Great Century, two missionaries came from the US to Korea. Although they are not the first Protestants (and I will term them *evangelicals*) to preach the gospel in Korea or to Koreans, they are the first two who were resident missionaries and remained in Korea for a longer period. The claim for, perhaps, pioneer missionary status goes to Karl F. A. Gützlaff (1803–1851), who visited the Korean coast on evangelistic missions.[136] The first Protestant (evangelical) martyr in Korea was Robert Jermain Thomas, a missionary to China, who was martyred in Pyeongyang on September 5, 1866, as a passenger on the USS General Sherman, an armed US naval vessel.[137]

The year prior to the arrival of Underwood and Appenzeller, a medical missionary, Dr. Horace N. Allen, arrived at Incheon on September 20, 1884, and at Seoul on September 22, 1884. Allen was the first resident missionary to enter Korea. In 1885, a Korean government hospital was established, with Allen in charge.

Both Underwood and Appenzeller were active members of the Student Volunteer movement (founded in 1886), their motto being: "The evangelization of the world in this generation." Horace G. Underwood (1859–1916) was born in England

---

135 Don Baker, *Catholics and Anti-Catholicism in Chosŏn Korea* (Honolulu: University of Hawaii Press, 2017), x–xi. On Korean Catholic history, see also Jai-Keun Choi, *The Origin of the Roman Catholic Church in Korea: An Examination of Popular and Governmental Responses to Catholic Missions in the Late Chosŏn Dynasty* (Norwalk, CA: The Hermit Kingdom Press, 2006).
136 See Jessie Gregory Lutz, *Opening China: Karl F. A. Gützlaff and Sino-Western Relations, 1827–1852* (Grand Rapids: Wm. B. Eerdmans, 2008).
137 Allen D. Clark, *A History of the Church in Korea* (Seoul: Christian Literature Society of Korea, 1971), 61–64.

and migrated with his family to the United States in 1872. The family joined the Dutch Reformed Church, and Horace began his studies as an undergraduate at New York University and at the New Brunswick Theological Seminary (Dutch Reformed). While he was a seminary student, his family was concerned about Horace's involvement with the Salvation Army, for it appeared he was ready to transfer to such work. After 1884, he was frequently called "the Methodist preacher of the Presbyterian mission." Henry G. Appenzeller (1858–1902), the first Methodist (North) missionary, was raised in the Reformed Church, being of Swiss-German ethnic heritage, and later became a Methodist while pursuing undergraduate studies at Franklin and Marshall College. He would later complete his seminary studies at Drew Theological School prior to his departure for Korea.[138]

Because of their unique spiritual backgrounds, both reflecting a "crossing over" from one side of evangelicalism to the other, Underwood and Appenzeller were uniquely prepared to work together in mission as fellow evangelicals. A sense of cooperation rather than competition between the two largest Protestant denominations resulted from the Methodist and Presbyterian missionaries arriving in Korea at the same time.

Underwood and Appenzeller arrived together, landing at Incheon (Jemulpo) on Easter morning, April 5, 1885. Appenzeller was accompanied by his wife, while Underwood was a bachelor when he began his mission work in Korea. "Underwood had studied medicine for a year, before leaving the States, and this made it possible for him to be of immediate help to Dr. Allen in the hospital."[139] While Underwood and Appenzeller had primary responsibilities for evangelism and church planting, the first generation of evangelical missionaries to Korea was responsible for the start of Western hospitals and Western

---

138 Daniel M. Davies, "Building a City on a Hill in Korea: The Work of Henry G. Appenzeller," *Church History*, Vol. 61, No. 4 (December 1992): 422–435.
139 Clark, *A History of the Church in Korea*, 91.

education. In 1886, Horace Underwood opened a boys' orphanage, which grew into present-day Yonsei University. Underwood was greatly assisted financially by his older brother, the affluent businessman John Thomas Underwood (1857–1937), inventor and owner of the Underwood typewriter.

There may seem to be a delay in the ministries of evangelism and church planting, but this is easily explainable. The new missionaries did not speak Korean at the onset of their ministries, and did not have language textbooks, grammars, dictionaries, or language institutes. Also, the Korean government did not officially look with favor on evangelistic activities. Evangelism and church ministry remained the primary purpose for both Underwood's and Appenzeller's arrival and their continued residency in Korea.

The first Sunday worship service was conducted on June 28, 1885, with the Allens, Scrantons, and Herons present. On April 25, 1886, again with the Methodists, the first baptism was held (infant daughters of the Appenzellers and Scrantons). A Methodist religious custom of gathering for prayer on New Year's Eve (December 31, 1885) turned into a season of crying out to God for souls. God answered this prayer on July 11, 1886, when Noh Dosa was baptized. Dosa had read a Chinese book, which was anti-Christian, but which sparked a deep interest in this new religion. Later, he would read the Gospels of Mark and Luke, borrowing the Chinese versions from Dr. Allen. While the Korean government was restricting evangelism and church ministries of Underwood and Appenzeller to Koreans, it placed no restrictions on the evangelism of Japanese people in Korea. On Easter Sunday 1886, one Japanese candidate was baptized. A second was baptized the following year. Other baptisms followed, both in Seoul and in North Korea.[140]

---

140 For further reading on early evangelical mission to Korea, see Everett N. Hunt Jr., *Protestant Pioneers in Korea* (Maryknoll, NY: Orbis, 1980) and L. George

The first Presbyterian church was organized on September 12, 1887 (Saemunan), and the first Methodist church was organized on October 9, 1887 (Jeongdong Church). After the beginnings of Methodist and Presbyterian faith missions to Korea, other churches would also start ministries there. Among those recent arrivals were Australian Presbyterian (1889), Church of England (1890), American Presbyterian Church (1892), American Baptist (1895), Methodist Episcopal Church, South (1896), Canadian Presbyterians (1898), Seventh-day Adventist (1905), Oriental Missionary Society (1907), and the Salvation Army (1908).

While we continue to view the last two decades of the nineteenth century as evangelical prolegomena for the twentieth century, one essential theological formulation rises to the forefront: the fourfold gospel. This topic is not well known by all Christians, and only a minority of evangelicals are even familiar with the term *fourfold gospel*. We will be using "fourfold gospel" to mean the four cardinal teachings of Christ as Savior, Sanctifier, Healer, and Coming King. These pillars were known as early as Irenaeus (ca. 130–200) in relation to the four canonical New Testament Gospels: Matthew, Mark, Luke, and John.

Our attention is upon the four teachings as they were collected and popularized by Albert Benjamin Simpson. Van De Walle calls these four teachings "Simpson's christocentric gestalt."[141] In broader terms, Donald Dayton describes these four "themes of the 'four-fold gospel' [as being] so pervasive in late nineteenth-century evangelicalism that one could almost speak of them as defining and indicating the boundaries of that subculture."[142] Dayton's claim should be taken seriously

---

Paik, *The History of Protestant Missions in Korea 1832–1910*, 2nd ed. (Seoul: Yonsei University Press, 1971).

141 Bernie A. Van De Walle, *The Heart of the Gospel: A. B. Simpson, the Fourfold Gospel, and Late Nineteenth-Century Evangelical Theology*, Princeton Theological Monograph Series (Eugene, OR: Pickwick Publications, 2009), 21.

142 Donald W. Dayton, "The Four-Fold Gospel: Key to Trans-Pacific Continuities," in *From the Margins: A Celebration of the Theological Work of Donald W. Dayton*, ed. Christian T. Collins Winn (Eugene, OR: Pickwick Publications, 2007), 362.

and will be the step upon which we stand to move to the next claim: that as evangelicalism reaches back through the centuries beyond the nineteenth and eighteenth centuries to the sixteenth-century Reformation, so the teachings of the fourfold gospel can be identified in antecedent theological formulations. Further, it will be noted that we can fit the fourfold gospel within Christology—a broader theological category that includes Christ's person and work. Although A. B. Simpson's name within evangelical history is not as prominent as that of Moody, Torrey, or Machen, the seeds he sowed more than 130 years ago have brought forth an abundant harvest in global mission among both radical evangelicals and radical holiness. He contributed much to where we stand today as evangelicals in the twenty-first century—theologically through the fourfold gospel, educationally via Nyack College, and organizationally through the start of the Christian and Missionary Alliance.

The fourfold gospel remains the evangelical foundation of the Korea Evangelical Holiness Church (KEHC). But the KEHC did not invent these four basics or even codify them. They arose and ascended from the rich spirituality of transpacific evangelicalism. The fourfold gospel tells in beautiful and rich language where both the KEHC and OMS are from, what these organizations believe today, and where they are headed together in the future. Yes, start with the basics and you can go the furthest distance.

In some ways, the fourfold gospel is like the Apostles' Creed; it's not written word-for-word in the Bible, but it flows entirely from the Bible, expressing clearly and powerfully what the whole Bible teaches. *The Fourfold Gospel* was originally a series of sermons preached in 1887 in New York, published as *The Fourfold Gospel* within *Tabernacle Sermons*, Volume 5. Though *The Fourfold Gospel* was the title of a book written by A. B. Simpson in 1890, he would have been the first to admit that he did not coin the term. You could say that Simpson just wove the rich threads together into one beautiful tapestry, or he was like a collector who arranges multiple treasures together in a single room. Simpson would later (1891) write an article titled "Fourfold Unity," where he compared the fourfold gospel to music sung in four parts.

The end of the nineteenth century marked a big shift in the Wesleyan-Holiness movement when people began to change their millennial views from postmillennial to premillennial. This may sound like a mere technicality, but the change to "pre" signaled a shift from trusting human-inspired visions and dreams to placing faith solidly in God's Word that promised Pentecostal visions and dreams (Acts 2:17).

In the 1890s, holiness Christians began taking the Great Commission (Matthew 28:19–20) seriously by looking at the fields "white already to harvest" (John 4:35 KJV); they were at the same time keeping an eye on the eschatological clock. One verse which maintained this focus was Matthew 24:14: "And this gospel of the kingdom will be preached in the whole world as a testimony to all nations, and then the end will come" (NIV). Waiting for the second coming did not mean hiding in a monastic cave, praying and fasting until Christ's return; it meant going to the nations and preaching to bring about the end. For many true believers, it was now the "eleventh hour"; time was running out, and the mission still remained to bring in the harvest from the farthest nations. Christ told his disciples that no one, not even himself as the Son of God, knew the exact hour when he would return, but that we could all prepare for that time. Indeed, getting ready for the second coming became a theme of the Holiness movement as it shifted from the nineteenth century to the twentieth century. The urgency of Christ's second coming became vivid to the point of seeming imminent. Since Christ could return any day, evangelicals were determined to train workers for the end-time harvest fields. This shows the connection between the first item (Savior, regeneration) and the final one (returning King, second coming).

As the fourfold gospel is in position, the church can survey means and ways of accomplishing the Great Commission to bring revival. For the radical holiness/evangelical, looking up meant understanding the events of the past simply as preparation for our current mission, and asking questions such as, Where is our vision today? What is the focus of our affections? Are you so much in love with the Lord that your gaze is upon him alone, the bride looking for her bridegroom? Now, we move to the second item: holiness/sanctification.

One of the New Testament texts on holiness is 1 Peter 1:13–16. It tells us we are to "be holy." It might appear as a common greeting in English, like "be nice" or "be happy." But "be holy" is a command, in the imperative mood. You *must* be holy, holy or else. William Baxter Godbey (1833–1920), an evangelical Methodist, wrote *Holiness or Hell?*[143] Hebrews 12:14 states clearly that "without holiness no one will see the Lord" (NIV). Not only is holiness a "must do," or a command, but it is also for all Christians, including all evangelicals.

We continue the fourfold gospel with the third point: healing. Right after Jesus is tempted in the desert, he emerges with a message and a ministry. Matthew 4:23 outlines the full ministry of Jesus Christ. "Jesus went throughout Galilee, teaching in their synagogues, proclaiming the good news of the kingdom, and healing every disease and sickness among the people" (NIV). Very simply, his ministry was preaching, teaching, and healing. The rules for his kingdom are set up in Matthew 5–7, called the Sermon on the Mount. Now that the new standards are announced, he begins putting them into practice. Jesus begins to display his authority, to take back

---

143   W. B. Godbey, *Holiness or Hell* (Atlanta: Foote & Davies, 1893).

from Satan, and to demonstrate his power to rule over all the person: body, soul, and spirit. He pushes back sin, Satan, and sickness to bring healing and wholeness to hurting people. We will be looking at the healing ministry of Jesus more closely below in Matthew 8.

But this is not just a story about what happened two thousand years ago; it is what we believe today and must also practice in our lives. Hebrews 13:8 says very clearly, "Jesus Christ is the same yesterday and today and forever" (NIV). He hasn't changed, and his Word remains true forever. We can witness the same Jesus, the Savior, the Sanctifier, and the Healer, as he ministers through us as his body. We can say with confidence today in churches that affirm the truth of his Word and the power of the Spirit, "Jesus the Healer is in the house today." Is a physician available for all of us: spirit, soul, and body? Yes, his name is Jesus.

First, Christ heals our bodies. Matthew 8 begins with healing. A man came to Jesus with leprosy. Jesus touched the unclean man, the kind you are not supposed to touch. Next, a centurion came to Jesus. His servant was sick at home. Jesus was ready to go there, but the centurion stopped him, saying, "Lord, I do not deserve to have you come under my roof. But just say the word, and my servant will be healed" (8:8 NIV). The third healing in Matthew 8 happens when Jesus goes to Peter's house: "He saw Peter's mother-in-law lying in bed with a fever" (8:14 NIV). Already three healings have happened in Christ's ministry, within only fifteen verses.

Today, in thinking of Christ the Healer, three groups of people appear: First, the nonbelievers among Christian liberalism who affirm neither the miracles of healing nor the historical record of the Bible or in the world today. Second, the people who affirm the historical record of the miracles in the past but believe these ceased a long time ago, either with the completion of the New Testament or the death of the last apostle. We call this group "cessationists." Third are the people who believe all the miracles recorded in the Bible (Old and New Testaments) and hold to the reality of miracles today. We call this group "fourfold gospel believers," "full gospel believers," or even "whole gospel believers."

After healing of bodies comes healing of spirits and souls. First Thessalonians 5:23 describes God's will for our entire sanctification. His will is also for our total healing. Many people today suffer from mental and spiritual illnesses. Jesus was able to drive out evil spirits and heal with his word. In the twenty-first century, people, at least those people in parts of the world where such care is available and affordable, find bodily healing in medical science. But the real challenge for the church today remains the ministry of healing to the spirits and souls of hurting people in a broken world. The church today needs to minister divine healing to the whole person, with a renewed emphasis on soul healing.

Rick Warren, pastor of Saddleback Church (Lake Forest, California) and author of *The Purpose Driven Life*, was absent from the pulpit for four months. A terrible tragedy struck him and his family. In 2013, Rick and Kay Warren's youngest child, Matthew, committed suicide at the age of twenty-seven. Matthew had struggled with depression his whole life.[144] Pastor Warren's message communicates how we in the church no longer should be ashamed of mental illness, and how we can learn to minister Christ's healing to all those suffering from these horrible diseases. Although soul or mental/emotional healing is not something talked about much in the church or

---

144 Michelle Boorstein, "Suicide of star pastor Rick Warren's son sparks debate about mental illness," *Washington Post*, April 10, 2013, www.washingtonpost.com/local/suicide-of-megapastor-rick-warrens-son-sparks-debate-about-mental-illness/2013/04/10/322e4910-a148-11e2-9c03-6952ff305f35_story.html?utm_term=.2fcfdf20616e. Accessed 20 March 2019.

in Christian colleges, it has always been part of divine healing, because Christ continues to make whole the entire person—healing bodies, souls, and spirits.

We conclude the fourfold gospel with the fourth point: second coming. In our earlier discussion about radical holiness, we looked at the shift from postmillennial to premillennial views of Christ's second coming. Within radical holiness (and radical evangelicalism) in North America, that shift birthed a fervency in world mission. Indeed, the fourfold gospel allows us to look at the second coming from the Lord's perspective, hearing again his words in Matthew 24–25. By reminding ourselves of these words, we will become ready to make an important switch, to view the second coming as a matter of priority, as the first event that will lead to all events rather than the last event that ends everything.

To show that OMS (at that time Oriental Missionary Society) held to the fourfold gospel, affirming each and every point of the four, we will study an essay published in *Electric Messages* with the aim of bringing about theological clarity for the public who questioned OMS's stance on holiness and other evangelical doctrines.

The title of the article is "What We Teach at the Central Gospel Mission and Bible Training Home: Tokyo, Japan," published after a mere two years on the mission field in Japan. Let us read first the part about holiness, noting that this article clearly affirms the Wesleyan view of entire sanctification:

> We believe that the Blood of Jesus cleanseth from all sin and not simply represses or covers up sin. We have heard some say that you were Keswick in your doctrine and so kindly ask you to tell us concerning your views on that subject. I do not know as I make it clear what I mean, but will you tell us

what you think entire sanctification does for one. Please write me a little note explaining.

We are rejoiced to be able to answer this question. We *do not* hold the Keswick doctrine, but rather the John Wesley doctrine, or better still the *Bible* doctrine of heart *purity,* not merely *imputed* but *imparted.* The following statement we trust will help this sister and any others who are unacquainted with our teaching to know us better.

First—We believe and teach the *birth* of the Spirit is an absolute necessary qualification for *entering* the Kingdom of God. "Jesus answered, Verily, verily, I say unto thee, except a man be born of water and of the Spirit, he cannot *enter* into the Kingdom of God." John 3:5.

We believe and teach that this "new birth" is not "baptism," but that it is a *radical* change of heart and *life,* according to the Scriptures: "Therefore if any man be *in* Christ, he is a new creature: (or, new creation) old things are passed away; behold, all things are become new." 2 Cor. 5:17.

Second—We believe that the *"root"* of sin, *"carnal* mind," "Old man" or, the "flesh" ("Sarx") which remains in the heart of every believer at and after conversion until he or she is sanctified wholly in a second definite work of grace, is removed, eradicated, burnt out by the "Baptism with the Holy Ghost and fire."

Our Japanese translation brings this out much stronger than the English, and this enables us in the Japanese language to preach it much stronger, leaving no room for our "suppression theory," or, "Jack in the box" friends to *guess* at what we mean. . . .

Third—We believe and teach, and all our students are so full of it that it crops out in almost every sermon and many testimonies: "The imminent pre-millennial return of our Lord." "Even so, come Lord Jesus."

Fourth—Divine healing as purchased in the atonement. "Himself took our infirmities, and bare our sicknesses." Mat. 8.17.

There can be no doubt that this text refers directly to physical healing. . . .We would not stop with merely a *fourfold* Gospel, but we believe the Bible as a whole from Genesis to Revelations [sic] to be God's inspired record of His dealings with man. There are many important subjects:

For example: *Conversion* does so much for a man that his heart *burns* to tell others, while Sanctification or the Baptism with the Holy Ghost and fire, blows *every thing* [sic] else out of him and so *constrains* him that it is "Woe is me if I *preach* not the gospel." If he doesn't stand in the *pulpit* (they won't let you in many places except you have a *title*) he stands in the *streets:* If he don't [sic] *go* to foreign lands, he *sends.*

> Salvation provides a pair of "field glasses" and says "Lift up your eyes and look on the *fields*"—note that word is in the plural—"fields" (John 4:35.) thus *forbidding* one to look merely on his own county, state or country but emphatically states "Ye shall receive power after that the Holy Ghost is come upon you; and ye shall be witnesses unto me BOTH in Jerusalem, and in all Judaea, and in Samaria, *and unto the uttermost part of the earth.*" Acts 1:8.[145]

The Cowmans and Kilbournes affirm the fourfold gospel, noting that the order set by Simpson has been changed and that the fourfold has become flexible to include other doctrines from the Bible, especially world evangelism. The inclusion of Acts 1:8 at the end of this extended passage further clarifies that revival and evangelism are the warp and woof of the fabric of evangelicalism within the Oriental Missionary Society at the beginning of the twentieth century.

Our survey of the last several decades of the nineteenth century, including endings and beginnings, should help us see again some "turning points" that positioned the twentieth century to become both Vinson Synan's "Century of the Holy Spirit" and Scott Sunquist's "Unexpected Christian Century." In addition, we can add a journal article by Grant Wacker that goes beyond the usual divide between evangelical and ecumenical, or the two-party system of conservative versus liberal. Rather than the standard reading ("distortions") which view this time as a faith divided over both theology and spirituality, Wacker views the period 1880–1910 as holding together American

---

145 *Electric Messages from Japan: A Monthly Holiness Missionary Journal (Unsectarian)*, C. E. Cowman and E. A. Kilbourne, Publishers, Vol. 2, No. 1 (November 1903): 4.

Protestantism.[146] For Wacker, the division between conservative and liberal or fundamentalist and modernist came in the 1920s. While there were venues in which both conservative and liberal would unite to hear preaching or to do ministry, within the Holiness movement, among radical holiness folk, the time of division had already come in the 1880s and 1890s. Separating sometimes meant leaving the church of one's birth or even being thrown out (*come-outers* and *put-outers* were the preferred terms of radical holiness at the end of the nineteenth century). We turn now to global revivals of the first decade of the twentieth century to see the role of the Holy Spirit in the forming of worldwide evangelicalism.

---

146 Grant Wacker, "The Holy Spirit and the Spirit of the Age in American Protestantism, 1880–1910," *The Journal of American History*, Vol. 72, No. 1 (June 1985): 45–62.

5

Global Revivals in the New Century

The larger portion of this textbook will be devoted to chapters 5 to 10 covering the entire twentieth century, decade by decade, and closing with the first decade of the twenty-first century. Since this time remains substantially larger, it is not possible to have comprehensive coverage of all that has happened in transpacific evangelicalism for an entire century; gaps will remain. As there are some persons and events not covered and others not completely explained, the purpose of any textbook proves not to have the final word but is instead to initiate a conversation, providing beginning statements. It is my hope and prayer that these first words will connect with the many cultural and social contexts represented in our own Wesleyan-Holiness Summer Study Program and will produce many following words, a variety of discussion, and will allow continuing conversation. While you read about what happened in one hundred years, please consider what has happened with your church and mission and nation for that same time period. Perhaps we will find ourselves related even more, connected through both space and time in the one body of Christ.

The attention of this chapter will focus on Los Angeles and

Pyeongyang, continuing in pursuit of revival and evangelism themes as two major components in the identity and mission of evangelicalism in America and Korea. In addition to the revivals in Los Angeles and Pyeongyang, we will look at the start of revivals in the new (twentieth) century in Topeka, Kansas, as well as other seasons of revival with Holy Spirit visitations in Wales and India.

At the turn of the century, two events that have been disconnected theologically for a long time will be compiled in our narrative of revival and evangelism. The Azusa Street Mission in Los Angeles and the Central Presbyterian Church in Pyeongyang were connected through the Spirit in 1906 and 1907, even when neither one knew of the other. It was as if Pyeongyang did not exist on the same planet as Los Angeles, and vice versa. Putting the two together for the purpose of this chapter creates a comparison that never historically existed one century ago, but it opens the possibility of a theological dialogue that can prosper unity within the larger evangelical family. That is my prayer.

Before we go to either Los Angeles or Pyeongyang, it will be necessary to look at the first year of the new century (1901) and see how two historically unconnected persons and two theologically disconnected movements can combine for the purpose of creating dialogue and prospering evangelical unity. So, let us go to Iowa, the birth state of two significant religious leaders, and consider how they might become connected enough to turn toward unity and together affirm the evangelical identity they share.

It was the marking of two persons and two movements, both born in Iowa, that would lead in different directions, one to faraway Japan and the other to Kansas. Who are these two persons? What are their two movements? Lettie Burd Cowman (1870–1960), born in Afton, Iowa, and Charles Fox Parham

(1873–1929), born in Muscatine, Iowa. The two respective ministries that became integral partners in global evangelicalism, although they never connected and remain disconnected with one another, are the Oriental Missionary Society (1901) and the Topeka Revival (1901). We will see other related ministries and persons within the global evangelical family that work together but are not always included in the record or history of evangelicalism. The larger tent includes all the people God has called and commissioned for evangelism and the mighty wind of the Spirit that blows in revival to all the nations. Again, we might exclude some, but God has already called them; and his record book includes everyone who has responded to the gospel, opening their hearts and inviting the Savior to come in.

The Oriental Missionary Society was positioned to begin strategic ministries in the years of significant revivals. In 1901, OMS began its first century in Japan, far from Iowa (Lettie Burd Cowman) and Illinois (Charles Cowman), and even Ontario (E. A. Kilbourne), the birthplaces of three of the four founders, though the fourth founder (Juji Nakada) called Japan home. In 1907, the year of the Great Pyeongyang Revival, OMS entered Korea as its second nation for mission revival and evangelism, two legs that need to be coordinated to step forward together; for mobility's sake, the two must cooperate. My prayer is that, as we look at the initial decade of the twentieth century with a focus on revival, we will begin to see the connections with revival that OMS must make in order to move ahead into its second century, to continue to "keep in step with the Spirit," just as we are born of the Spirit and must live in the Spirit (Galatians 5:25 NIV).

Let us begin the new century on its official first day: January 1, 1901. Here, the new century of the Holy Spirit commenced, not in New York or London, or even Chicago, but in Topeka, the state capital of Kansas, a state only forty years old by this time. Now, when we look at the series of global revivals, even by using several surveys by church historians, we find that Topeka and Los Angeles are missing from the narrative.

Charles F. Parham was a former Methodist pastor who joined with the Holiness movement and later became the theological parent of Pentecostalism. Parham was born in Muscatine, Iowa, in the southeastern corner of the state. He had numerous physical struggles and challenges growing up, and the family relocated to Cheney, Kansas, when Charles was only five years old. Charles's physical disabilities made it difficult for him to do even light farm duties. At the age of thirteen, Parham stood at the close of a church service and formally registered his own conversion experience. This was at the local Congregational church, a far cry from the Apostolic Faith/Pentecostal church that would be his home for the remainder of his life.

Parham preached the fourfold gospel and opened the Bethel Healing Home, and later Bethel Bible College, to train missionaries for the worldwide harvest. As students did their homework assignments and searched through the book of Acts for the Bible evidence of Spirit baptism, Parham departed the school in order to conduct some revival meetings in Kansas City.[147]

Sarah Parham tells the story of how the Spirit visited Topeka on January 1, 1901, the very day on which some have marked the start of global Pentecostalism, or, as we would dare say, global evangelicalism, knowing that Pentecostals are part of the evangelical family as much as Baptists, as much as Holiness, and even as much as Presbyterians. Here's the report of what happened on January 1, 1901:

---

[147] The term "Bible evidence" was used by early Pentecostals to express their belief that speaking in tongues was the initial, physical manifestation proving a person had received the baptism in the Holy Spirit. The very moment that speaking in tongues was experienced, the act of Spirit baptism had occurred.

> Sister Agnes N. Ozman (now LaBerge) asked that hands be laid upon her to receive the Holy Spirit as she hoped to go to foreign fields. At first I refused, not having the experience myself. Then being further pressed to do it humbly in the name of Jesus, I laid my hand upon her head and prayed. I had scarcely repeated three dozen sentences when a glory fell upon her. A halo seemed to surround her head and face, and she began speaking in the Chinese language, and was unable to speak English for three days. When she tried to write in English to tell us of her experience she wrote the Chinese, copies of which we still have in newspapers printed at that time.[148]

It would be only two days later, on January 3, 1901, that Parham himself would receive the missionary gift of Spirit baptism and speaking in tongues. He described his own experience as "a slight twist in my throat, a glory fell over me and I began to worship God in the Sweedish [sic] tongue, which later changed to other languages and continued so until the morning."[149] From Topeka, Parham and his students would carry the message of Pentecost to Kansas City, Lawrence, Galena, and further south to Houston, Texas. As these Midwestern Pentecostals moved south geographically, James Goff estimated that their numbers multiplied as well. Within five years (summer of 1906) there were eight to ten thousand members of the Apostolic Faith.[150]

---

148 Sarah E. Parham, *The Life of Charles F. Parham, Founder of the Apostolic Faith Movement* (Joplin, MO: Hunter Printing Co., 1930), 52–53. Other sources for the life and teachings of Charles Fox Parham include James R. Goff, *Fields White Unto Harvest: Charles Fox Parham and the Missionary Origins of Pentecostalism* (Fayetteville: University of Arkansas Press, 1988) and a section in Douglas Jacobsen, *Thinking in the Spirit: Theologies of the Early Pentecostal Movement* (Bloomington: Indiana University Press, 2003), 18–50.
149 Parham, *The Life of Charles F. Parham*, 54.
150 Goff, *Fields White Unto Harvest*, 115.

The man who would be perhaps the most significant student at Parham's Bible school in Houston was not allowed to sit in the classroom with the other students who were all white, due to the Jim Crow laws. William Joseph Seymour (1870-1922) had already interacted with radical holiness saints and was a student in Houston for only five weeks before he departed to Los Angeles. What happened in Los Angeles after Seymour's arrival in 1906 is historically known as the Azusa Street Mission and Revival (1906-1909).[151] We will turn our attention to that as the third revival location in the first decade of the twentieth century, but only after we visit Wales.

The 1904-1906 revival in Wales was not the first time Wales had experienced revival. In fact, it seemed that whenever anyone, and that would be anywhere in Great Britain (United Kingdom), experienced revival, it spread quickly to Wales. For the revival in Wales, we have the preaching and praying leadership of Evan Roberts, which acted as a catalyst that began the move of the Spirit.

According to popular coverage of the revival, it erupted in November 1903 at a church pastored by Joseph Jenkins at New Quay, Cardigan Bay. One of the first converts was Evan Roberts (1878-1951), a miner/blacksmith who turned evangelist. As a lay preacher, Roberts was assisted by Alexander A. Boddy (1854-1930), an Anglican, and Seth Joshua, a Calvinistic Methodist.[152] Again, we can see a multiconfessional or multidenominational cooperation for the sake of a greater revival.

---

151 While Azusa Street is the name that is more commonly used by scholars, the actual building had the name "Apostolic Faith Gospel Mission" painted on the exterior of the formerly Methodist church building at 312 Azusa Street. For further reading on Azusa Street, see Gastón Espinosa, *William J. Seymour and the Origins of Global Pentecostalism: A Biography and Documentary History* (Durham, NC: Duke University Press, 2014) and Cecil M. Robeck Jr., *The Azusa Street Mission and Revival: The Birth of the Global Pentecostal Movement* (Nashville: Thomas Nelson, 2006).

152 Two of the accounts of the Welsh Revival are J. Vyrnwy Morgan, *The Welsh Revival, 1904-5: A Retrospect and a Criticism* (London: Chapman & Hall, 1909)

On October 29, 1904, a group of young people went with Rev. Seth Joshua (the main evangelist of the Forward movement in Wales) to hear his preaching at Blaenannerch. They joined together in one voice to sing a simple song with a powerful message: "It is coming; it is coming; the power of the Holy Ghost. I receive it; I receive it; the power of the Holy Ghost."

At a 7:00 a.m. service, Pastor Joshua preached these words: "Bend us, O Lord." This became Evan's prayer. Although the revival in Wales was part of the global awakening in the first decade of the twentieth century and a key catalyst for revival in other places, including India, Korea, China, and the US, there is a disconnect theologically between Wales and Azusa, even when the terms are shared. For example, the phrase "filled with the Holy Spirit" contains differences in meaning and application.

People came from other countries (India, China, Japan, Germany, France, US, and Russia) to the Welsh revival. Next, the revival fire spread from Wales to India, Korea (1907), North China, and Latin America. Our next stop in global revivals is India. By 1905, news of the Welsh revival was spreading to America, as people who had visited Wales returned to the US and shared their own experiences. Many more read the accounts by W. T. Stead (1849–1912), S. B. Shaw (1854–1900), and G. Campbell Morgan (1863–1945), all stalwart evangelical leaders at the turn of the new century.

F. B. Meyer (1847–1929) and Joseph Smale (1867–1926), pastor of First Baptist Church in Los Angeles, kept the vision burning with their accounts of the Welsh revival. Frank Bartleman also added to the excitement over Wales and the expectation that God could do the same in Los Angeles.

When we begin to examine the revival in India, we find several locations, but all seem connected in a networking of the

---

and W. T. Stead and G. Campbell Morgan, *The Welsh Revival* (Boston: Pilgrim Press, 1905).

Holy Spirit. One of the first places to experience revival in India was northeast India (Khasi Hills); and it was welcomed at the Mukti Mission (located in Kedgaon in southwest India). At the Mukti Mission, thirty women were meeting daily to pray for the power of the Holy Spirit. Minnie F. Abrams (1859–1912) had been ministering at the Mukti Mission since 1898, and in India from the time she sailed as a faith missionary for Bombay in 1887. She was a graduate of Mankato Normal School (Minnesota) and the Chicago Training School for City, Home, and Foreign Missions.[153] She described in her book the outpouring of the Holy Spirit on June 29, 1905:

> "[A]t 3:30 A.M., the Holy Spirit was poured out upon _____, one of these volunteers. The young woman sleeping next to her awoke when this occurred, and seeing the fire enveloping her, ran across the dormitory, brought a pail of water, and was about to dash it upon her, when she discovered that _____ was not on fire. In less than an hour nearly all of the young women in the compound gathered around, weeping, praying, and confessing their sins to God."[154]

At the end of her book, she constructs a form of spiritual geography, describing the revival in Wales and how it should be extended farther to the nations of the world:

> Prayer is ascending for a world-wide revival. The Spirit was first poured out upon Wales. There, in

---

153 Stanley M. Burgess, ed. *Christian Peoples of the Spirit: A Documentary History of Pentecostal Spirituality from the Early Church to the Present* (New York: New York University Press, 2011), 248.

154 Minnie F. Abrams, *The Baptism of the Holy Ghost and Fire: Matthew 3:11*, 2nd ed. (Kedgaon, India: Mukti Mission Press, 1906), 5–6.

places, they all prayed at once, or sung the same chorus a hundred times over, or quietly listened to the Word and exhortation as the Spirit led. Eye witnesses have described the scenes at Keswick last year (1905), when people were weeping, making confessions, and praying in apparent confusion. Yet there was no confusion in the mind of the infinite God. In Assam and India trembling under the power of conviction, loud crying in prayer, the pouring forth to God in loud confession the sins of a life-time, sudden falling on the ground, writhing, being twisted and violently thrown down when an unclean spirit has been cast out as the person has cried for deliverance, have been frequent scenes.[155]

Many twenty-first-century readers of this report of revival from more than one hundred years ago might be critical of the behavior at the revival meetings, but at the time and in the original context there was no confusion. As Abrams declared, people were clear on how the Spirit manifests himself and how other spirits are manifested. This report is from Minnie Abrams at the Mukti Mission, who would later send a copy of her book, *The Baptism of the Holy Ghost and Fire*, to one of her classmates from Chicago, Mary Hoover, who was now a Methodist missionary in Chile. Her husband, Dr. Willis C. Hoover (1856–1936), read the book and turned from being a Methodist who rejected Pentecost to one who received the fullness of Spirit baptism and speaking in tongues. Word of Hoover's new Pentecostal experience reached the US. The Methodist Church charged Hoover and his group with being "unscriptural, irrational, and anti-Methodist." They were all kicked out. Hoover and thirty-seven of his followers began a new church, The Methodist

---

155 Abrams, *The Baptism of the Holy Ghost and Fire*, 77–78.

Pentecostal Church (La Iglesia Metodista Pentecostal). It is one of the largest Pentecostal denominations today, and, until the construction of Yoido Full Gospel Church in Seoul in 1973, the Jotabeche Methodist Pentecostal Church in Santiago was the largest single congregation in the world.[156]

The Mukti Mission was originally founded under the spiritual direction of Pandita Ramabai (1858–1922). While Minnie Abrams can be identified as a Methodist or Wesleyan-Holiness, the founder, Pandita Ramabai, cannot fit easily within one category, whether evangelical or ecumenical. This is especially true of some evangelicals within Asian nations who were members of mainline denominations and reached out to adherents of other world religions, and in addition, engaged in social ministry beyond evangelism. As we saw earlier, there is no simple way to define evangelicalism. When cultural issues related to language and ethnicity join the mix, the complexity continues to develop. Our next topic moves us from India back to the US for our look at the Azusa Street Revival.

William Joseph Seymour was born in 1870 in Centerville, Louisiana, the son of former slaves, fully aware of the struggles of his people in America. After five weeks at Parham's Bible school in Houston, Texas, Seymour accepted a call to pastor a Holiness church in Los Angeles. Seymour's first sermon at the Holiness church was a message on the Bible evidence of Spirit baptism, namely speaking in tongues. His new congregation was unwilling to accept this new message, forcing Seymour to find yet another new congregation. While the initial group of custodians and domestic workers who first attended Seymour's prayer meetings was African American, more and more whites were attracted to the message and to all the manifestations

---

156 Vinson Synan, *In the Latter Days: The Outpouring of the Holy Spirit in the Twentieth Century*, 2nd ed. (Fairfax, VA: Xulon Press, 2001), 57–62. See also Allan Anderson, *Spreading Fires: The Missionary Nature of Early Pentecostalism* (Maryknoll, NY: Orbis Books, 2007), 201–204.

that become standard for those advocating the Latter Rain and Pentecost. The new building was located at 312 Azusa Street, a former church building used as a warehouse. In the initial issue of *The Apostolic Faith* (September 1906), the building was first described as so small that it was overlooked. This issue also said, "Many churches have been praying for Pentecost, and Pentecost has come. The question is now, will they accept it? God has answered in a way they did not look for. He came in a humble way as of old, born in a manger."[157] The same issue of *The Apostolic Faith* transitioned from describing the Azusa Street Mission as being too small to calling it too big. "Jesus was too large for the synagogues. He preached outside because there was not room for him inside. This Pentecostal movement is too large to be confined in any denomination or sect. It works outside, drawing all together in one bond of love."[158] The multitudes came to 312 Azusa Street from 1906 until nearly 1909 to watch or to study and argue, and, finally at the altar, many would surrender and receive baptism with the Holy Spirit and tongues.

Seymour's major contribution to the Holiness/Pentecostal movement was his preaching and leadership at Azusa. As a pastor concerned with maintaining biblical spirituality, Seymour tended to temper the revival movement not with a call to quench the Spirit, but with an emphasis on creating balance and integrity. Because Seymour's extant writings are very limited, adequately and comprehensively describing his theology is difficult. It is possible, however, to highlight one distinct area of Seymour's theological concern: biblical holiness and unity.

Holiness and unity, according to Seymour, were grounded in the Word of God. Revival and miracles were "wrought by the power of the Holy Ghost flowing through His sanctified

---
157 *The Apostolic Faith* (September 1906): 1.
158 Ibid.

humanity."¹⁵⁹ Once these sanctified people gathered, whether the one dozen that began at Azusa or the thousands who stopped by in pilgrimage, the call to unity would not be "we can be one in spirit." Instead, Seymour exclaimed that "we cannot all be one, except through the Word of God."¹⁶⁰

Holiness required consecration and resulted in humility. It was impossible to exhibit pride in the gifts of the Spirit, if they were genuine. One powerful illustration of humility was the way Seymour understood his own ministry. It was like that of John the Baptist, pointing away from himself and toward the greater one. "Jesus Christ is the archbishop of these assemblies, and He must be recognized. Also, we must recognize the Holy Spirit in all of His office work."¹⁶¹

The Apostolic Faith movement began in Kansas and spread from Missouri to Texas and within five years to California. While parked at 312 Azusa Street, the missiological vehicle would pick up enough pilgrims to spread the message to every region of the United States and to every inhabited continent. But the evangelical missionaries in Korea would not be looking at the Azusa Revival as they prayed and prepared for revival in Pyeongyang; rather, their vision was set on India and Wales.

Korea was marked by changes in the first decade of the twentieth century, specifically within two areas: the advent of Japanese colonization and the ongoing openness to the West, assisted especially by the increasing popularization of Christianity. As previously noted, a number of studies have examined the relationship between religious revivals and social,

---

159   W. J. Seymour, "The Baptism of the Holy Ghost," *The Apostolic Faith* (May 1908): 3.

160   W. J. Seymour, "Christ's Messages to the Church," *The Apostolic Faith* (October–January 1908): 3.

161   W. J. Seymour, "The Holy Spirit Bishop of the Church," *The Apostolic Faith* (September 1907): 3.

economic, and political change; we will be focused on revival as a spiritually intense movement.[162]

Prior to the beginning of the Pyeongyang Revival in 1907 were preparatory meetings for prayer. Jonathan Goforth wrote how "the revival which began in 1903 and had continued to increase, now flowed on in increasing volume, from the Ping Yang [Pyeongyang] center, all over Korea."[163] Young-hoon Lee views "the origin of the revival" as "a prayer meeting of Methodist missionaries at Wonsan in 1903." The leader of the prayer meeting in 1903 was R. A. Hardie. Originally an independent missionary from Canada, he was a member of the Methodist mission by this time. Hardie was assisted by Miss M. C. White, a missionary from China, and he taught on prayer for this eight-day retreat.[164] This brief study will give primary attention to the revival meetings in Pyeongyang in January of 1907.

Without mentioning the earlier date of 1903, Methodist missionaries George Heber Jones (1867–1919) and William Arthur Nobel (1866–1945) described the special prayer meetings in 1906 as preparations for revival.

During the month of August 1906, the missionaries at Pyeongyang sought a deeper experience of God's power in their own lives, and for this purpose meetings for Bible study

---

[162] The following studies present the relationship between religious revivals/movements and social change: Donald W. Dayton, *Discovering an Evangelical Heritage* (New York: Harper & Row, 1976); Nathan O. Hatch, *The Democratization of American Christianity* (New Haven: Yale University Press, 1989); Frank Lambert, *"Pedlar in Divinity": George Whitefield and the Transatlantic Revivals, 1737-1770* (Princeton, NJ: Princeton University Press, 1994); Timothy L. Smith, *Revivalism and Social Reform in Mid-Nineteenth-Century America* (New York: Abingdon, 1957); Harry S. Stout, *The Divine Dramatist: George Whitefield and the Rise of Modern Evangelicalism* (Grand Rapids: Eerdmans, 1991); and George M. Thomas, *Revivalism and Cultural Change: Christianity, Nation Building, and the Market in the Nineteenth-Century United States* (Chicago: University of Chicago Press, 1989).

[163] Jonathan Goforth, *When the Spirit's Fire Swept Korea* (Grand Rapids: Zondervan, 1943; Elkhart, IN: Bethel Publishing, 1984), 12.

[164] Young-hoon Lee, *The Holy Spirit Movement in Korea: Its Historical and Theological Development*, Regnum Studies in Mission (Oxford: Regnum Books, 2009), 25.

and prayer were held for eight days. During these meetings a special burden for the Korean church was laid upon them and in response to their suggestion, hundreds of the Korean Christians covenanted to spend one hour a day in prayer for the outpouring of the Holy Spirit. This concert of prayer continued through the autumn and winter, when in the first week of January 1907, the Holy Spirit was literally poured forth on the people and the fire of his presence spread rapidly throughout the whole city and the surrounding country. This was the outbreak of that revival which can best be likened to a storm.[165]

As early as the 1890s, both Methodist and all four Presbyterian missions were cooperating at a level above and beyond the comity agreement. Although organic union never became a reality, it nonetheless remained a manifestation of the revival that people continued fervently praying for one another.

"Pyeng Yang is praying for all Korea—and it is praying as one man, 'shoulder to shoulder,' missionaries, their servants, Presbyterians, Methodists, school boys, school girls, teachers, church officers, men and women from every class and condition. Unofficially, but organized thoroughly as by the Spirit, they are interceding for thousands of people in the other parts of the land of Korea and the world."[166]

The actual Great Revival took place in the Central Presbyterian Church during the Winter Bible Training Class for Men (January 2–15, 1907), with fifteen hundred present, Methodists and Presbyterians together.[167] The revival began Monday night

---

165 Jones, George Heber, and W. Arthur Noble, *The Korean Revival: An Account of the Revival in the Korean Churches in 1907* (New York: The Board of Foreign Missions of the Methodist Episcopal Church, 1910), 5.

166 W. B. Hung, "Impressions of an Eye Witness," *The Korea Mission Field* (March 1907): 38.

167 For further reading on the Pyeongyang Revival, see Jonathan Goforth, *When the Spirit's Fire Swept Korea* (Elkhart, IN: Bethel, 1984); George Heber Jones, *The Korean Revival* (New York: The Board of Foreign Missions of the Methodist Episcopal Church, 1910); and Yong-Kyu Park, *Pyeongyang Daebuheung Undong* [The Great Revivalism in Korea: Its History, Character, and Impact, 1901–1910] (Seoul: Saengmyeong Ui Malseum Sa, 2000).

(January 14) and lasted through the next day and night. While the training class ended on January 15, the message of Pentecost was taken back to the provinces, cities, and villages in Korea by missionaries and Christians who had experienced the fire of confession and repentance in Pyeongyang. G. S. McCune's account of the revival proves helpful:

> It was estimated last night there were two thousand men crowded into that building, and there were no fewer in the building this evening, I'm sure. After Mr. Hunt's sermon Mr. Lee said a few words. The latter said, "Let us pray," and immediately the room full of men was filled with voices lifted to God in prayer. I am sure that most of the men in the room were praying aloud. It was wonderful! No man prayed with a loud voice, and yet, if you would listen, you could distinguish between the different ones. Some were crying and pleading God's forgiveness for certain sins which they named to Him in prayer. All were pleading for the infilling of the Holy Ghost. Although there were so many voices, there was no confusion at all. It was all a subdued, perfect harmony. I cannot explain it with words. One must surely witness such to be able to understand it. There was an absence of the sensational, the "emotional" (in the sense in which the word is so often used), and there was perfect concentration in the prayer of each one. And it is only the beginning! What great blessings are in store for us the coming days and evenings! . . . The men who preached were filled with the Holy Ghost, else they couldn't have spoken as they did and we wouldn't have seen and heard what I have related

above. I am sure you will join us in prayer for this same thing that we are praying for—that these men may take to their groups the power received here and that the work may increase more than we have ever seen work grow.[168]

Here is the testimony of another eyewitness, missionary William Newton Blair from Kansas: "I stood up and began to pray, 'Father, Father' and got no further. It seemed as if the roof lifted from the building and the Spirit of God came down in a mighty avalanche of power upon us. I knelt at Kim's side and prayed as I had never prayed before...Some threw themselves full length upon the floor, hundreds stood with their arms raised to heaven."[169]

In the popular accounts of revival exists a spiritual geography where one revival begins because of another, markers along the highway of spiritual outpouring. This testifies to the universal nature of revival, emphasizing the supernatural. At other times, it becomes a matter of revival succession to gain spiritual legitimacy. But when one attempts to map the connections between Azusa, Los Angeles, and Pyeongyang, Korea, no clear line appears from one to the other. At the most, the historical connection is indirect, one of a common thread that passed through Wales and India, nearly equivalent to the power of myth, yet one communicated by living witnesses who heard from others.

The writing of Frank Bartleman describes the strong connection between the Azusa Revival and the earlier Indian and Welsh revivals: "The present world-wide revival was rocked in the cradle of little Wales. It was 'brought up' in India, following;

---

168 G. S. McCune, "The Holy Spirit in Pyeng Yang," *The Korea Mission Field* (January 1907): 1–2.
169 Blaire, William, and Bruce Hunt, *The Korean Pentecost and the Sufferings Which Followed* (Edinburgh: Banner of Truth, 1977), 73.

becoming full grown in Los Angeles later."[170] The connection between Azusa and Wales, at least, was more than mythical. Joseph Smale (1867–1926), pastor of First Baptist Church, First New Testament Church, and the Upper Room Mission (in chronological sequence), traveled to Wales and met with Evan Roberts.[171] Frank Bartleman was corresponding with Evan Roberts, asking that the saints in Wales pray for the believers in Los Angeles.[172] The revivals in Wales and India were also reported to the church in Korea, noted as models Korea should repeat.

When we compared our results in Korea with those in China, Japan, and elsewhere, we saw that our ingatherings far exceeded anything in those lands, and we came to the conclusion that God probably did not intend to grant us greater blessings than we had already seen. But we got our eyes opened at Seoul, in September 1906, when Dr. Howard Agnew Johnston, of New York, told us of the revival in the Kassia Hills, India, in 1905–06, where they had baptized eighty-two hundred converts during the two years.[173] Johnston also reported the Welsh revival in his messages of September 1906, titled "Steps to Spiritual Power."[174] It is interesting to note that Wales is mentioned more in the US and India than it is in Korea.

Frank Bartleman wrote *How Pentecost Came to Los Angeles— As It Was in the Beginning* (1925), which remains the fullest account of the revival. Issues of *The Apostolic Faith* provide another source for understanding the events and interpretation of revival in Los Angeles. Two reports were written by missionaries who participated in the Pyeongyang Revival: William

---

170 Frank Bartleman, *Azusa Street* (S. Plainfield, NJ: Bridge Publishing, 1980), 19.
171 C. M. Robeck Jr., "Smale, Joseph" in *The New International Dictionary of Pentecostal and Charismatic Movements*, eds. Stanley M. Burgess and Eduard M. van der Maas (Grand Rapids: Zondervan, 2002), 1074.
172 Bartleman, *Azusa Street*, 31.
173 Jonathan Goforth, *When the Spirit's Fire Swept Korea* (Elkhart, IN: Bethel Publishing, 1984), 7.
174 "Recent Work of the Holy Spirit in Seoul," *The Korea Mission Field*, Vol. 3, No. 3 (March 1907): 41.

Newton Blair (1876-1970) and Jonathan Goforth (1859-1936). Blair's account was first published as *The Korea Pentecost -- And Other Experiences on the Mission Field* (1910). At the time of the Pyeongyang Revival, Blair was assigned to the Pyeongyang Station and had "pastoral charge of North church and charge of Anju and Yung You circuits."[175] Goforth was serving as a missionary in Manchuria and was visiting Korea at the time of the revival. His account was published as *When the Spirit's Fire Swept Korea* (1943).

Let us pause briefly to look at the life and ministry of Jonathan Goforth. He was born on a farm in western Ontario, Canada, the seventh of eleven children. After reading *The Memoir of Robert Murray M'Cheyne*, he committed himself to future ministry in the church. Later, when he heard a powerful message from George Leslie Mackay (1844-1901), a visiting Presbyterian missionary to Taiwan, Goforth dedicated himself to serve as a foreign missionary. While he completed his studies at Knox College (University of Toronto), he served in ministry with both the William Street Mission and the Toronto Mission Union, reaching out to people of the slums. During this ministry time in Toronto, he would meet his future wife, Rosalind (1864-1942), who was an art student at the time.[176]

At first, he was preparing to serve with the China Inland Mission because the Canadian Presbyterians did not have any mission work in China at the time. But the "missionary vision captured the Presbyterian Church of Canada as it never had before."[177] Soon the Goforths would be leaving Canada, sailing for China in 1888, and serving in Honan Province. They experienced many trials. They both suffered from illnesses, five of their eleven children died, and they passed through fires and

---

175 "Presbyterian Mission, North," *The Korea Mission Field* (September 1906): 231.
176 Rosalind Goforth, *Jonathan Goforth* (Grand Rapids: Zondervan, 1937; Minneapolis: Bethany House, 1986), 23-24.
177 Ibid., 36.

floods. In 1900 they survived the Boxer Rebellion, a popular revolt that targeted both foreigners and missionaries in China. In 1904 Goforth began hearing about the revival in Wales and started reading Charles G. Finney's *Lectures on Revivals of Religion* (1835). Both stirred within Goforth's spirit a desire to see and receive the blessings of divine revival. After his visit to Korea to witness firsthand the Great Revival in Pyeongyang, Goforth returned to China and told others of the wonderful grace the saints in Pyeongyang had received. While many heard Goforth's testimonies of revival in Korea, revival fires spread from Korea, through Manchuria, and on to China. Though Goforth became known as a revivalist, some criticized this Pentecostal style and said his views and personal expressions of revival were merely emotionalism. J. Herbert Kane, a China missionary turned missiologist, called Goforth "China's most outstanding evangelist."[178]

It appears the only transpacific connection that remains is the shared testimony of the earlier revivals in Wales and India. Otherwise, the many disconnections would indicate no common revival heritage between Azusa and Pyeongyang. This explains the absence of any Pyeongyang mention in historical accounts of early twentieth-century revivals. Obviously, the two revivals did not know of one another; yet a shared theology brings the two revivals, on opposite sides of the Pacific, under a close evangelical tent, meaning a cry for God to show his mercy and pour out his Spirit. For the radical holiness believers, Pentecost had come to Los Angeles in 1906. For the Korea missionaries, Pentecost had come to Pyeongyang in 1907.

Graham Lee's testimony reminds us of Pentecost's sounds in Pyeongyang:

---

178 Ruth A. Tucker, *From Jerusalem to Irian Jaya: A Biographical History of Christian Missions*, 2nd ed. (Grand Rapids: Zondervan, 2004), 201.

Some of us were praying for two men especially, Mr. Kim and Mr. Chu, for we felt that these two men had things in their lives that needed to be confessed. The climax came when Mr. Kim gained the needed strength. He was sitting on the platform and suddenly he arose and came forward and was immediately given an opportunity. He confessed to hatred in his heart for the other brethren and especially for Mr. Blair, and then he went all to pieces. It was terrible beyond description, the agony that man went through. He fell to the floor and acted like a man in a fit. When he broke down the whole audience broke out in a perfect storm of weeping and they wept and wept and wept. We missionaries were weeping like the rest, and we simply couldn't keep from it. While they were weeping Mr. Kang got up to pray, and that poor man agonized in prayer, and then he broke down completely and wept as if his heart would break. The brethren gathered around, put their arms about him, and soon he became quiet, then it was beautiful to see him go to Mr. Kim, put his arms lovingly about him, and weep with him. When Mr. Kim broke, he turned to Mr. Blair and said, "Pastor Blair, can you forgive me, can you forgive me?" Mr. Blair got up to pray, said the word "Father" twice and he could go no further, he was beyond words. The audience kept on weeping and it seemed as if they could not stop. At last we had to sing a hymn to quiet them, for we feared that some might lose control of themselves. During the singing they quieted down and then the confessions began again and so it went on until two o'clock.[179]

---

179 G. Lee, "How the Spirit Came to Pyeng Yang," *The Korea Mission Field* (March 1907): 34–35.

The power of religious experience at the Pyeongyang Revival was such that the spiritual language of confession expressed the deepest and most profound levels of repentance, while at the same time it showed the inability of language to express religious experience as being "beyond words."

Revival, as experienced in Pyeongyang, returned to Korea by waves, or "rhythmic tides of the sea." With periods of advance and recession, the Korean church was both reaching forward and retreating. Revival and Korean church growth have been joined together throughout the twentieth century. Donald Owens identifies these decades of growth and those of slackening. As we near the close of our look at the first decade of the twentieth century and revivals, let us see how the twentieth century was outlined to revival. From 1884 until 1904, these first twenty years were a time of steady rise in membership. Next were the Great Revival years, when the church experienced explosive growth (1905–1910), followed by a period of small growth (1911–1919). The first five years of the 1920s were a time of revival, followed by recession (1925–1928). The years right before World War II witnessed unusual progress (1929–1937), followed by recession during the years 1937 until 1945, which was followed by another advance (1945–1960).[180]

Beyond the schedule that tracked the decades of recession and growth, we can revisit the decade that saw revival from Topeka to Pyeongyang and add a final discussion on revival, as bookends. What happened in Topeka at the turning of the century from the nineteenth into the twentieth was difficult to explain to onlookers. It was as if the second chapter of Acts became reality again and moved from Jerusalem to the streets of Topeka, Kansas. That same year in another part of the Midwest,

---

180 Donald D. Owens, *Revival Fires in Korea* (Kansas City, MO: Nazarene Publishing House, 1977), 36.

in the city of Chicago, R. A. Torrey's how-to book on revival was published.[181]

Reuben Archer Torrey (1856-1928) was a Congregationalist, a graduate of both Yale University and Yale Divinity School. After a term pastoring churches in Ohio and Minnesota, he joined D. L. Moody in ministry. Moody first appointed Torrey to be principal of the Bible Institute of the Chicago Evangelization Society (now Moody Bible Institute), and later, for twelve years, he served as pastor of the Chicago Avenue Church (Moody Church). His ministry included times overseas as well as evangelistic crusades in Europe, Africa, Asia (including Korea in July 1921), and Australia, accompanied by his songleader, Charles M. Alexander (1867-1920).[182] Torrey and Alexander were the first revivalist team to completely circle the globe in evangelistic ministry.[183] We will revisit Torrey, as he later became dean of the Bible Institute of Los Angeles (Biola), pastor of the Church of the Open Door, and one editor of *The Fundamentals: A Testimony to the Truth* (1910-1915).

While we can fully embrace both Parham and Torrey as evangelicals, marked differences from Topeka to Chicago are undeniable in the aforementioned views of revival. One view was that God powerfully pours out his Spirit in revival, and the other was that people stir revival through prayer and preparation. In a way, the Topeka revival followed the pattern set

---

181 R. A. Torrey, *How to Promote and Conduct a Successful Revival: With Suggestive Outlines* (Chicago: Fleming H. Revell, 1901). A book critical of Torrey's view of revival was published three years later. See T. Rhondda Williams, *The True Revival Versus Torreyism* (London: Percy Lund, Humphries, 1904).

182 While Torrey did not visit Korea during his earlier "around the world" tour with Charles M. Alexander, he did eventually visit Korea from July 6 until July 11, 1921.

183 For a recent biographical study of Torrey, see Fred Sanders, *How God Used R. A. Torrey: A Short Biography as Told Through His Sermons* (Chicago: Moody Press, 2015); the older and still useful George T. B. Davis, *Torrey and Alexander: The Story of a World-Wide Revival* (New York: Fleming H. Revell, 1905); and J. Kennedy Maclean, *Triumphant Evangelism: The Three Years Mission of Dr. Torrey and Mr. Alexander in Great Britain and Ireland* (London: Marshall Brothers, 1907).

during the first Great Awakening, while Jonathan Edwards and the latter fit Charles G. Finney's new measures of "how to do" revival. But the possibility of viewing all revival as "revivalism" remains, to believe that somehow the human element of planning, preparing, conducting, and the follow-up work depend more upon people and less on God. Is it truly possible to have a God-sent and God-superintended revival where people are only receivers of the Spirit? That is a question we can continually ask, knowing theologically there is a difference between human and divine, and realizing how much the church has struggled to fully understand and proclaim Christ's incarnation and Scripture's total inerrancy and inspiration. That is an important question to not only ask, but also to answer. It has a lot to do with evangelicalism, just one introduction to the many hopefully begun by this book. Now, for the other side of the bookends, where revival is planned and prepared, let us go to the end of the first decade in Korea, from one side of the Pacific to the other.

We turn now to an article titled "A Call to Prayer for Korea." In 1910, only three years after the outbreak of the Great Revival in Pyeongyang, the combined evangelical missions, called the General Council of Evangelical Missions in Korea, were praying for one million to be converted in Korea during this one year. Considering evangelical missions had only been active on the peninsula since 1885, and that this is only twenty-five years after the group's very start, this is an amazing and bold expectation for evangelicals in Korea—whether you see grace or works more in play. The evangelical missionaries also saw not only that it was the right time for such prayer (three years after the Great Revival in Pyeongyang), but also that they were led by God to designate their prayers for specifically one million souls in one year. It was both the right year and the right number, but what about the right reason? They felt that the year 1910, remember, only twenty-five years after the very start of evangelical mission in Korea, was "God's opportunity for making Korea a Christian nation; and because Korea is the strategic point of the Far East, and to win Korea NOW means to help immeasurably in the evangelization of the East; we ask Christian people in all lands to observe Sunday, March 20 as a 'Day of Prayer' for the million movement in the onetime 'Hermit Land.' Pray that through the gracious outpouring of the Holy Spirit upon the missionaries, the Christian Koreans, and those who are still in the darkness of heathenism, the million may be more than realized."[184]

In addition to the prayer request for the "million movement," a song was composed and sung by Christians in Korea. It was called the "Million" song. The lyrics were: "A million souls for Jesus! Lord, this can surely be! A million souls for Jesus! 'Tis not too much for Thee! Is not Thy Word all powerful to touch the sinful heart? Is not the Spirit willing thy Word of Life to impart? A million souls for Jesus in this dark land of sin! A million souls for Jesus! Lord, now the work begin!"[185] The million movement involved a series of home visitations, publication and distribution of one million copies of the Gospel of Mark, and visits to Korea by prominent evangelical speakers. Already one year prior (1909), John Wilbur Chapman (1859–1918) and Charles M. Alexander had visited Korea as one stop on a global evangelistic tour. "Christian adherents, who were estimated at only two hundred thousand believers, gave approximately one hundred thousand days of work to the campaign."[186] The vision for one million was reported as being "led by God's Spirit" to the extent that "the committee suggested, that we ask of

---

184 "A Call to Prayer for Korea," *The Korea Mission Field*, Vol. 5, No. 3 (March 1, 1910): 54.
185 "A Million Souls for Jesus" *The Korea Mission Field*, Vol. 5, No. 11 (November 15, 1909): 181.
186 Kim and Kim, *A History of Korean Christianity*, 107.

God 1,000,000 souls in Korea this year. It was adopted unanimously, in deep solemnity while many were trembling at what seemed like temerity, yet not daring to limit God." In the end, they chose the Korean phrase as a motto: "This year a million souls"; in Korean, "Geum nyeon baek man myeong."[187] While the year 1910 was marked in the Korea missionary's calendar as a year of evangelism, with an expectation of converting one million, Korean history itself would record a more significant event: the annexation of Korea by the Japanese empire, beginning thirty-five years of Japanese colonialism on the Korean peninsula. Although historians can trace Japanese influence on Korea back to earlier centuries, the official date that began Japanese annexation was August 22, 1910.

Now, at the end of a decade of revivals, we turn to the increasing desire for the "younger churches" to become independent, even in the midst of the economic hardships of the global Great Depression and the social and cultural pressures from Japanese colonialism. In American evangelicalism, similar to a desire for independence, came a period of dividing and separating called modernism/liberalism. We'll look at both and try to understand the dynamic of transpacific evangelicalism through times of intense trial.

---

187 *The Korea Mission Field*, Vol. 5, No. 10 (October 15, 1909): 195.

6

Independence and the Three Selves

The popularity of the so-called "three selves" in North American and British missions in the late nineteenth and throughout the twentieth century meant that missionaries in Korea were committed to the rise and development of Korean pastoral leadership. But in addition to the nurturing of pastoral leadership was the call for financial independence and ecclesial independence for the purpose of national evangelism.

The phenomenal growth of Protestant Christianity in Korea faced setbacks during Japanese colonialism (1910–1945). In the 1930s, the Japanese government began to impose the Shinto shrine service, resulting in a large number of Korean church leaders compromising their positions. There were exceptions, of course, and the most stellar was Pastor Ju Gicheol.[188] By the next decade, with the forced repatriation of foreign missionaries from both the US and Great Britain during World War II, Korean leadership was in a sink-or-swim mode. Later, after

---

188 For the Shinto shrine issue, see Allen D. Clark, *A History of the Church in Korea* (Seoul: Christian Literature Society of Korea, 1971), 221–232; James Huntley Grayson, "The Shintō Shrine Conflict and Protestant Martyrs in Korea, 1938–1945," *Missiology: An International Review*, Vol. 29, No. 3 (July 2001): 287–305; and Timothy S. Lee, *Born Again: Evangelicalism in Korea* (Honolulu: University of Hawaii Press, 2010), 54–60.

national independence and the formation of separate regimes (1945–1948), the Korean War (1950–1953) and its aftermath became a crisis that fully tested the strength of the independent church in Korea. We will be looking at all these developments in the history of evangelicalism in Korea. First up is the issue of independence.

A delayed financial independence for the Korean church meant that Korean Christians could not manage their affairs through the traumas of colonialism and war without outside assistance. This aid was most visible in the postwar relief efforts of North American Protestant denominations, mission agencies, and the parachurch organization World Vision. Samuel H. Moffett wrote that the "overwhelming relief and reconstruction needs of Korea after the war made at least a temporary suspension of the principle of self-support inevitable."[189] While the Korean church had achieved independence in the areas of government and evangelization, financial dependence upon the West caused further disruptions and divisions in the Korean church.

As a means of viewing the Nevius Plan and its programming in Korea missions, we will look beyond the numbers, whether adherents or dollars. Filling in a graph with the numerical input to show the growth of a mission or church over a decade, or even a century, is an easy-enough task. Numbers, however, while they show growth or decline, cannot tell the historical narrative to include both the larger context and its theological significance. Along with the statistical analysis of missiology and church growth, we need to fill in the picture with the historical context and color it with theological analysis. Just as church history needs missiology to tell a bigger story, so also missiology needs church history to see beyond the numbers.[190]

---

189 Samuel Hugh Moffett, *The Christians of Korea* (New York: Friendship Press, 1962), 61.

190 For a look at how missiology can enhance church history, see Mark A. Noll, "The Challenges of Contemporary History, the Dilemmas of Modern History, and Missiology to the Rescue," *Missiology*, Vol. 24 (1996): 47–64.

INDEPENDENCE AND THE THREE SELVES

The purpose of this chapter is to fill in the blank spaces with the historical context that surrounded the Korea mission's decision in the late nineteenth century to become independent, along with adding some theological color to understand the impact of the Nevius Plan on global evangelicalism.

America was especially aware of the spread of independence movements into the nineteenth century, after having won its own war of independence against Britain in 1783. The call for revolution spread to France (1789–1799) and later back to the western hemisphere with declarations of independence in Haiti (1804), Chile (1810), Paraguay and Venezuela (1811), Mexico (1813), Argentina (1816), Columbia (1820), Venezuela (1821), Ecuador (1822), Bolivia (1824), and Uruguay (1825).[191] By 1850, the vast Spanish empire in the New World, which had covered two continents, had dwindled down to only two nations: Cuba and Puerto Rico.[192] At the same time that the Spanish empire was in decline, Belgian, British, Dutch, German, and French colonialism, and in the twentieth century, American and Japanese colonialism, were all expanding and consolidating power within Africa and Asia. With this larger historical context in play, the message of three selves seems an irony. For in the bigger picture, while the nations of this world are competing for territory, the kingdom of Christ is proclaiming independence to the new churches. Now, we turn to the formula itself: three selves.

Perhaps the most important mission theory that emerged in the early nineteenth century was the indigenization principle or the three selves: self-supporting, self-governing, and self-propagating. Among the group of British and American mission theorists who advocated the three selves were Henry

---

191 It is difficult to list accurately the independence movements in Latin America, since declarations of independence do not always equal the establishment of a separate and free government.
192 J. H. Elliott, *Empires of the Atlantic World: Britain and Spain in America 1492-1830* (New Haven: Yale University Press, 2006), 391.

Venn (1796–1873), Rufus Anderson (1796–1880), William Taylor (1821–1902), and John Livingston Nevius (1829–1893). A quick reading of the three mission leaders who predated Nevius will show similarities in both mission theory and practice.

Henry Venn is considered the actual "father" of the indigenous church principles. As a leader of the evangelical branch of Anglicans, he opposed the High Church view of episcopacy-dominated missions. He also opposed the civilizing model of Christian mission. The three Cs of commerce, civilization, and Christianity did not belong together in Venn's view of world mission. Venn became the secretary of the Church Missionary Society (founded in 1799) in 1841, representing the mission interests of the evangelical party within the Church of England. For Venn, the pattern for mission was the Antioch church, as it was described in the New Testament and through the first centuries of church history.[193]

As a Congregationalist, Rufus Anderson was given the responsibility of serving as senior secretary of the American Board of Commissioners for Foreign Missions (ABCFM) in 1832, working until he achieved emeritus status in 1875. Anderson stressed the need to have a "native ministry" capable of "self-propagation" and organized into churches, with one aim: "the conversion of lost men."[194] Just as with Venn, Anderson disagreed with the task of civilizing the world. He wrote, "The proper test of success in missions, is not the progress of civilization, but the evidence of a religious life."[195]

William Taylor questioned the institution-based methods

---

193 Wilbert R. Shenk, *Henry Venn Missionary Statesman*, American Society of Missiology Series, Vol. 6 (Maryknoll, NY: Orbis, 1983), 27–29.

194 R. Pierce Beaver, "Rufus Anderson 1796–1880, To Evangelize, Not Civilize," in *Mission Legacies: Biographical Studies of Leaders of the Modern Missionary Movement*, eds. Gerald H. Anderson, Robert T. Coote, Norman A. Horner, and James M. Phillips (Maryknoll, NY: Orbis, 1998), 549.

195 R. Pierce Beaver, ed. *To Advance the Gospel: Selections from the Writings of Rufus Anderson* (Grand Rapids: Wm. B. Eerdmans, 1967), 102.

of nineteenth-century Methodist missions and began to follow a biblical model of "self-supporting missions."[196] After thirty years of mission experience, Taylor wrote his *Pauline Methods of Missionary Work* (1879). Following Paul's apostolic ministry, Taylor listed six items in the plan: "to plant nothing but pure gospel seed," native leadership, the unity of the Holy Spirit, "without purse or scrip" (faith mission), indigenous communities of faith, and an itinerant ministry (staying only long enough to "develop the Christian character of each member up to the standard of holiness").[197]

All three advocates of indigenous missions stressed the need to develop pastoral leadership within the cultural context of each mission. William Taylor cited Paul's selection of both Timothy and Titus as examples of this pattern. All three mission theorists pointed back to the New Testament or the early church as being the correct standard for all contemporary mission.

The New Testament and apostolic pattern of the indigenous church promoted by these nineteenth-century mission leaders would be further developed by John Livingston Nevius and carried to the Korea field in 1890. This was the ideal of the emerging mainstream of Protestant conciliar and evangelical mission theology. Indigenous missions would be carried through the meetings of the ecumenical movement in Edinburgh (1910), Jerusalem (1928), Tambaram (1938), Bangkok (1973), and on to the Lausanne Congress on Evangelism (1974).[198]

---

196 William Taylor, *Ten Years of Self-Supporting Missions in India* (New York: Philips & Hunt, 1882), 92–99.

197 David Bundy, "William Taylor 1821–1902, Entrepreneurial Maverick for the Indigenous Church," in *Mission Legacies: Biographical Studies of Leaders of the Modern Missionary Movement*, eds. Gerald H. Anderson, Robert T. Coote, Norman A. Horner, and James M. Phillips (Maryknoll, NY: Orbis, 1998), 464.

198 Robert Wuthnow, *Boundless Faith: The Global Outreach of American Churches* (Berkeley and Los Angeles: University of California Press, 2009), 52–53. One alternative to the three selves is the idea of "full circle." It has been used by missiologists who study the growth of third-world missions. See C. Peter Wagner, "Full Circle: Third World Missions," in *Readings in Third World Missions: A Collection of Essential Documents*, ed. Marlin L. Nelson (South Pasadena, CA: William Carey Library, 1976), 57–66.

The real advocate of mission independence through the three selves was John Livingston Nevius, born near Ovid, New York.[199] He attended Union College in Schenectady, New York, and for a while taught school in Georgia. During his time as a teacher, he attended an Old School Presbyterian church, which influenced his choice of Princeton over Union for theological studies. While at Princeton, Nevius arose daily at 4:00 a.m. to spend time in prayer. At Princeton, he received his call to missions.[200] Studying under both Archibald Alexander and Charles Hodge, Nevius graduated with a bachelor of divinity degree (now master of divinity) in 1853.

He was ordained by the New Brunswick presbytery (New Jersey) in May of that year and married in June to Helen Coan.[201] The newly married couple departed for China on the Bombay ship on September 19, 1853.[202] The journey lasted six months, and upon their arrival, the Neviuses began studying the Chinese language. After one year, John Nevius was proficient enough in Chinese to preach on the streets of northeastern China. From this early period in Nevius's mission to China, he envisioned the need for both a theological school and a synod, both as essential components of a growing and developed indigenous church.[203] After nearly four years in the United States, the Neviuses returned to China in 1869 with his new ministry of teaching at the theological seminary in Hangchow.[204]

---

199 The biographical sources on the life of John Livingston Nevius include a biography written by his wife, Helen S. Coan Nevius, *The Life of John Livingston Nevius: For Forty Years a Missionary in China* (New York: Fleming H. Revell, 1895), and an article by Everett N. Hunt Jr., "The Legacy of John Livingston Nevius," *International Bulletin of Missionary Research*, Vol. 15, No. 3 (July 1991): 120, 122–124.

200 John Halsey Wood Jr., "John Livingston Nevius and the New Missions History," *The Journal of Presbyterian History*, Vol. 83, No. 1 (Spring/Summer 2005), 26.

201 Wood, "John Livingston Nevius," 28.

202 Everett N. Hunt Jr., "The Legacy of John Livingston Nevius," *International Bulletin of Missionary Research*, Vol. 15, No. 3 (July 1991): 122.

203 Wood, "John Livingston Nevius," 29.

204 Hunt, "The Legacy of John Livingston Nevius," 122.

While in the United States, his book *China and the Chinese* was published by Harper and Brothers.[205] This book portrays Chinese culture in positive terms, with the only negatives given for Chinese religions, which he equates as "idolatrous and superstitious."[206]

The next year, the Neviuses requested to relocate to Chefoo. There John continued itinerant ministry, visiting preaching points on horseback. From June to August of each year, around forty young men would come to the Nevius home for an intensive time of Bible instruction. As a means of training church leaders, Nevius wrote his *Manual for Inquirers*; it included Bible study methods, guidelines on prayer, the Apostles' Creed, and memory verses.[207]

During this latter period of mission, he also developed the ideas which later would become a series of articles in the 1885 *Chinese Recorder*. These articles turned into the Nevius Plan, published as *Methods of Mission Work* (1886) and later as *The Planting and Development of Missionary Churches* (1899). On the basis of his work on mission theory and methodology, Nevius was invited to address the missionary conference in Shanghai (1889) and a small group of Presbyterian missionaries in Korea for two weeks (1890). Nevius's mission principles were not accepted by all of his colleagues in China. One of his most critical opponents was a fellow Presbyterian missionary to China, Calvin Wilson Mateer (1836–1908).[208] What Nevius considered to be the "new" method of mission was rejected by proponents of what was termed the "old" methods. Old methods represented a more traditional (and institutional) view on

---

205 John Livingston Nevius. *China and the Chinese: A General Description of the Country and Its Inhabitants* (New York: Harper and Brothers, 1869).
206 Wood, "John Livingston Nevius," 33.
207 John Livingston Nevius, *The Planting and Development of Missionary Churches* (Philadelphia: Presbyterian and Reformed Publishing Company, 1958), 38.
208 See Daniel W. Fisher, *Calvin Wilson Mateer, Forty-Five Years a Missionary in Shantung, China* (Philadelphia: Westminster Press, 1911).

the hiring and funding of Chinese evangelists. Mateer insisted that Nevius's methods failed to bear fruit in Shantung, where he had ministered for a decade.

After a visit to Japan, the Neviuses returned to the United States, coming back to China in 1892. John continued his hectic schedule of visiting the churches in the Shantung area. This ministry pace continued only until October 19, 1893, when John died from a heart attack; he was only sixty-four years old.[209] Out of nearly four decades of mission to China, our gaze is fixed upon a short term of only two weeks, when Nevius began to share his heart and his principles with a small group of young missionaries in Korea.

Though he was only in Korea for a brief sojourn, Nevius's legacy carries on beyond a century later. Helen Nevius described the scene in June 1890 where "the young missionaries clustered around [John] as round a father, with affection and deference, asking his advice on many questions."[210] In 1890, Horace Underwood was only thirty-one years old; Nevius at that time was sixty-one. Among the less than a dozen young missionaries was twenty-six-year-old Samuel A. Moffett.[211] Indeed, the torch was being passed, and the principles would be planted both in policy and planning of the Korean Presbyterian Church.

Horace G. Underwood described the decision of the mission:

> After careful and prayerful consideration, we were led, in the main, to adopt this, and it has been the policy of the Mission first, to let each man "Abide in the calling wherein he was found," teaching that each was to be an individual worker for Christ and

---

209   Hunt, "The Legacy of John Livingston Nevius," 122.
210   Helen S. Coan Nevius, *The Life of John Livingston Nevius: For Forty Years a Missionary in China* (New York: Fleming H. Revell, 1895), 447.
211   Charles Allen Clark, *The Nevius Plan for Mission Work: Illustrated in Korea* (Seoul: Christian Literature Society, 1937), 84.

INDEPENDENCE AND THE THREE SELVES

to live Christ in his own neighborhood, supporting himself by his trade.

Secondly, to develop church methods and machinery only so far as the native Church was able to take care of and manage the same.

Third, as far as the Church itself was able to provide the men and the means to set aside those who seemed the better qualified, to do evangelistic work among their neighbors.

Fourth, to let the natives provide their own church buildings, which were to be native in architecture, and of such style as the local church could afford to put up.

In addition to the training strategy itself was the textbook. The study of the Bible, according to Underwood, was the real source of the Korean church's growth.[212]

After the Nevius Plan was accepted as standard procedure for Presbyterian mission in Korea, it was decided that a copy of Nevius's book would be handed to every new missionary who arrived in Korea. After one year, each new missionary would be examined on his/her knowledge of the Korean language and Nevius's book.[213]

By 1929, when Charles Allen Clark completed and successfully defended his PhD dissertation at the University of Chicago, it seemed that the Nevius Plan would sustain exponential growth of the Korean church through the century. Clark noted that,

---

212 Horace G. Underwood, *The Call of Korea: Political—Social—Religious* (New York: Fleming H. Revell, 1908), 109–111.
213 Charles Allen Clark, *The Korean Church and the Nevius Methods* (New York: Fleming H. Revell, 1930), 76.

among all the mission fields of the Presbyterian Church, the Nevius Plan was only being followed consistently in Korea.[214] In his conclusion, Clark noted the "Fundamental Factor making success possible was the self-support element." Second was "self-propagation," and third was "self-government."[215] With the financial side emphasized as being the most important, it deserves closer attention.

Financial independence can mean a small amount or a large amount, depending upon the size of the overall budget. For Calvin Mateer, it included a church building with a full-time pastor on salary who was able to administer the sacraments and preach. Nevius's view of self-support was on a smaller scale, with unpaid and voluntary staff meeting together in someone's house, which might or might not be subsidized by the community.[216] Self-support would only come after the church had grown. For that reason, Roy Shearer noted the differences between the phenomenal growth in the northwest of Korea (Pyeongyang) and the slower growth in Seoul. He stated bluntly: "It is clearly incorrect to say that the Church will grow wherever the Nevius Method is used." He further cites Chun Sung Chun and George Adams who expressed their view that "the Nevius principle of self-support not only did not fit well with the poverty-ridden tenant farmer population in the south, but it, in fact, retarded growth there."[217] Following the Nevius Plan for the entire nation simply meant there would be places where it worked and places where it failed.

As we mentioned above, Nevius had envisioned the need

---

214 Charles Allen Clark, *The Korean Church and the Nevius Methods* (New York: Fleming H. Revell, 1930), 219.
215 Clark, *The Korean Church and the Nevius Methods*, 242.
216 Nevius, *The Planting and Development of Missionary Churches*, 31–35.
217 Roy E. Shearer, "The Evangelistic Missionary's Role in Church Growth in Korea," *International Review of Mission*, Vol. 54, No. 216 (October 1965): 467. See also Roy E. Shearer, *Wildfire: Church Growth in Korea* (Grand Rapids: Wm. B. Eerdmans, 1966), a work that grew out of Shearer's studies with Donald A. McGavran (1897–1990) at the Institute of Church Growth (Eugene, Oregon).

for both a theological seminary and a synod in China, and he served on faculty at a seminary for the last eight years of his life. But, as a graduate of Princeton Theological Seminary, was Nevius thinking of building another Princeton in China?

In his *The Planting and Development of Missionary Churches*, Nevius mentioned "Bible or Training Classes," not seminaries or schools of theology. Nevius criticized the very idea of a professional class of church leaders as being "introduced by missionaries from the Church at home." For Nevius, it was a "prevailing disposition in western lands, noticeable in Protestant communions as well as in the Romish Church." In summary, it was "ecclesiasticism." Self-support then downgraded the ministry from a profession to a service, from leader to common member. One cannot help but notice the influence of the free church and the American ideal of the "democratization" of Christianity being carried across the Pacific.[218]

Looking at Protestant Christianity in Korea today, one can easily consider 1890 and proclaim that the Nevius Plan worked. It "was the key to the institutional growth that made the Presbyterian denomination the largest Christian body in Korea from the beginning of the century."[219] But why did the Nevius Plan work in Korea so well when it did not work in China? G. Thompson Brown helps our understanding of the unique context that was Korea over one hundred years ago.

The first factor was nationalism. The colonial power in Korea was Asian, not European, and the Christian missionaries were seen as friends, not enemies of independence. In China, Christians were viewed as being on the other side of a progressive independence movement.

---

218 See Nathan O. Hatch, *The Democratization of American Christianity* (New Haven: Yale University Press, 1989). It should be noted that the religious movements which became more "of the people" discarded Reformed theology (Calvinism) to get there.
219 Donald N. Clark, *Living Dangerously in Korea: The Western Experience 1900-1950* (Norwalk, CT: EastBridge, 2003), 127.

The second factor was the development of a national church by the missionaries. In China, missionaries themselves set up presbyteries composed of their own membership. In Korea, the first Koreans were ordained only twenty-three years after the first missionaries arrived.

The third factor is the smaller number of Protestant missions in Korea as compared with China. China had 130 missions by 1919, while Korea had only four Presbyterian missions and two Methodist missions.

Finally, Brown lists a number of cultural and religious features unique to Koreans themselves. In the end, it seems it was not the Nevius Plan but rather the Korean people who made for the success story of evangelicalism into the twentieth century.[220] But what about the next century? What about looking further ahead into the third millennium?

We know church historians are not allowed to predict the future; that remains the territory of prophecy, not history. Yet generations must look ahead if they are to grow in their understanding of the past.

When we consider updating Nevius for a global church, we have to ask, Is it possible for an independent, indigenous, and successful three-selves church to become a global church that is evangelical in both confession and lifestyle?

I can think of three possible relationships between sending churches and receiving churches: dependence, independence, and interdependence. The "old" churches were all dependent, the "new" churches were independent, but the global evangelical church calls for churches that are interdependent. In the area of missions and money, this idea is simply called "partnerships."[221]

---

220 G. Thompson Brown, "Why Has Christianity Grown Faster in Korea Than in China?" *Missiology: An International Review*, Vol. 22, No. 1 (January 1994): 82–85.

221 See Mary T. Lederleitner, *Cross-Cultural Partnerships: Navigating the Complexities of Money and Mission* (Downers Grove, IL: IVP Books, 2010).

Interdependent churches are globally connected beyond cultural borders, in spite of racial and ethnic differences, and they express the full beauty of all God's children. How can that be achieved? It is not a least-common-denominator union of everyone everywhere who believes anything.

In the third millennium lies a need for each culture to express what it means to be truly evangelical. This calls for contextualized evangelical theologies. The continuing "brain drain" from the East to the West, and from the South to the North, makes establishing an indigenous evangelical identity increasingly difficult. Even in the case of South Korea, with its numerous theological seminaries and Christian universities, the direction remains as the East going out to the West and not so much the West coming to the East. Can we learn from one another, being interdependent members of one body? We will revisit this question in our conclusion: "Being Evangelical, Doing Gospel, and Going Global."

While ecclesiastical independence was the drive for Korean Christians, the political situation in Korea cried out for independence, heard especially on the streets of Seoul in 1919. The words ringing loudly on the streets were "Manse Dongnip," or "Long live independence." As we consider the history of the late nineteenth-century independence movement in Korea, some key dates arise. First, 1884 was the time of the Kapsin Revolt, which sought reform in Korea through the implementation of Japanese-style political events. In 1894, the Donghak Peasant Revolt spread from the southeast of Korea to the entire peninsula. Two wars, involving China and Japan, and Russia and Japan, were fought on Korean soil (Sino-Japanese War and Russo-Japanese War). Right after the end of the Russo-Japanese War, Japan took Korea in as a protectorate. Second, Korean annexation was official and complete by Japan in 1910. Already independence movements in Asia were taking off after the

Paris Peace Conference and US President Wilson's encouraging words which incited people to not only desire independence but also to demand it. While the March First movement was not the first or last struggle for independence from Japan, it would set the standard for decades to come of how a people have the right to be free from colonialism.[222] On March 1, 1919, a group of thirty-three signers made the Korean Declaration of Independence official and would stand or fall with this cry for independence. Of that total, sixteen out of the thirty-three were Christians (Protestant). Most significant among the sixteen Christians was Kil Seonju. In addition to Kil Seonju, we will discuss the end of Rev. John Thomas's ministry in Korea, as the victim of a Japanese assault shortly after the shouts for independence on March 1.

First, we will see Rev. Kil Seonju (1869–1935) as a people's representative who turned again to revivalism.[223] Born in Anjoo, near Pyeongyang, North Korea, on March 15, 1869, he was raised by a traditional Confucian family and had his own avid interest in religions (Taoism and Buddhism). Seonju was what we would call a "spiritual seeker." When he was twenty-eight, he received a copy of the Chinese Bible and John Bunyan's *The Pilgrim's Progress*. After his readings in Christian literature, Seonju decided to pray to the Christian God to ask for forgiveness of sins and for salvation. At first his prayer was in formal language:

> "Dear Heavenly Lord, take pity on me. I have come to have doubts about Seondo, which I have

---

[222] For further reading on the March First movement, see Timothy S. Lee, "A Political Factor in the Rise of Protestantism in Korea: Protestantism and the 1919 March First Movement," *Church History*, Vol. 69, No. 1 (March 2000): 116–142.

[223] Chong Bum Kim, "Preaching the Apocalypse in Colonial Korea," in *Christianity in Korea*, eds. Robert E. Buswell Jr. and Timothy S. Lee (Honolulu: University of Hawaii Press 2006), 149–166.

devotedly believed in and studied for many years; yet I do not understand whether that seemingly righteous teaching of Christianity is indeed the truth leading to eternal life; I am so distraught I am at the edge of death. Please take pity and give me peace in my heart."

But after several days of praying in this manner, late at night, he was on his knees, hunched over and alone, earnestly in prayer. He was engaged in a wrestling—the wrestling of life and death that Jacob had engaged in with God to be confirmed by an answer to his prayer. Before Kil—in earnest, with sweat streaming down his face—had uttered, "Tell me whether Jesus is the true savior of humankind," the inside of the room reverberated with a ringing sound of a jade flute, followed by thunderous gun noises that seemed to shake the room. In the instant when Kil was startled and astonished, he heard above the din three times—"Kil Seonju, Kil Seonju, Kil Seonju"—which so terrified and shook him up that he did not dare raise his head. In prostration he prayed, "My father who loves me, please forgive my sins and save me." In that moment, his heart finally burst forth and his mouth opened, enabling him to call God "father." On his own, Kil realized he was a sinner and wailed loudly. His body grew hot like a ball of fire; he prayed harder and louder. For a long time, Kil's prayer continued. He reached a state of ecstasy. Joy gushed forth from his heart; tears of gratitude overflowed like spring water. As if in a state of frenzy or intoxication, he felt nothing but joy filling up his heart. His mind was peaceful. His pessimism toward the world was overcome by joy; his nickname "the Hercules" would be replaced by another, the "Madman of the Gospel." The moment he prayed to the Heavenly Lord seeking enlightenment as to whether Jesus was the savior, calling God "father," Kil himself had become a captive of Christ.[224]

The reason for this lengthy account of Kil Seonju's conversion is to show the strong parallels with both the biblical text (Jacob is mentioned by name, but there is also a similarity with Saul/Paul's conversion narrative) and evangelicalism. This is a classic account of evangelical conversion; one could place it next to John Newton or Charles G. Finney and not lose any power of the text.

Soon Kil was baptized by the Presbyterian missionary Graham Lee, and he would later join with the six students to begin studying at the Presbyterian Theological Seminary, established in 1901 in Pyeongyang. His ordination would follow his graduation in 1907. One of the remarkable traits of Kil's revivalism was this: "the gospel was not escapist but transformational."[225]

While doing ministry in Pyeongyang, Seonju played a crucial role in the Pyeongyang Revival (1907). He was a pioneer in the daybreak prayer meetings, holding them at 4:00 a.m. But then his life took a seemingly different turn toward politics and not ministry. In March 1919, Seonju would become one of the thirty-three who signed the Declaration of Independence. Because of his involvement, he was imprisoned for two years. During his time in prison, Seonju read the Old Testament 30 times, the New Testament 100 times, and the book of Revelation 10,200 times.

After his release, he never returned to political issues but devoted himself to evangelism and revival services. During his thirty years of ministry, Seonju planted sixty churches, preached twenty thousand sermons, baptized three thousand, and led seventy thousand to saving faith in Jesus Christ. He was known

---

[224] Robert E. Buswell Jr., ed. *Religions of Korea in Practice*, Princeton Readings in Religions (Princeton, NJ: Princeton University Press, 2007), 402–403.

[225] Mark Shaw, *Global Awakening: How 20th-Century Revivals Triggered a Christian Revolution* (Downers Grove, IL: InterVarsity, 2010), 43.

as a revival preacher, turning to the book of Revelation for many of his sermons. He died shortly after having suffered a major stroke in the middle of preaching at a revival meeting in 1935. Now, we turn briefly to an incident where a foreign missionary in Korea was wrongly beaten and how the independence movement signaled his return to the US.

John Thomas (1868–1940) and his older brother David Thomas (1860–1930) were established financially through David's clothing business in London. The two brothers worked together, "tarried" for sanctification together, and finally ministered together through Reader Harris's (1847–1909) Pentecostal League of Prayer, though David never preached, but remained a member of the laity. Later, in 1906, after a disagreement with Reader Harris over his interdenominational ministry where ministers and missionaries remained members of other denominations and served together, David Thomas started the Holiness Mission in Battersea, London. Renamed the International Holiness Mission, it became a fellowship or association of ministers that took the place of established churches until it merged with the Church of the Nazarene in 1952.

John Thomas was ministering at the Star Hall in Manchester when the call for mission to Korea came. John and Emily Thomas sailed for Korea and arrived in 1910, and the next year commenced leadership of the Bible school.[226] Gyeongseong Bible Academy became the one and only place of theological education for the growing Holiness Church, later called the Korea Evangelical Holiness Church.

John and Emily Thomas were in their ninth year of mission in Korea when—during a mission trip to South Chungcheong Province to inspect some mission property—John was physically assaulted by the Japanese police, mistaken for an American and

---

226 "Our Call to Korea" by Brother and Sister John Thomas; "Native Missionaries" by Cowman & Kilbourne, Japan, *God's Revivalist and Bible Advocate* (July 7, 1910): 12.

thought to have led the local independence demonstrations. A signed statement officially gave a report to the government of his physical assault on March 20, 1919, and was published with other documents by the Federal Council of Churches in the US. The official account of John Thomas's attack was stated as follows:

> "On March 20th the Rev. John Thomas, a missionary of the Oriental Missionary Society, was attacked by soldiers at Kokei, and severely beaten. When he produced his British passport, it was thrown on the ground and stamped on, as was also a preaching permit which had been given him by the authorities."[227]

In addition to the official report was John Thomas's own sworn testimony of what happened. He saw a group of five young men race by as they yelled out "Mansei," meaning "ten thousand lives," generally a Korean expression that denotes support of a cause. A few minutes after the young men passed by Thomas, four soldiers came with two police officers. They began to beat John Thomas "and kicked us mercilessly, refusing to hear of explanation, and started to take us to the police station."[228] Later, the five Korean young men who had shouted aloud "Mansei" were questioned and admitted no knowledge of John Thomas, not even being aware that there was a foreigner in the village that afternoon/evening. The police then realized they were

---

227 The Commission on Relations with the Orient of the Federal Council of the Churches of Christ in America, *The Korean Situation: Authentic Accounts of Recent Events by Eye Witnesses* (New York: Commission on Relations with the Orient of the Federal Council of the Churches of Christ, 1919), 19.
228 The Commission on Relations with the Orient of the Federal Council of the Churches of Christ in America, *The Korean Situation: Authentic Accounts of Recent Events by Eye Witnesses*, 35.

mistaken in assuming a connection between John Thomas and the five young Korean protesters.

John Thomas was later asked to leave Korea and to never return, due to an amount of financial reparations paid on his behalf to the British government. While some reports exaggerated his injuries to the point of describing them as nearly death-causing, his own statement did not mention physical wounds or injuries of that extent, but rather mentioned others having received more severe beatings. Further, we can surmise from reading a 1922 article in *The Way of Faith* (Columbia, South Carolina) that Thomas was still alive and well, serving as an itinerant evangelist not in his native Britain (Wales), but in the US, based in Wilmore, Kentucky. And, when one considers the schedule he kept for evangelism, one could assume the requirement of strength that a person nearly dead would have trouble finding.[229]

Holiness, being separate from the world and consecrated to God, was the call in America, as we turn toward the second and third decades of the twentieth century. Perhaps no evangelist represents this move more than Billy Sunday. As separation was the new standard for fundamentalism, it took several forms, some culturally separate, others theologically separate in what they believed/confessed. The old religion became the standard for the decades and centuries ahead.

William "Billy" Ashley Sunday (1862–1935) was born on a farm near Ames, Iowa. He was known as the "baseball evangelist" because he had played for the major league. With little formal education but a radical conversion and a passion for evangelism, Sunday headed to the small towns of the Midwest to preach the gospel and speak against alcohol. Later, his crusades would make it to major cities of America.[230] Sunday is given credit for

---

229 John Thomas, "The Gospel is Still the Power of God," *The Way of Faith* (Columbia, SC), Vol. 33, No. 42 (October 19, 1922): 5–6.
230 For a biographical study of Billy Sunday, see Lyle W. Dorsett, *Billy Sunday and*

having helped pass the Prohibition Amendment (Eighteenth Amendment to the US Constitution). This restriction on alcohol would later be repealed with the Twenty-first Amendment in 1933. Since we are taking a closer look at Prohibition in the US, we can observe that both liberals and fundamentalists were united in their opposition to the manufacture, sale, and consumption of alcoholic beverages in America. Many social problems were related to the abuse of alcohol, and advocates of both social reform (liberals) and evangelism (conservatives) were opposed to the use of alcohol. During this time in America, many criminals (gangsters) began to make and sell liquor illegally. As crime increased, many citizens said that it was impossible to "legislate morality."

While the efforts to battle alcohol in the US were a unified front, the next decade would witness some of the more seemingly stable denominations start to unravel as they prepared to divide, usually between "fundamentalists" and "moderates." Moderates (liberals) had control and an apparent monopoly on higher education and theological education. Still, the conservatives had to show absolute commitment to theological orthodoxy and conservative Christianity.

One of the first and perhaps most significant seminaries to usher in the separation of the 1920s and 1930s was Princeton Theological Seminary. In our section on theological education in America, we viewed Princeton as a seminary that started to combat the liberalism of Yale Divinity School (and Yale University). The new founding of Westminster Theological Seminary by Rev. J. Gresham Machen (1881–1937) marked the beginning of evangelical/fundamentalism and the increase

---

the Redemption of Urban America, Library of Religious Biography (Grand Rapids: Wm. B. Eerdmans, 1991), and for a look at the religious cultural context of the time, see Douglas W. Frank, *Less Than Conquerors: How Evangelicals Entered the Twentieth Century* (Grand Rapids: Wm. B. Eerdmans, 1986).

in theological seminaries and Bible colleges.[231] In addition to Westminster, Machen would start the Independent Board for Presbyterian Foreign Missions (1933) and the Orthodox Presbyterian Church (1936).

Since Machen represents the start of a new seminary, new mission board, and a new church (denomination), we can study him more carefully as a representative of the move away from Protestant liberalism toward evangelicalism. We find even more in Machen by viewing him as a mentor: "Three of his students, Harold Ockenga, Carl McIntire, and Francis Schaeffer, for instance, were instrumental in shaping some of the most pivotal later movements."[232] Further, with the publication of Machen's *Christianity and Liberalism*, the view of Protestant liberalism would shift to find that liberalism had become a separate religion, as different from Christianity as Buddhism or Islam.

Machen underlines the radical divide between Christianity and liberalism when he writes, "The Christian religion which is meant is certainly not the religion of the modern liberal Church, but a message of divine grace, almost forgotten now, as it was in the middle ages, but destined to burst forth once more in God's good time, in a new Reformation, and bring light and freedom to mankind."[233] The book is a theological survey of evangelicalism's primary beliefs, or fundamentals, as we will discuss them. They include doctrine, God and man, the Bible, Christ, salvation, and the church. While Machen is no doubt an evangelical, he refused the title "fundamentalist" (in currency during his time) and preferred to be known as a confessional Presbyterian. As an indication of the distance between Machen and fundamentalists (and even evangelicals to some

---

231 See D. G. Hart, *Defending the Faith: J. Gresham Machen and the Crisis of Conservative Protestantism in Modern America* (Philipsburg, NJ: P&R Publishing, 1994), and an important work by Machen himself is J. Gresham Machen, *Christianity and Liberalism* (New York: Macmillan, 1923).
232 Marsden, *Understanding Fundamentalism and Evangelicalism*, 183.
233 Machen, *Christianity and Liberalism*, 15–16.

extent), Machen saw premillennialism as a "false method of interpreting Scripture," but because of this, Machen states his agreement with both postmillennialist and premillennialist fundamentalists on their shared high view of Scripture:

> Yet how great is our agreement with those who hold the premillennial view! They share to the full our reverence for the authority of the Bible, and differ from us only in the interpretation of the Bible; they share our ascription of deity to the Lord Jesus, and our supernaturalistic conception both of the entrance of Jesus into the world and of the consummation when He shall come again. Certainly, then, from our point of view, their error, serious though it may be, is not deadly error; and Christian fellowship, with loyalty not only to the Bible but to the great creeds of the Church, can still unite us with them.[234]

Machen continues to extend the analogy of holding different views but remaining within evangelicalism (or in his words, the Christian religion). He includes views on the sacraments, church polity (apostolic succession), and Calvinist or Arminian views on the atonement. Machen concludes with these wise words: "[T]rue evangelical fellowship is possible between those who hold, with regard to some exceedingly important matters, sharply opposing views." As wide as the tent of evangelicalism is spread according to Machen, there is even room potentially for Roman Catholics, since they hold to the "common heritage" of Scripture and the early creeds.[235]

But as we read through *Christianity and Liberalism*, we

---

234 Machen, *Christianity and Liberalism*, 49.
235 Ibid., 51–52.

realize there is no room at all for liberalism, which remains Christianity's chief modern rival.[236] Reading the chapter titles in Machen's book can help show what is important to him, one could say: Machen's fundamentals. While he is patient with differing views of eschatology, ecclesiology, and even soteriology, he has established a "bottom line" of what is essential to Christianity. We all have our own lists of what we hold as essential, or the basic doctrines that make one an evangelical. At times, our list matches exactly our denomination's or mission's statement of faith, sometimes too neatly. We need to discern the core of evangelicalism, but how do we sort out the many different areas of belief and all the views of each doctrine? I have found church history/historical theology to supply some helpful resources, meaning the communion of the saints. First, let us look to the early church for guidance. When we go back to the fifth century for clarity in the twenty-first century, we find Vincent of Lérins (d. 445). He contributed his "canon" to the church for the purpose of measuring orthodoxy. It says, in Latin, "quod ubique, quod semper, quod ab omnibus creditum est," or in English, "that faith which has been believed everywhere, always, by all."[237] Jaroslav Pelikan calls the Vincentian canon an "insistence upon continuity and universality."[238] When we look at some key representative theologians of the nineteenth and twentieth centuries, we find John Henry Newman (1801–1890), as an Anglican, supportive of the Vincentian canon, but Karl Barth (1886–1968), Yves Marie-Joseph Congar (1904–1995), and Joseph Ratzinger (1927–) unwilling to use it in defining contemporary theology.[239] Although not always popular with

---

236 Ibid., 53.
237 *A Commonitory*, 2.6. In *A Select Library of Nicene and Post-Nicene Fathers*, eds. Philip Schaff and Henry Wace, Series 2, Vol. 11 (Grand Rapids: Wm. B. Eerdmans, 1998), 132.
238 Jaroslav Pelikan, *Development of Christian Doctrine: Some Historical Prolegomena* (New Haven: Yale University Press, 1969), 39.
239 Thomas G. Guarino, *Vincent of Lérins and the Development of Christian Doctrine*,

Protestant and Catholic theologians, the canon helps us relate the three areas of concern to orthodoxy: universality, antiquity, and consent. If we are doing historical theology, we need to combine the two major directions of research (global and historical) into a beautiful tapestry that has both warp and woof (universality and antiquity) and the color of "consent." Indeed, globalism in historical theology is not an innovation or novelty but remains consistent with the teachings of the church fathers and the Reformers.

From later centuries, during the Reformation and modern periods, we can hear first the words of Richard Baxter (1615–1691), the Puritan pastor who talked about "mere Christianity." In the same way, three hundred years later, C. S. Lewis (1898–1963) would use the same expression to mean "the faith which was once delivered unto the saints" (Jude v. 3 KJV). Baxter made another Reformation saying popular, although he was not the original source: "In things necessary, there must be unity; in things less than necessary, there must be liberty, and in all things, there must be charity." The earlier form is found this way: "In essentials unity, in non-essentials liberty, and in all things love," and it comes from the German Lutheran theologian Peter Meiderlin (1582–1651).

Now, of course, the challenge is to determine what the essentials (major doctrines) and the non-essentials (minor doctrines) are. Evangelicals hold a spectrum of views regarding all the doctrines of Christianity. *Across the Spectrum: Understanding Issues in Evangelical Theology* discusses debates over inerrancy, providence, foreknowledge, genesis (creation), divine image, Christology, atonement, salvation, sanctification, eternal security, destiny of the unevangelized, baptism, the Lord's Supper, charismatic gifts, women in ministry, millennium, and hell.

Foundations of Theological Exegesis and Christian Spirituality (Grand Rapids: Baker Academic, 2013), 2–3.

That is only seventeen issues, but others have both divided evangelicals and been the basis for starting a new church or denomination.[240]

Certain key beliefs have been connected with the creeds and confessions of the church through the centuries, so those have been held firmly, and to deny one of them or to place it in the minor category would be losing one's evangelical identity. We will look at these "fundamentals," or key evangelical doctrines a little later, when we begin to look at the Presbyterian Church and its struggle in the early twentieth century to remain evangelical.

By the late nineteenth century, American evangelicals in both the sanctuaries and the classrooms were facing several social and ideological challenges to the Christian faith. They included biological evolution, higher criticism, the immigration of new (non-Protestant) groups, and rapid urbanization. In the midst of these challenges, some denominations began to list essential beliefs or fundamentals. The 1910 Presbyterian General Assembly issued a list of five fundamentals for ordinands, meaning what you must believe in order to be ordained for Christian ministry. The five essentials or basic doctrines were the inerrancy of Scripture, the virgin birth of Christ, Christ's substitutionary atonement, Christ's bodily resurrection, and the authenticity of Christ's miracles. Three of the five are in the Apostles' Creed, but while substitutionary atonement and Christ's miracles are not mentioned there, we find both in the pages of the Bible, along with the other three. These fundamentals were kept current by later General Assemblies in 1916 and 1923. But in 1923, a group of Presbyterians met together and decided it was not in the spirit of the Reformed Faith to require belief in any set of doctrines. This group then issued its

---

[240] Boyd, Gregory A., and Paul R. Eddy, *Across the Spectrum: Understanding Issues in Evangelical Theology*, 2nd ed. (Grand Rapids: Baker Academic, 2009). Another helpful resource is J. I. Packer and Thomas C. Oden, *One Faith: The Evangelical Consensus* (Downers Grove, IL: InterVarsity Press, 2004).

Auburn Affirmation (1924), a victory for the modernists against the fundamentalists in the Presbyterian Church.[241]

The Auburn Affirmation had six sections, with statements the exact opposite to the clearly held positions of evangelicalism. They were:

1. The Bible is not inerrant. The individual believer, or the "reader," determines the actual value of Scripture.

2. The General Assembly has no power to dictate doctrine.

3. The General Assembly's prior actions were not in keeping with the rules of the Book of Discipline.

4. None of the five essentials (fundamentals) that were presented in 1910 and reaffirmed in 1916 and 1923 should be used as a test of ordination. It is okay to believe differently.

5. Liberty of thought is important (valued).

6. Division is deplored, unity and freedom are commended.

The first statement on the Bible not being inerrant has skewed the entire list that follows it. Thus, the nature of Reformed theology and the rules of the Book of Discipline are now reigning over the church's beliefs and practices.

As we continue exploring evangelical doctrines and what we should believe, it is good to revisit Bebbington's quadrilateral. The four sides are: conversionism (the belief that lives need to be changed), activism (the expression of the gospel in effort), biblicism (a particular regard for the Bible), and crucicentrism (a stress on the sacrifice of Christ on the cross). But what is

---

241 David O. Beale, *In Pursuit of Purity: American Fundamentalism Since 1850* (Greenville: Unusual Publications, 1986), 161.

"biblicism"? Some people use the word *bibliolatry*. What does that mean? Webster defines it as "excessive reverence for the Bible as literally interpreted." Is that what evangelicals really believe about the Bible? Do we worship the Bible? You can compare Christian regard for the Holy Bible with the Muslim devotion to the Quran, or Hindu devotion to the Rig Vedas, or the Buddhist devotion to the Sutras. Rather, when I hear *biblicism*, I think of inspiration, illumination, and interpretation, three steps through which the Spirit guides Scripture in its writing and reading. I also think about the spiritual reading of Scripture (Lectio Divina), meditation (quiet time), and even preaching and the hymns of the church (especially of the Psalter).

The year 1909 held a desire to respond to the modernist changes of what the church believed in Christ and what the church communicated to the world outside of Christ. That desire was embodied with the writing of *The Fundamentals: A Testimony to the Truth*. Before any mention of the editors or the many authors of the twelve volumes of *The Fundamentals*, we need to introduce their financial sponsors and the role they played in guiding evangelicalism toward a renewed emphasis on taking a stand, on stating clearly what they believe, and doing so to gain intellectual respectability both in the church and in society.

Milton Stewart (1838–1923) and Lyman Stewart (1840–1923) were two brothers who co-founded Union Oil of California after having left Pennsylvania, where they couldn't control the fast-growing oil business. The younger brother, Lyman Stewart, birthed the idea of publishing *The Fundamentals* initially in 1909, while Milton Stewart contributed one-third of the money needed to both publish and distribute the books. The two brothers were able to fund the collection of names to make a phenomenal list of three hundred thousand persons in ministry (pastors and missionaries). In addition to compiling this vast number of missionaries, pastors, and teachers came distributing three million copies of the books between 1910 and 1915. The Stewarts will bypass the liberal Protestant-oriented John D. Rockefeller in the long run.[242] In recognition of Lyman Stewart as the visionary and benefactor of this publishing project, R. A. Torrey began his preface to the twelve volumes with this one sentence: "In 1909 God moved two Christian laymen to set aside a large sum of money for issuing twelve volumes that would set forth the fundamentals of the Christian faith, and which were to be sent free to ministers of the gospel, missionaries, Sunday School superintendents, and others engaged in aggressive Christian work throughout the English speaking world."[243]

This is not the first case of affluent business leaders committing to mission with their own money; it joins an already lengthy record of evangelical philanthropists. Along with the Stewarts are two other oil-business families who gave financially to support religious causes of their own confession. So, we can see John D. Rockefeller Sr. (1839–1937) contributing millions to start the University of Chicago (1890) and Central Philippine University (1905). The University of Chicago's Divinity School and all the faculty teaching Bible and religion are notoriously liberal and present views that are not only open to higher criticism, but are also ones that continue the tradition of assaulting the Bible's authority. Rockefeller's son John D. Rockefeller Jr. (1874–1960) and the noted liberal pastor Harry Emerson Fosdick (1878–1969) planned and constructed the Riverside Church in New York City, always an edifice committed to liberal Protestantism.

---

242 B. M. Pietsch, "Lyman Stewart and Early Fundamentalism," *Church History*, Vol. 82, No. 3 (September 2013): 618.
243 Torrey, R. A., and A. C. Dixon, eds. *The Fundamentals: A Testimony to the Truth*, 2 vols. (Los Angeles: Bible Institute of Los Angeles, 1917; Grand Rapids: Baker Books, 2003), Preface.

A third oil-business family that contributed significantly to religious projects, most of them within the Disciples of Christ tradition, was Thomas Wharton Phillips (1835–1912). After his death, the new school in Oklahoma was named Phillips University (1906–1998) in his honor.

The list might appear endless when you consider how many affluent evangelicals have contributed to support both missions and church ministries and have even gone so far as to birth new missions. One final example is Henry Parsons Crowell (1855–1944), founder of Quaker Oats, who gave generously to support Moody Bible Institute.[244]

After the preface, when one opens the table of contents for the two volumes, is a long series of articles in the first volume related to the "battle for the Bible," meaning a total of nineteen chapters are devoted to the polemical task of resisting "higher criticism." Initially, *The Fundamentals* was comprised of a twelve-volume set of books with two editors, R. A. Torrey and A. C. Dixon. It was published from 1910 to 1915 by Biola. The reprint edition (2003) is only two volumes, published by Baker Books. The first volume, roughly half of the original twelve volumes, is a collection of essays written by highly respected and highly qualified evangelical writers, some of whom we would refer to today as "mainline" or "mainstream" Christians, not evangelicals. So, when we look back at one hundred years from the time of initial publication, *The Fundamentals* set a high standard of writing that spoke powerfully to the challenges the church was facing at the beginning of the twentieth century. The twin challenges of higher criticism and biological evolution had placed the church in a position where apologetics was a vital part of the evangelical message, with a focus on Genesis

---

[244] The Moody story can be heard by reading Timothy Gloege, *Guaranteed Pure: The Moody Bible Institute, Business, and the Making of Modern Evangelicalism* (Chapel Hill: University of North Carolina Press, 2015).

as the creation account and the Pentateuch as written by Moses and Isaiah as one unified book.

The second volume is filled with articles focused on theological or doctrinal themes, ranging from sin to the incarnation, with essays on evangelism, world missions, and prayer (spirituality). The authors in the second volume contributed toward the standardization of two theological views: premillennial dispensationalism and Keswick (or Higher Life) spirituality. Despite the nearly celebrity status of many of the theological authors in *The Fundamentals*, according to Ernest Sandeen, they all failed in their primary task: to stop the spread of modernism.[245] Perhaps the task was too large to accomplish with only a book, or perhaps they needed to build seminaries and churches and fill them all with a new generation of evangelicals who could only preach the pure/full gospel.

In the same year that R. A. Torrey wrote his preface and congratulated the two Presbyterian laity (Stewart brothers) who were moved by God to give millions, a reference Bible was being published by Oxford University Press. It was called *The Scofield Reference Bible* (1909). This proved a popular and wide window through which the public could view premillennial dispensationalism. Premillennial dispensationalism has a longer history than *The Scofield Reference Bible*, going back to an Irish attorney turned Anglican priest in 1826 named John Nelson Darby (1800–1882). Darby was born in London and educated at Trinity College (Dublin) in the classics (Greek and Latin). After meeting with like-minded brethren, he left the Anglican priesthood and began ministering with the Plymouth Brethren, developing his views of Christian eschatology (dispensationalism).[246] Darby went on extensive missions

---

245 Ernest R. Sandeen, *The Roots of Fundamentalism: British & American Millenarianism, 1800–1930* (Chicago: University of Chicago Press, 1970), 206–207.

246 The Plymouth Brethren are also known as Christian Brethren or either Open

to Europe where he planted churches and worked on French, German, and English translations of the New Testament. He also traveled to North America, Australia, and New Zealand to teach the Bible.

After *The Scofield Reference Bible* was published, the hidden hermeneutics became heralded to the ends of the earth in a missionary movement that made evangelicalism (after World War II especially) a new religious power with which to be reckoned. Premillennial dispensationalism transitioned to the new standard way of reading the Bible for most evangelicals, along with Keswick Holiness as the more standard (or majority) view of sanctification.

The end harvest of the popular system of premillennial dispensationalism was the publishing and sale of *The Late Great Planet Earth* and the *Left Behind* series. Hal Lindsey's *The Late Great Planet Earth* (1970) within twenty years sold a total of twenty-eight million copies. The *Left Behind* series of novels penned by Tim LaHaye and Jerry Jenkins have sold a total of eighty million copies. But what appeared to be a "win" for evangelical beliefs and their expression in society turned into an understanding by the rest of society to defuse the religious rhetoric and place the real religious emphasis not on what we believe, but on how we live our religion. A popular saying of the second half of the twentieth century was "doctrine divides,

---

or Exclusive Brethren. While having its origins in the United Kingdom in the early nineteenth century, they have gone global and their influence is far beyond their actual numbers. In addition to the hermeneutical system of premillennial dispensationalism, the Plymouth Brethren are well known for their weekly meetings for breaking bread (Eucharist/Holy Communion) and their lack of religious titles and rituals. They are extreme Congregationalists who are viewed as being nondenominational or undenominational. For further reading on their history, see Henry Pickering, *Chief Men Among the Brethren* (London: Pickering & Inglis, 1918) and Harold H. Rowdon, *The Origins of the Brethren 1825–1850* (London: Pickering & Inglis, 1967). Two of the more "famous" persons associated with the Plymouth Brethren are Anthony Norris Groves (already mentioned in association with "faith missions") and George Müller (1805–1898), who was born in Prussia and ministered in England where he was well known for directing an orphanage in Bristol as a faith mission.

missions unite." For some people, doctrine should be secondary to the main work of reaching out to the poor and proclaiming peace and justice. As a result of this new emphasis, a clear shift occurred in the twenty-first century, one where the new "in" word is *spirituality*, and *theology* is out.

But what may be true today has not always been true of the church through the centuries. The early church, for example, was a community that "devoted themselves to the apostles' teaching" (Acts 2:42 NIV). As evangelicals, we must have doctrinal agreement (unity) on the essentials in order to do ministry in the power of the Spirit. So, we should know the foundational beliefs that are for all evangelicals, not only in North America or even Europe, but also in all of Asia.

A high view of Scripture will certainly provide a platform for the examination of theological matters to discern which are major and which are minor. Many of the evangelical creeds and confessions hold such a high view of Scripture, stating that it is inerrant in its original autographs (manuscripts). Let us look at a few evangelical statements on Scripture.

First, we see the statement on Scripture from *Christianity Today*. As we consider the later birth and development of American evangelicalism, or neo-evangelicalism, four stated pillars exist. They are: Billy Graham (1918–2018), the National Association of Evangelicals (1942–), Fuller Theological Seminary (1947–), and *Christianity Today* (1956–).[247] *Christianity Today* affirmed "The sixty-six canonical books of the Bible as originally written were inspired of God, hence free from error. They constitute the only infallible guide in faith and practice."[248]

The Evangelical Theological Society was founded in 1949 as

---

[247] Brian Stanley, *The Global Diffusion of Evangelicalism: The Age of Billy Graham and John Stott*, A History of Evangelicalism: People, Movements, and Ideas in the English-Speaking World, Vol. 5 (Downers Grove, IL: IVP Academic, 2013), 36–38.

[248] Packer, J. I., and Thomas C. Oden, *One Faith: The Evangelical Consensus* (Downers Grove, IL: InterVarsity Press, 2004), 42.

a scholarly community of evangelicals, meeting together once a year in a conference (usually a little in advance of American Thanksgiving, or mid-to-late November) where academic papers are read and discussed. Nine years later (1958), the *Journal of the Evangelical Theological Society* (*JETS*) would begin its publishing history with an article by Ned Stonehouse, "The Infallibility of Scripture and Evangelical Progress."[249] The ETS statement on Scripture reads: "The Bible alone, and the Bible in its entirety, is the Word of God written and is therefore inerrant in the autographs."[250] ETS, like many organizations and institutions related to neo-evangelicalism, has had its share of controversy over stated positions on doctrinal issues, especially those on Scripture.

This statement was later amended to add a short statement on belief in the Trinity or the triune God. I have been a member since 1997, the first year of my doctoral studies at Trinity Evangelical Divinity School (Deerfield, Illinois). In order for a person to have full-member status, he or she must have at least a master of theology degree (ThM) and must sign the statement on Scripture and the Trinity on an annual basis. I have also been a member of the Korea Evangelical Theological Society (KETS) since around 2005, and I know they do not require a signature on any doctrinal statement or position as a test for membership. As a result, for good or ill, the membership does appear to be more theologically diverse in Korea, meaning there is a fuller spectrum of evangelicals and they are open to mainline Christians (ecumenical).

We could have added a lot more of the creeds and confessions

---

249 Ned B. Stonehouse, "The Infallibility of Scripture and Evangelical Progress," *Journal of Evangelical Theological Society*, Vol. 1, No. 1 (1958): 9–13. For a fuller view of ETS and *JETS*, see Andreas J. Köstenberger, ed., *Quo Vadis Evangelicalism? Perspectives on the Past, Direction for the Future: Presidential Addresses from the First Fifty Years of the Journal of the Evangelical Theological Society* (Wheaton, IL: Crossway Books, 2007).

250 Packer and Oden, *One Faith*, 51.

of evangelicalism, especially since 1945. Among those most prominent within evangelicalism are *The Lausanne Covenant* (1974), *The Gospel of Jesus Christ: An Evangelical Celebration* (1999), and *The Amsterdam Declaration: A Charter for Evangelism in the 21st century* (2000).

While we continue to look at evangelicalism in the 1920s to 1930s, we ask one simple question: What is the purpose of faith statements? Are they not merely "window dressing" to make an organization appear more evangelical? I have prepared an analogy that might help explain the place and purpose of statements of faith. First, we need guardrails to keep us on the road, to keep us from driving off into the ditches and ravines. Jesus answered, "I am the way and the truth and the life" (John 14:6 NIV). The Bible, then, acts as a road map and creeds/confessions as guardrails. But what happens when there's a crash, when a denomination departs from the standards of either the Bible or the historical creeds/confessions? The crash is a separation or a division. We can revisit the divisions that came during the 1920s and 1930s, and even some in the 1940s. But before we look at the twentieth century, it should be noted that the nineteenth century already witnessed the American Civil War (1861–1865) and the separation of national denominations into both a northern church and a southern church.

The issue that divided the nation was not directly over the view of the Bible (infallible or inerrant or not), but rather over the interpretation of whether or not the Bible endorses (or allows) human slavery. The three major Protestant denominations divided; the first was the Presbyterian Church's split between Old School and New School in 1837, followed by a more geographical divide in 1861. The two Presbyterian denominations would not reunite until 1983. The Methodists divided between North and South in 1844 and later reunited in 1939. The Baptists divided in 1845. While both Presbyterians and

Methodists reunited, as noted above, there is one exception to the rule of reuniting, and that is the Baptists. They remain divided over a war that ended in 1865. The Northern Baptists are now called the American Baptist Churches USA, and are members of both ecumenical organizations: the World Council of Churches (WCC) and the National Council of the Churches of Christ in the USA (NCCC). On the other side remains the SBC, the largest Protestant denomination in America with anywhere from sixteen to eighteen million members.[251] Kansas City, my hometown, is a border region for the Baptists because both major Baptist denominations have a denominational seminary in Kansas City. The Southern Baptists have Midwestern Baptist Theological Seminary, and the American Baptist Churches USA have Central Baptist Theological Seminary. No other city/location in the US has the dubious "honor" of having two Baptist seminaries representing a still-divided church. Now, we turn to the divisions of the 1920s and 1930s.

While we have looked at J. Gresham Machen and the birth/division of the Presbyterians and the formation of Westminster Theological Seminary, included here are some reminders of names and dates to help us remember what is probably the most infamous division in the twentieth century. The first division related to Machen and conservative Presbyterians (read evangelical Presbyterians rather than fundamentalists) was in 1929, when Machen and others left Princeton Theological Seminary to form Westminster Theological Seminary in Philadelphia. The second date was 1933, when Machen's group formed the Independent Board for Presbyterian Foreign Missions. The year 1936 brought the formation of a separate denomination called the Orthodox Presbyterian Church.

The rise of separatist fundamentalism in the US south and

---

251 A good historical source for the divisions is C. C. Goen, *Broken Churches, Broken Nation* (Macon, GA: Mercer University Press, 1988).

north is more easily noted among the Baptists, not only in the separation but also in the formation of new denominations and mission boards in the 1920s and 1930s. It is significant that the challenges to evangelicalism were being made on foreign soil by foreign missionaries. We can mention two Baptist denominations that separated from the Northern Baptist Convention and in general emerged from the modernist/fundamentalist controversy of the 1920s: Conservative Baptist Association of America, which is now known as CBAmerica (1947, but a separate mission organization was started in 1943), and General Association of Regular Baptist Churches (1932). The Conservative Baptists later merged with evangelicalism and left the margins of fundamentalism in America. The General Association of Regular Baptist Churches was founded because a mission organization was formed first and caused the Northern Baptist Convention to disfellowship anyone linked with the new mission.

Separation over beliefs and practices also happened on the mission field with the Christian Church/Disciples of Christ. For them, the line that should not be crossed was "mode of baptism." On the mission field, pastors and missionaries were beginning to accept other forms of baptism (sprinkling and pouring) as being valid or equivalent to immersion. For some denominations, mode of baptism was never a major theological issue, but for the Christian Church/Disciples of Christ, it was an integral part of the conversion process and mattered significantly, whether it was as a believing adult and whether or not it was by immersion.

We mentioned two newly emerging denominations and their related mission boards, but in order to see the picture more clearly, we need to include a few faces in passing. To see balance, we are mentioning one from the south and one from the north: John Franklyn (J. Frank) Norris (1877–1952), whose leadership centered in Texas, and William Bell Riley (1861–1947), whose leadership centered in Minnesota.[252] With all the attention we paid to the Presbyterian J. Gresham Machen, we can find more balance by mentioning Robert Reynolds (Bob) Jones Sr. (1883–1968), a one-time Methodist who separated and formed a leading fundamentalist university named, of course, after himself: Bob Jones College (later University).[253] With a very short list of prominent figures among evangelicals and fundamentalists in the 1920s and 1930s, we turn to what more people know about than the pastors, teachers, and theologians of a growing religious tradition: a trial in the small city of Dayton, Tennessee.

The trial in 1925 in Dayton was a symbolic battle between biological evolution and the biblical creation account from Genesis. It was called, in jest, the Monkey Trial. From this perspective of nearly one hundred years in the future, we now see that the entire trial by jury was a setup, meaning John Scopes's crime of teaching humans' biological evolution in the public high school science classroom was deliberately planned to bring about a trial and provide a public forum for the science-versus-religion debate. John Scopes was represented by the American Civil Liberties Union and trial attorney Clarence Darrow. The fundamentalist (or biblical view) side was represented by William Jennings Bryan (1860–1925), three-time democrat candidate for US president and former member of the US Congress and Secretary of State. Although Bryan's fundamentalist side won the guilty verdict for John Scopes, they lost the publicity war, and the people who had supported Bryan as a real commoner were not switching sides.[254]

---

252 Two academic studies include: Barry Hankins, *God's Rascal: J. Frank Norris and the Beginnings of Southern Fundamentalism* (Lexington: University Press of Kentucky, 1996) and William Vance Trollinger, *God's Empire: William Bell Riley and Midwestern Fundamentalism* (Madison: University of Wisconsin Press, 1990).

253 See Mark Taylor Dalhouse, *An Island in the Lake of Fire: Bob Jones University, Fundamentalism, and the Separatist Movement* (Athens: University of Georgia Press, 1996).

254 For a study of the Scopes Trial, see Edward Larson, *Summer for the Gods: The*

In a 1920 article in *The Watchman-Examiner* by the Reverend Curtis Lee Laws (1868–1946), a Baptist minister and the magazine's editor, Laws selected the term *fundamentalists* to describe advocates for the traditional faith. Other terms were *conservatives, premillennialists,* and *Landmarkers*. In the twenty-first century, the word *fundamentalist* has come to express the worst of any religious tradition. Because there are fundamentalist expressions of all major world religions, the real understanding of fundamentalists and what they believe can become distorted as people compare them with the extreme Muslim fundamentalists, whose cries for Jihad are heard as terrorism.

While there are Christian fundamentalists, Jewish fundamentalists, Hindu fundamentalists, and Islamic fundamentalists, this does not bring any measure of clarity in understanding the meaning of the term and its actual usage. First, a quick comparison with the other side: Christian liberalism. Fundamentalists are seen as narrow-minded, only caring to preserve or conserve the truth in their doctrines, and opposing anyone and everyone different from themselves. Liberals, on the other hand, are seen as tolerant and open, embracing those different from themselves.

In North America is a growing movement of people who have become "antifundamentalists." Images on TV screens and movies in America portray fundamentalists and, by association, evangelicals, as being intolerant and hypocritical. A few popular Hollywood movies and a TV program feature evangelicals as no different than fundamentalists. Among these popular movies, standing out as examples of intolerance and hypocrisy, are *Elmer Gantry* (1960), *Inherit the Wind* (1960), *The Mosquito Coast* (1986), and *At Play in the Fields of the Lord* (1991). The

Scopes Trial and America's Continuing Debate Over Science and Religion (New York: Basic Books, 2006). Also, for a short summary of the events that summer, see Jon R. Stone, *On the Boundaries of American Evangelicalism: The Postwar Evangelical Coalition* (New York: St. Martin's Press, 1997), 64–66.

movie *Elmer Gantry* is based upon the novel by Sinclair Lewis (1926) that is a satire on evangelical Christianity, with many parallels between Lewis's fiction and the real-life minister Aimee Semple McPherson. *Inherit the Wind* was a re-enactment on film of the Scopes Monkey Trial of 1925.

In addition to the movies, the character Ned Flanders on the TV show *The Simpsons* stands out as a religious bigot. These are only a few examples, but with the American media's less than respectful view of evangelicalism, it is no surprise that some fundamentalists and evangelicals choose not to watch television or to attend the cinema.

While there is a historical basis for viewing the appearance of the word *fundamentalists* with Curtis Lee Laws above, George Marsden offers a new definition. His definition of *fundamentalism* is "militantly anti-modernist evangelicalism." Further, he states it is a "loose, diverse, and changing federation of co-belligerents united by their fierce opposition to modernist attempts to bring Christianity into line with modern thought."[255]

Francis Schaeffer wrote *The Mark of the Christian*. The "mark" of the Christian is to express (to live) the truth of John 13:34–35. "A new command I give you: Love one another. As I have loved you, so you must love one another. By this everyone will know that you are my disciples, if you love one another" (NIV).

The primary reason for separating from liberals was that evangelicals (conservatives or traditionalists) saw liberals as having abandoned the historical Christian beliefs and having replaced those traditional views with an openness to newer ones, including higher criticism and biological evolution. Another part, which was more transpacific, was the emerging interest in world religions. When westerners became aware more of Eastern philosophies and religions, an openness emerged and

---

[255] George M. Marsden, *Fundamentalism and American Culture: The Shaping of Twentieth-Century Evangelicalism, 1870–1925* (New York: Oxford University Press, 1980), 4.

they saw them as more than mere paganism, as representing highly developed world civilizations (China and India). Once this shift occurred, then the transition from an exclusive view of Christian revelation and salvation to an accommodating view of one revelation among many was possible. Reading two Scripture texts from the New Testament should make an evangelical position clear: "Jesus answered, 'I am the way and the truth and the life. No one comes to the Father except through me" (John 14:6 NIV), and "Salvation is found in no one else, for there is no other name under heaven given to mankind by which we must be saved" (Acts 4:12 NIV). Even with the clarity of those two verses from the New Testament, there have arisen three theological positions concerning salvation in the name of Jesus alone: pluralist, inclusivist, and exclusivist. Some do not use the term *exclusivist*, as it sounds more negative than positive, and instead prefer *particularist*.[256] Even though *exclusivist* has less than positive connotations, it was the majority opinion among evangelicals through the past centuries. Only in the twentieth century, with the growth of interreligious dialogue, have evangelicals adopted an inclusivist view of salvation. The pluralist view has not been used by evangelicals; it remains the domain of liberal/progressive/ecumenical Christians.

We will pass through the beginning of interreligious dialogue and the demise of mainline Protestant evangelism in the nations of Asia, especially China. And while mainline or ecumenical Protestants were leaving evangelism behind, evangelicals were looking for new forms of evangelism in an effort to expand their efforts at world mission. We will look at the changing

---

[256] Some helpful books on this subject include Ronald H. Nash, *Is Jesus the Only Savior?* (Grand Rapids: Zondervan, 1994); Dennis L. Okholm and Timothy R. Phillips, eds., *Four Views on Salvation in a Pluralistic World* (Grand Rapids: Zondervan, 1995); John Sanders, *No Other Name: An Investigation into the Destiny of the Unevangelized* (Grand Rapids: Wm. B. Eerdmans, 1992); and Terrance L. Tiessen, *Who Can Be Saved? Reassessing Salvation in Christ and World Religions* (Downers Grove, IL: InterVarsity, 2004).

views of evangelism among missionaries and mission boards of mainline Protestantism as one side of the Pacific. Indeed, what happened in China had a strong effect on the sponsoring churches in the US. But before we go to China and look at the changing views of missionaries and their American sponsors (mission boards), we will first visit Chicago.

The first real attempt at meeting one another was not on the mission field but on American soil. It came in 1893 with the World's Parliament of Religions, held in Chicago at the same venue and on slightly later dates as the World's Columbian Exposition or what would later be called the World's Fair. Present at the Parliament were representatives from the following world religions: Jain (Virchand Gandhi), Theravada Buddhism (Anagarika Dharmapala), Zen Buddhism (Soyen Shaku), Pure Land Buddhism (an address by Kiyozawa Manshi was read to those gathered in his absence), Hinduism (Swami Vivekananda), Islam (Mohammed Alexander Russell Webb), Bahai Faith (Henry Jessup), Theosophical Society (William Quan Judge), and Christian Science (Septimus J. Hanna).

The original planning for the World's Columbian Exposition had set the date at 1892, to celebrate the four hundred years that had passed since Columbus's voyages to the New World. It did not begin, however, until 1893, but the dream was extended beyond Columbus to connecting all the world religions with one another in dialogue. Historians have traced the very genesis of interfaith or interreligious dialogue back to this Parliament in 1893.

While the president of the World's Parliament of Religions was Charles Bonney, not an evangelical, since he was a member of the Swedenborgians or New Jerusalem Church, there were evangelical voices giving speeches that were pure gospel. One of them was the Reverend George F. Pentecost (1842–1920), who had worked with D. L. Moody. His address to the Parliament sounded more like a sermon. Here are the first five sentences, his introduction fully evangelical:

> Christianity is a fighting religion. Christ came not to send peace but a sword—not the sword of a Mohammed, but the sword of the Spirit, which is the word of God. Christianity recognizes the absolute freedom of the human will and conscience. It condemns all violence in its conflict with other religions, appealing only to the intelligence, the conscience and the heart of men, by the Word of God with the Holy Ghost sent down from heaven. It is not intolerant of other religions, except as light is intolerant of darkness, but will in no case compromise with error, or enter into fellowship with any religious system or philosophy that is not built on the Rock of Ages.[257]

In addition to Pentecost's sermon, R. A. Torrey presented a talk on "Instruction in [the Bible's] Use in Personal Work," again showing a real evangelical presence at the Parliament.[258] Marcus Braybrooke gives some figures on the actual numbers involved who were evangelical.

> A total of seventy-nine out of the one hundred and ninety-four people who presented papers were clearly outside the evangelical mainstream. Add to this the Swedenborgians, members of Eastern Orthodoxy, Armenians, Universalists, African Methodist Episcopalians, Christian Scientists, Quakers, Shakers and one member of the Salvation

---

257 George F. Pentecost, "The Invincible Gospel" in *The World's Parliament of Religions*, Vol. 2 (Chicago: Parliament Publishing, 1893), 1166.
258 *The World's Parliament of Religions*, 1448.

Army, then the total of non-evangelicals comes to one hundred and two. It is not surprising that some evangelical Christians viewed the Parliament with alarm. Those who took part tended to love the sinner and hate the sin. They affirmed their brotherly feeling for the Asians, but condemned other religious as they did not offer salvation.[259]

The Parliament also had congresses representing all the major world religions, including Christianity, and among that group were some evangelicals. The Evangelical Alliance Congress was comprised of W. E. Dodge, W. S. Rainsford, George A. Gates, Russell H. Conwell, Charles H. Parkhurst, and Josiah Strong. Subjects for the presentations and groups were focused on social issues, as this was reflective of the era when urbanization and immigration brought the church face to face with new and challenging areas of ministry. Another listed "object" of the Evangelical Alliance was to promote religious liberty. As you read the entire program, you see that "religious liberty" was seeking an absence of religious persecution, but not merely that which Protestants (evangelicals) had suffered from Roman Catholics and Orthodox Christians. The Evangelical Alliance affirmed it was committed to religious liberty for all and would seek equal freedoms for Catholics, Jews, Muslims, Buddhists, and Hindus.[260]

While the World's Parliament of Religions signaled a transpacific relationship with the arrival of Asian representatives from the world's religions, another relationship, one of recommendation and reform, was forming through a book published in the United States. Based upon reports from concerned Christians,

---

[259] Marcus Braybrooke, *Pilgrimage of Hope: One Hundred Years of Global Interfaith Dialogue* (New York: Crossroad, 1992), 27. It is interesting to note that Braybrooke identifies the Salvation Army as not being evangelical.

[260] *The World's Parliament of Religions*, 1441.

it was titled *Re-Thinking Missions: A Laymen's Inquiry After One Hundred Years*, edited by William Ernest Hocking (1873-1966) and published in 1932.

The *Laymen's Inquiry*, as the overall project was called, began in January 1930 with a meeting of Baptist laymen that had been called by John D. Rockefeller Jr., and that was addressed by the Methodist layman John R. Mott. Subsequently, on the strength of Rockefeller's financial backing and a tentative blessing from seven of the major denominational boards, the Institute for Social and Religious Research was commissioned to conduct interviews and collect data in India, Burma, Japan, and China.[261]

As the title indicates, the book was not the sole research and writing of Hocking, then a professor of philosophy at Harvard, but was published after long discussion sessions that reviewed the impact of Christians missions in Asia. In summary, the "report" recommended that missionaries no longer evangelize, but rather concentrate all their efforts on education as social reform. In one chapter of the *Laymen's Inquiry* titled "Problems of Administration," Hocking lists a series of reasons missionaries are missing the mark. The areas listed include salaries, children's education, furloughs, and turnover of personnel. While these are all valid areas in which missionaries can make adjustments, the tone of the report is severely critical and puts blame on missionaries for failing to make enough changes. Within this chapter on "Problems of Administration" is an interesting section titled "Doctrinal discord."

We can read easily the tensions between the progressives and the conservatives that existed in China and other Asian nations. The recommendation of the author is that they refrain from "sending to the field persons who insist upon emphasizing divisive dogmas or who have a narrow and rigid conception

---

261 William R. Hutchison, *Errand to the World: American Protestant Thought and Foreign Missions* (Chicago: University of Chicago Press, 1987), 158.

of the scope of mission." "Narrow and rigid" is pointing at "individuals who foment theological discord or endeavor to defeat the programs of social reconstruction advocated by their broader-minded associations."[262] One can easily read here the struggle between evangelicals and Protestant liberals.

After the report was published, the final critical evaluation of Hocking toward Protestant missions, both mainline and evangelical, was that one thing needed to be eliminated.

What must not remain, Hocking thought, is a parochialism that in effect denies the God-given right of others to hold a similar loyalty to their own religious systems. In that respect, he said, to boast about a unique or superior grasp of religious truth is not only unnecessary, but it also constitutes a "humiliating mistake."[263]

With the wealth and power of Christian liberalism, it might be difficult to view an evangelical response or how evangelicals could even survive in the midst of this intense competition for Christian ascendency, especially on the mission field, and specifically in China, where the Hocking report was the latest authority that ruled. But we turn to find a young man named John Sung from China.

John Sung (Song Shangjie, 1901–1944) was born the son of a Methodist pastor in Fujian, China.[264] With both family encouragement and some limited financial aid, John was able to study in America, earning three degrees (bachelor's, master's, and PhD) in five years. His major was chemistry. After he earned his PhD from Ohio State University, he began studies at Union Theological Seminary (New York). This was partly to relieve his uneasy conscience for having traveled to the US

---

262 The Commission of Appraisal, *Re-thinking Missions: A Laymen's Inquiry After One Hundred Years* (New York: Harper & Brothers, 1932), 299.
263 Hutchison, *Errand to the World*, 161–162.
264 For a biography of Sung, see Leslie T. Lyall, *A Biography of John Sung* (London: China Inland Mission, 1961).

and never studying theology, in preparation for the ministry, as many of his father's parishioners back home had expected. Right after his first semester at seminary, Sung had a spiritual experience on February 10, 1927. He called it the "baptism with the Holy Spirit." His spiritual renewal placed him on the side of fundamentalism in a liberal Protestant seminary context. There were outbursts in class when John would preach repentance and conversion to his professors.[265] Finally, due to his evangelical zeal, the authorities (by some accounts, including Union's President Henry Sloane Coffin) at Union had him committed to a mental asylum.[266] He spent 193 days there, which turned into the time when he read the Bible multiple times, and which formed his ministry.[267] When Sung returned to China, he began an evangelistic ministry with the "Bethel Bands" of the Bethel Mission in Shanghai until 1934, when he was asked to leave, and from that time until his death in 1944, he traveled and preached as an independent evangelist.

Philip Yuen-Sang Leung has studied the Chinese context of Christianity and calls evangelicals like John Sung, Watchman Nee, Andrew Gee, and Wang Mingdao all "Marys," meaning "they were God-centered and Scripture oriented and emphasized prayer rather than social action; they were more interested in the spiritual life than in social engagement."[268] No doubt, all these martyrs would be pleased with their description as

---

265 John Sung, *The Diaries of John Sung: An Autobiography*, translated by Stephen L. Sheng (Luke H. Sheng and Stephen L. Sheng, Publishers, 1995), 15–16.
266 The official records of Union Theological Seminary and the memoirs/records of President Henry Sloane Coffin do not mention John Sung's experience either as a student or as a patient.
267 For a study of Sung's experience in New York, see Jonathan Seitz, "Converting John Sung: UTS Drop-Out, Psychiatric Patient, Chinese Evangelist," *Union Seminary Quarterly Review*, Vol. 62, Nos. 1–2 (2009): 78–92.
268 Philip Yuen-Sang Leung, "Conversion, Commitment, and Culture: Christian Experience in China, 1949–99," in *Christianity Reborn: The Global Expansion of Evangelicalism in the Twentieth Century*, edited by Donald M. Lewis (Grand Rapids: Wm. B. Eerdmans, 2004), 89.

"Marys" who were God-centered, Scripture-oriented, and emphasized prayer.

China, in the early twentieth century, was spiritually influenced by its neighbor Korea, through the revival reporting and leadership of Jonathan Goforth. There was also a transpacific influence in China when Paul Rader, a revival speaker from Chicago who had connections with both the Christian and Missionary Alliance and the Moody Church, visited China and "preached intensely on 'sin, only sin' as the obstacle to a full Christian life, and often 'the whole audience would be in tears.'"[269]

In addition to Sung's call for people to repent and make restitution, "[h]is meetings were often quite emotional, even spectacularly so. But he also did not hesitate to denounce the pastors and leaders of denominational churches even as they sat before him in his meetings in their churches. Yet Sung must be reckoned probably the single-most-powerful figure in Chinese revivalism in the mid-1930s. Although eventually barred from some churches, he was highly esteemed by many others."[270] Sung boldly preached the cross, repentance, and the blood. By 1936, more than one hundred thousand Chinese were converted through his ministry, and many were healed of physical disease. During the final years of his ministry, Sung made trips to preach to the Chinese diaspora in Indonesia, Malaysia, the Philippines, Taiwan, Singapore, and Thailand. Sadly, this great evangelical died from cancer and tuberculous at the early age of forty-two.

While the older traditions among Protestants (Baptists and Presbyterians) were dividing in the 1920s and 1930s, there was a repositioning and posturing for growth among Pentecostals.

---

269 Daniel H. Bays, "Christian Revival in China, 1900–1937," in *Modern Christian Revivals*, edited by Edith L. Blumhofer and Randall Balmer (Urbana and Chicago: University of Illinois Press, 1993), 165.

270 Bays, "Christian Revival in China," 173.

Although there was some resistance to organizing denominations and becoming like other churches, the process was inevitable. No one exhibits the "charisma" of Pentecostal leadership more in the 1920s and 30s than Aimee Semple McPherson (1890–1944). In many ways we can refer to Sister Aimee as a Pentecostal celebrity, but in the biography by Edith Blumhofer, we see that she is "Everybody's Sister."[271] There is some crossover between Aimee's life story and that of Jonathan Goforth. Both were born on farms in Ontario, Canada. Both were called revivalists. Aimee's mother was active in the Salvation Army. She met and married a young preacher named Robert Semple, originally from Northern Ireland, and they would serve together in Hong Kong, having been ordained (January 2, 1909) and sent out by William Durham's North Avenue Mission in Chicago.[272] The time of the Semples' mission in Hong Kong was tragically cut short when Robert Semple contracted malaria and died only ten weeks after their arrival in China. Aimee, his widow now, remained in Hong Kong until the birth of their daughter, Roberta Star, after which she returned to the United States and later to Canada.

During this time of transition, Aimee Semple joined the Assemblies of God (AG) but later began her own evangelistic association and denomination. Along the way in her ministry, Aimee remarried in 1912. Her new husband was Harold McPherson. Aimee began traveling throughout North America as an evangelist, preaching the finished-work doctrine. She and

---

[271] Edith L. Blumhofer, *Aimee Semple McPherson: Everybody's Sister*, Library of Religious Biography (Grand Rapids: Wm. B. Eerdmans, 1993). Another more recent study is Matthew Avery Sutton, *Aimee Semple McPherson and the Resurrection of Christian America* (Cambridge: Harvard University Press, 2007).

[272] "The last missionaries going out from us were Mr. and Mrs. R. J. Semple and Miss Phoebe Holmes, who left us last winter and are now situated in Hong Kong, China, which will be their field of labor for the present or till the Lord leads them elsewhere." From "Our Foreign Missionaries," *Pentecostal Testimony*, Vol. 1, No. 5 (July 1, 1910): 10.

Harold divorced in 1921, partly as a result of the demands from her itinerant ministry.

From 1921, Aimee Semple McPherson began to preach "full gospel evangelism," very similar to A. B. Simpson's *The Fourfold Gospel*, and she titled her teachings "foursquare gospel." McPherson preached her foursquare gospel as Jesus the only Savior, Jesus the great physician, Jesus the baptizer with the Holy Spirit, and Jesus the coming king. Interestingly, she does not claim any knowledge of Simpson's fourfold gospel, testifying rather that God directly revealed the foursquare gospel to her, with Ezekiel 1 as the key text.

Here is McPherson's foursquare gospel: "Gazing upon the four-square Gospel, which comes to us from the cloud of Grace, flashing, blazing, burning, glowing, the first glimpse of revelation of our blessed Redeemer that appears to our adoring eyes is that of the face of the Man." She further sees "the face of a lion—Jesus Christ, the baptizer with the Holy Ghost," "the face of the Ox—Jesus Christ, the great physician," and "the face of the eagle—Jesus Christ the coming king."[273] In an insightful article, Kristy Maddux presents the "Foursquare Gospel of Aimee Semple McPherson: McPherson the prophet, evangelist, performer, and storyteller," showing both Sister Aimee's breadth (populist rhetoric) and depth (evangelical spirituality).[274]

Continuing on through ministry in the Los Angeles area, Aimee would start a new church in the Echo Park area. With the construction of the building completed, Angelus Temple opened on January 1, 1923. It had seating for fifty-three hundred people but often would accommodate seventy-five hundred. A week's schedule included: Sunday—9:30 a.m. Sunday school, and 10:30 a.m., 2:30 p.m., and 7:30 p.m. preaching services. Meetings

---

273 Aimee Semple McPherson, "The Foursquare Gospel," *The Bridal Call* (January 1923): 103–105.

274 Kristy Maddux, "The Foursquare Gospel of Aimee Semple McPherson," *Rhetoric and Public Affairs*, Vol. 14, No. 2 (Summer 2011): 302.

were held every night of the week and many afternoons. In the first six months there were eight thousand conversions and fifteen hundred baptisms by immersion.[275] Sister Aimee was one of the first women to preach on the radio in 1924. She was also the first woman to hold a radio license in 1934. But all is not perfect in Los Angeles.

On May 16, 1926 (Sunday), Aimee Semple McPherson was not present to preach during the services at Angelus Temple. Instead, her mother, Minnie Kennedy, stepped to the pulpit and made an announcement: "Sister is with Jesus."[276] It was reported first as a drowning and then as a disappearance, possibly a kidnapping. The June 5, 1926, issue of the *Pentecostal Evangel* published a two-page obituary without any clear evidence, no body, and no witnesses. The *Pentecostal Evangel* began: "Aimee Semple McPherson was a gift from God."[277] The kidnapping and death story was later proved to be false. This scandal marked her ministry for a while, making her reputation less than stellar. In 1927, she formed the International Church of the Foursquare Gospel, making herself lifetime president. She was married a third time to David Hutton, an actor and musician, in 1931. They divorced in 1934. Aimee died in 1944; some speculate that it was a suicide or possibly an accidental drug overdose. All in all, Sister Aimee was a dynamic preacher and church leader. Indeed, she was the first Pentecostal celebrity in America. We turn now to the next chapter, when battle lines are drawn (again) and cold wars are waged.

---

275 Blumhofer, *Aimee Semple McPherson*, 247. For a fuller narrative of the services at Angelus Temple, see *This is That: Personal Experiences, Sermons, and Writings* (Los Angeles: Foursquare Publications, 1996), 562–589.
276 Sutton, *Aimee Semple McPherson*, 93.
277 "Aimee Semple McPherson," *The Pentecostal Evangel* (June 5, 1926): 2–3

7

Battle Lines and Cold Wars

The emergence of neo-evangelicalism happened during the 1940s and into the 1950s. While agreements and partnerships among evangelicals, including comity agreements on the mission field, existed, the real cooperation in the twentieth century came with the founding of the National Association of Evangelicals. Of course, not everyone joined or even attempted to be part of this "new evangelicalism." One group that resisted membership was Westminster Theological Seminary, represented by Paul Woolley, professor of church history. Wooley had said there was a choice for any organization between "many members and much money and read[ing] about itself in the newspapers" or retaining Reformed identity, but it could not have both.[278] The Orthodox Presbyterian Church, with roots going back to J. Gresham Machen, also changed its mind about joining the American Council of Christian Churches and remained unconnected with either fundamentalism or evangelicalism. We should note that while the current membership and the historical membership of the NAE is not Reformed but rather

---

278 D. G. Hart, *Defending the Faith: J. Gresham Machen and the Crisis of Conservative Protestantism in Modern America* (Phillipsburg, NJ: P&R Publishing, 1994), 167.

Arminian, three Reformed churches have joined from the 1980s: the Evangelical Presbyterian Church (1982), the Presbyterian Church in America (1986), and the Christian Reformed Church in North America (1988).

This chapter is titled "Battle Lines" because unity is never complete on this side of heaven, and the body of Christ continues to be divided throughout its two millennia of history. The larger Christian church continues to have three groups (one will count four): Roman Catholic, Eastern Orthodox, and Protestant. The fourth group would be non-Chalcedonian churches, including the Coptics in Egypt and Ethiopia as examples of that ancient tradition. In addition, Protestants are divided into at least three ideologies: ecumenical, evangelical, and fundamentalist. Some would place evangelical and fundamentalist together and see Pentecostals as a "third force" of Christian experience, therefore deserving of a separate position.[279] While we have explained the divisions somewhat evenly and "cleanly," the segmenting into new churches/denominations continues, and there are more denominations now than ever. The global count of Protestant denominations is forty thousand and counting. Because of the separating and diversity of Protestantism, we will consider three global organizations called "alliance," "fellowship," or "council." The level of unity among these three was sometimes "organic unity" but, for the most part, was a partnership of like-minded denominations or churches working together for the kingdom of God.

To remind ourselves again of the four pillars of American evangelicals, we add three more to the NAE: Billy Graham, Fuller Theological Seminary, and *Christianity Today*. We will look at each of the four pillars and the historical context in which they emerged during the 1940s and 1950s. After an orientation on the

---

279 See Paul A. Pomerville, *The Third Force in Missions: A Pentecostal Contribution to Contemporary Mission Theology* (Peabody, MA: Hendrickson, 1985).

state of evangelicalism in the 1940s and 1950s, we will move on to the ecumenical movement, the one global church with a new address in Amsterdam and later Geneva. Finally, we will see the global spread and the connections among fundamentalists.

The actual shift from fundamentalism to evangelicalism (read neo-evangelicalism) would become clearer in the 1950s, as there was still some fellowship through the 1940s. When we look at the history of the NAE, we notice some fundamentalists who were invited and even participated at the earliest stages, but would later separate and refuse membership. An example was a meeting called and hosted by Will Houghton, president of Moody Bible Institute, in October 1941. The meeting's purpose was to start a national organization similar to the regional one in New England. Sixteen leaders were called, and one of them was Carl Curtis McIntire Jr. (1906–2002). The same Carl McIntire, only a few weeks prior, had established the American Council of Christian Churches, a fundamentalist/separatist organization known for its belligerent attitude toward the rest of Christendom. But there seemed to remain a shared identity of affirming the historic creeds and confessions of traditional Christianity. Was it possible that the ACCC and the New England Fellowship (a regional precursor to the NAE) could be united and share a common witness and vision? It was hoped certainly that the ACCC would begin to gather membership and supporters, gain a sufficient power base, and become an influence for righteousness in the midst of a secularized America. However, there would be no unity, not even a consideration of having a shared witness, at the next planning session of the New England Fellowship. Instead, McIntire became aware that the NAE had an openness to all evangelical denominations, including Pentecostals. McIntire had studied under Machen at Westminster, was a conservative Presbyterian, and viewed all Pentecostals (and Wesleyans) as failing to affirm the correct theological view (Reformed/Westminster standards), while on the other hand, both J. Elwin Wright and Harold J. Ockenga had Wesleyan roots and viewed evangelicalism as large enough to hold both Wesleyans and Pentecostals.[280]

Part of the dynamic of change was forced on evangelicalism by a changing culture and not so much by a changing Christianity, but fundamentalists saw both (church and culture) falling down a slippery slope of "accommodation" to one another. So, we can say that the actual changes between evangelicals and fundamentalists should become more distinct. A look at the history and identity of the NAE will help in this direction.

The National Association of Evangelicals was birthed in 1942 at a meeting in St. Louis, Missouri. As we will see later, the NAE was formed after the other church councils in the United States (ACCC and NCCC). Some of its leaders at the earliest stages of organization were actually fundamentalists who would later separate from the NAE. Among that group were Bob Jones Sr. (1883–1968), John R. Rice (1895–1980), and Charles Woodbridge (1902–1995). Leaders who would remain within the neo-evangelical community were Harold John Ockenga (1905–1985), William Henry Houghton (1887–1947), James Elwin Wright (1890–1973), and Paul Stromberg Rees (1900–1991).

As the organization was planned for in Chicago and birthed in St. Louis, the Midwest markings remained strong until the office moved to Washington, DC, showing the desire to dialogue with, or at least be present as salt and light in, the halls of government and power in the US. Early on, the name changed (1943) from National Association of Evangelicals for United Action to simply National Association of Evangelicals. Also, from an early date there was an invitation to meet with

---

280 Garth M. Rosell, *The Surprising Work of God: Harold John Ockenga, Billy Graham, and the Rebirth of Evangelicalism* (Grand Rapids: Baker Academic, 2008), 93–95.

President Eisenhower, showing a trend for the most powerful office in the world to grant favor to the NAE. In a nation that made separation of church and state a point of law based on its Constitution, it seemed that evangelicalism would remain part of the national religious landscape. Of course, not all US presidents would extend that hand of blessing or welcome. One president who not only welcomed but also addressed the NAE was President Ronald Reagan, who in 1983 gave his "Evil Empire" speech/sermon at its annual meeting.[281] George H. W. Bush would be the third US president to speak before the NAE.

In addition to having a national voice on both religious and political matters, the NAE created agencies that would serve both church and society in America. In late 1944, around 150 broadcast ministries joined together to form the National Religious Broadcasters (NRB). The NRB was first a collective organization to join vision and engage in united action; part of the new action was protecting the free speech of evangelical ministries. Mainline Christianity was under the watch and care of the NCCC (national ecumenical organization in the US). In the late 1940s and into the 1950s, radio, and later television time slots were available to churches for religious purposes, but the mainline (liberal) churches wanted to keep these free and desired to claim all the spots for their own religious broadcasters. Thus, an attempt was made to block evangelical ministries by silencing their spokespersons. NAE preferred having radio time slots "for rent," rather than as public service announcements, meaning religious broadcasting would be for sale to the highest bidder. The US government was initially in support of mainline churches and did not allow radio/television time to be for sale, thus excluding evangelicals from the airwaves. That governmental stance would be changed, thanks to the NAE/

---

281 Rowland, Robert C., and John M. Jones, "Reagan's Strategy for the Cold War and the Evil Empire Address," *Rhetoric & Public Affairs*, Vol. 19, No. 3 (2016): 427–463.

NRB's efforts. Having radio and television (and now internet) time is very significant for evangelical ministries, both as a source of income (offerings) and as a means of spreading the evangelical mission. The issues of religious persecution and fair treatment were most recently made alive, not in the majority world, but within the US. In 2019, at their seventy-fifth annual meeting, the NRB declared its commitment to fight against censorship of social media and digital media, wherever there was a threat to freedom of speech and religion. Of course, much of the censorship referenced in this meeting occurs in the US, against evangelicals who are expressing conservative viewpoints in public through social networking service media such as Facebook, Twitter, Google, and Apple.

In the same year that evangelical radio was emerging (1944), the NAE created the Chaplains Commission to help evangelical chaplains in the military have a voice and to ensure equal treatment of all evangelicals. Again, the older traditional denominations had voices, but evangelicals were removed from the centers of power. All military chaplains were required to have denominational endorsement in addition to graduate studies in theology and ordination for ministry. Although he never served in the military, Billy Graham viewed it the way he, indeed, saw the whole world: as a mission field. Graham referred to military chaplaincy as "one of the greatest missionary undertakings." Therefore, graduate theological education was now a necessity. With optimism, the NAE Chaplains Commission was prepared to go for the long-range goal of "taking enough graduate theological work so that we, within four years, can adequately supply chaplains for this great mission field."[282]

The smaller evangelical denominations and the multitude of independent churches did not have anyone at a high-enough

---

282 Ronit Y. Stahl, *Enlisting Faith: How the Military Chaplaincy Shaped Religion and State in Modern America* (Cambridge: Harvard University Press, 2017), 181.

level of government to help them in matters related to equal treatment and equal pay. That was the role of the Chaplains Commission. But, even with that special assistance, actual levels of influence and ability to be promoted and recognized by the military was never equal in practice.

Again, the real situation imposed itself on the dreams and spiritual ambitions of evangelical military chaplains. Chaplains from mainline denominations were promoted more quickly and rose to higher levels of leadership in the military. One example is the chief of chaplains in the US Army, a position started in 1920. Since that time, nearly one hundred years, there have been almost equal numbers of Protestants and Catholics represented in this leadership role, but there was no evangelical until 2007, when the first Southern Baptist clergy/chaplain was selected to be chief of chaplains (major general, or two-star general).[283] The current chief of chaplains (appointed May 31, 2019), Major General Thomas Lynn Solhjem (25th chief of chaplains), is an Assemblies of God minister and the second evangelical and the first Pentecostal to serve in this position. That means in one hundred years and among twenty-five chiefs, only two have been evangelicals.

A third NAE-related agency was formed in 1944 to assist in compassion ministries around the globe. First called the War Relief Commission, it aimed to assist Europeans who lost everything during and after World War II. Later, the name was changed to World Relief Commission (WRC). OMS's former Korea field director James Elmer Kilbourne (1920–2017) served as its director for both South Korea and, in the late 1960s, for Vietnam.[284] WRC continues to assist persons who have lost

---

[283] If you count Seventh-day Adventists (SDA) as evangelicals, then Barry Black, an SDA navy chaplain, served as chief of chaplains from 2000 until 2003, when he became the chaplain of the US Senate. Rear Admiral Barry Black was also the first African American to serve as chaplain of the US Senate.

[284] For further reading on the World Relief Commission, see Elmer Kilbourne

everything from war, disasters, and persecution. It is supported by churches and individuals, but most notable are the financial grants offered from the US government.

A fourth agency is now called Missio Nexus. It began in 1945 and was originally called the Evangelical Foreign Missions Association. The name changed later to simply Evangelical Foreign Missions. The name changes can be difficult to understand, or even remember, since so many occurred in such little time. The first name it received was the Evangelical Fellowship of Mission Agencies (EFMA), then later it was called The Mission Exchange, and finally Missio Nexus. The birth of Missio Nexus was celebrated on February 6, 2012, at Tabernacle Church (Salem, Massachusetts) in conjunction with the bicentennial celebration of American overseas missions (the sending of Adoniram and Ann Judson to Southeast Asia). Perhaps the more significant ecumenical event was that Missio Nexus was more than an update or renaming of EFMA; it marked a joining together of the two evangelical mission organizations that had existed separately and had distinctive doctrinal statements. The Interdenominational Foreign Mission Association (IFMA) was founded in 1917, and represented an earlier evangelical move away from Protestant liberalism to form foreign mission associations independent from mainline denominations. Although an earlier proposed merger failed in 1946, the newer names of CrossGlobal Link (formerly IFMA) and The Mission Exchange (formerly EFMA) were united and remain committed to the greater *Missio Dei* (mission of God).[285]

The initial reason for making a foreign mission agency in 1945 was to "provide a medium of voluntary united action

---

and Ed Erny, *Missionary Maverick* (Greenwood, IN: OMS International, 2009), 125–141.

285 For further reading, see Bradley A. Coon, "From Adoniram Judson to Missio Nexus: Celebrating Two Hundred Years of North American Missions," *Evangelical Missions Quarterly*, Vol. 48, No. 3 (July 2012): 362–364.

among evangelical foreign missionary agencies, without, however, exercising executive or legislative control over the constituent members."[286] At the very start of EFMA history, OMS was a charter member. We can see now a definite NAE/OMS connection.

After all the name changes and mergers, today "Missio Nexus is the largest and most inclusive expression of Great Commission oriented evangelicals in North America (US and Canada) that fosters shared learning, opportunities for collaborative action, and produces increased effectiveness through its many mission-orientated products, programs, and services."[287]

Another project of the NAE is English Bible translation. While a growing number of fundamentalists claim a King James Version-only view of Bible inspiration and preservation and do not use or endorse any modern translations of the Scriptures, both evangelical and ecumenical Christians today engage in Bible translation to ensure that modern audiences understand ancient text. The NCCC acquired the copyright of the American Standard Version Bible (1901) and made a revision, completing it in 1952. A copy of the Revised Standard Version Bible (RSV) was presented to President Harry S. Truman that same year, oddly enough, the first time a Bible was given to a president of the United States. But amid the new translation arose "two categories: opposition to Bible revision in general, and opposition to Bible revision by liberals."[288]

Only three months after the publication of the RSV, the NAE's *United Evangelical Action* "editorialized the need for a more conservative translation, without naming the NAE

---

286 James DeForest Murch, *Cooperation without Compromise: A History of the National Association of Evangelicals* (Grand Rapids: Wm. B. Eerdmans, 1956), 102–104.
287 From their website: https://missionexus.org/who-we-are. Accessed 14 July 2019.
288 Peter J. Thuesen, *In Discordance with the Scriptures: American Protestant Battles over Translating the Bible* (New York: Oxford University Press, 1999), 87.

as a possible sponsor."[289] It would take five years for the first step to be taken. In 1957, a committee was formed to consider sponsoring a new translation of the Bible in English. Within eight years, the NAE's committee joined a group from the Christian Reformed Church to become the Committee on Bible Translation, with the New York Bible Society (later called International Bible Society) as their sponsor. The translation was first published in 1978, with a revision in 1984 and, most recently, a 2011 revision.

We should mention why the Revised Standard Version was rejected by many evangelicals. It all hinged on only one word, which was translated differently than in the King James Version (1611) and other revisions in the Tyndale Version tradition. It was merely one word mistranslated, but a cardinal doctrine. A major belief of traditional Christianity was on the line, with just a single incorrect word.[290] The one Hebrew word was *almah*, rendered by the RSV in Isaiah 7:14 as *young woman*, rather than *virgin*. *Young woman* is retained, surprisingly, in the Catholic edition of the RSV and in the New Revised Standard Version (1989).

A final few sentences on English Bible translations in the US: If we were to identify a Protestant in America by the Bible he or she carries, we could simply say that a fundamentalist has the King James Version, an evangelical reads the New International Version (NIV), and an ecumenical Christian (liberal) uses the New Revised Standard Version. That, of course, is simplified, not taking into account various exceptions. Not all evangelicals use the NIV, since the 2011 revision employs some gender-neutral or gender-inclusive language; some more-conservative evangelicals

---

289 Peter J. Thuesen, *In Discordance with the Scriptures: American Protestant Battles over Translating the Bible* (New York: Oxford University Press, 1999), 123.
290 We can remember the Auburn Affirmation (1923–1924) which rejected the Five Fundamentals (or Doctrinal Deliverance of 1910) for Presbyterians, one of them being "virgin birth of Christ."

in the area of gender roles in the church (complementarians, or in other words, those against the ordination of women) are switching to the English Standard Version, among others.

After looking at the birth and growth of the NAE in the US, we can connect with the World Evangelical Alliance (WEA) on a global scale. We can say the WEA was founded in 1846 as the Evangelical Alliance in Britain, with American and other English-language church memberships. But the American Civil War (1861–1865) and the Christian division over slavery made it difficult to have reconciliation and continue forward as one church, so the Evangelical Alliance would have to wait until 1951 for its rebirth. The World Evangelical Fellowship (as it was originally called, WEF) had its first General Assembly at Woudschoten (Zeist) in the Netherlands. The name was changed after the General Assembly in Kuala Lumpur (2001) from "Fellowship" to "Alliance." The previous leader was Canadian, Geoff Tunicliffe. Now, the Alliance is led by Secretary-General Efraim Tendero (since 2015) of the Philippines, and, since 2010, the Alliance offices have been in New York City.

As we mentioned, the first life of the Evangelical Alliance, in 1846 Britain, came to its demise and division over slavery. The British membership decided to exclude any slaveholders from the Alliance, and the American church leaders from the South opposed this. The Alliance still existed through all those tensions, but not as a united front of mission and evangelism. Not until it was "reborn" in 1951 in the Netherlands did we see it shine. The planning that led up to its rebirth in 1951 was conducted by J. Elwin Wright and Clyde W. Taylor, both of the NAE. Brian Stanley lists three shortcomings of the WEA in *The Global Diffusion of Evangelicalism*. The first is the difference between American evangelicals and British and continental evangelicals. Americans were members of conservative denominations, whereas many of the British evangelical members were conservatives in liberal churches. The second fault is that funding of the WEA was from America almost exclusively. In November 1976, "it was reported that 98.5% of income of the WEF international office for the past year had been supplied from the United States and that membership fees from other WEF national bodies made up of less than 0.5% of total income."[291] Third and finally, because most of the financing and leadership was either American dollars or American pastors, the international alliance appeared to be a branch office of the NAE, rather than an autonomous and global alliance. The list of WEA leaders includes an almost equal list of British and American secretaries-general, with two Canadians and two Filipinos. However, it is difficult to see the WEA as a healthy, nearly independent organization with so much dependence on the US. It seemed the WEA had hoped to go forward in 2014 when it had planned for a General Assembly in Seoul, South Korea. But the General Assembly was never held and no alternative was announced. Considering this lack of communication, the WEA appears to be less than vibrant, possibly even awaiting another resurrection.

Before we move on to Billy Graham as the second of four pillars of evangelicalism in America, we can be reminded that there was a vast difference between the evangelical experience in America in 1943 and that in Korea the same year. For Americans, World War II began on December 7, 1941, with the Japanese bombing of the US naval base at Pearl Harbor, Hawaii. But in Korea, being a colony of the Japanese empire since 1910 (annexation) led the Korean church to struggle against control, seeking not only independence or the three selves as churches (see chapter 6), but as a nation and people, also crying aloud for independence on March 1, 1919. These

---

291 Stanley, *The Global Diffusion of Evangelicalism*, 71.

two moves toward independence combined within the one heart of Korean evangelicals.

During the time when the churches were becoming self-governing, self-propagating, and self-supporting (1930s), the malevolent control of the Japanese government over churches (and in fact, all religions except Shinto, the de facto faith of the Japanese empire) made Shinto shrine rituals compulsory for Christians as "citizens" of the empire. Only a few of the evangelical denominations strongly opposed any compromise and refused—to the point of death/martyrdom—to bow before what they viewed as a religious idol rather than a civic symbol. Among the major evangelical groups, only the Presbyterians related to the Australian missionaries and those from the Presbyterian Church US (Southern Presbyterians) were consistent in their resistance. The Canadian Presbyterians, US Northern Presbyterians, and both Methodist churches accommodated the practice for the purpose of keeping their Christian schools open and remaining in Korea as a Christian presence.[292] These issues of bowing or not bowing would be settled, not during the war years, but after independence (1945), when the Korean church experienced its own form of truth and reconciliation.

While there was pressure from 1937 on, to bow before the Shinto shrine, there was, from 1940 on, pressure to merge all evangelical (Protestant) denominations into one united church which was controlled and monitored by the Japanese government. In 1939, the Japanese Diet passed the Religious Organizations Law, which became practiced as the law of the land in 1940. By 1945 (after the surrender of the Japanese empire), the new constitution established by the occupation powers allowed for freedom of religion, thus there was a Religious Corporations Ordinance.

---

292 For a detailed discussion of the history, see Sang Gyoo Lee, *To Korea with Love: Australian Presbyterian Mission Work in Korea, 1889-1941* (Melbourne: Presbyterian Church of Victoria, 2009), 170–213.

One unplanned move toward the three selves (self-government) was when the Japanese empire forced foreign missionaries in Korea (US American, Australian, British, and Canadian) to return to their home countries. Some were able to return safely, but others were confined or imprisoned; even some who tried escaping to North America were intercepted as their ships were captured by the Japanese Navy in the Pacific Ocean.[293]

The Japanese empire had targeted three evangelical churches more than any of the mainline churches. It should also be remembered that all Protestant denominations were required to join the Kyodan (United Church of Christ in Japan). There was, however, concern over three churches/denominations, as the majority of them joined together to form the United Church.

The three congregations under close watch were the Holiness Church, the Salvation Army, and Malcolm Fenwick's East Asia Church of Christ. All three churches/denominations were not allowed to meet during the last two years of the Pacific War. The Holiness Church was dissolved by the government on December 29, 1943. All the Holiness buildings were taken over by the Japanese government and used for military purposes (barracks and training). During the almost two-year period that the Holiness Church was illegal, everyone had to attend either a Presbyterian or Methodist church. The East Asia Church of Christ (later combined with the Southern Baptists/Korea Baptist Convention) was not allowed to meet because of its emphasis on the second coming of Jesus Christ. Likewise, the Seventh-day Adventists were disbanded by Japanese authorities on December 27, 1943. The most dangerous doctrine to the Japanese colonial government was the second coming of Jesus Christ. Is the second coming viewed as a threat to civil/secular government today? Maybe a better question is, Do evangelicals

---

293 Roy E. Shearer, *Wildfire: Church Growth in Korea* (Grand Rapids: Wm. B. Eerdmans, 1966), 77–79.

today wait eagerly for Christ's coming, our Bridegroom, our blessed hope, or have we moved on to other relationships and other hopes? The political contexts in America and Korea differed drastically from one another during the 1930s as well, but one constant was the blowing of the Holy Spirit's wind through both nations. In America, as we saw already, Billy Sunday and other evangelists traveled the breadth of America, and evangelicalism continued to both expand its numbers and extend its territory. In fact, no other single evangelist had as much of an impact on unsaved America as Billy Sunday until at least the 1950s and beyond, with the global evangelistic ministry of Billy Graham. Revival and evangelism were united in this period as evangelists continued to preach the gospel and the Holy Spirit brought revival to those same meetings. Once again, healing services combined with the proclamation of the gospel emerged, just as had occurred in the first century.

Through the 1920s and into the 1930s, Korea experienced ongoing waves of revival from the evangelistic ministries of three pillars of Korean evangelicalism: Kil Seonju (1869–1935), Lee Yongdo (1901–1933), and Kim Ikdu (1874–1950). We do not have the time to fully introduce these three pillars, but we can note the distinctives of each one.[294]

Kil Seonju was associated with both the Great Revival in Pyeongyang (1907 and beyond) and the Korean Independence movement, but, after his imprisonment by the Japanese, he emerged as a preacher of eschatological themes, focused especially on the book of Revelation.[295]

Our second pillar is viewed by many scholars of Korean

---

[294] The majority of writings on these three Korean pillars of revival and evangelism remain in the Korean language only. For an introduction to their ministries and their methods, see Kim and Kim, *A History of Korean Christianity*, 139–143.

[295] Chong Bum Kim, "Preaching the Apocalypse in Colonial Korea: The Protestant Millennialism of Kil Sŏn-ju," in *Christianity in Korea*, eds. Robert E. Buswell Jr. and Timothy S. Lee (Honolulu: University of Hawaii Press, 2006), 149–166.

religions as an evangelical mystic.²⁹⁶ Lee Yongdo was a Methodist pastor who suffered much during his life, but the pains of life were transformed into power for ministry. Lee also had a ministry of preaching baptism with the Holy Spirit, intercessory prayer, and the ministry of spiritual warfare, or casting out demons. Lee remains controversial, as some indicate he went beyond the boundaries of orthodoxy and became more than a mystic by challenging both established religious structures and doctrines. My own limited reading of Lee causes me to think of him as a Korean evangelical version of the Roman Catholic Saint Thérèse of Lisieux (1873–1897).

The third pillar is the evangelical Kim Ikdu. Kim had a radical conversion experience, similar to that of Billy Sunday or Charles Finney. His revival and evangelistic ministries were combined with prayer for divine healing. He "led 776 revival meetings, peached 28,000 times, established 150 new churches, healed thousands of the sick, and inspired more than 200 to become ministers. It is estimated that more than two million people turned to Christ as a result of his preaching."²⁹⁷ Victor Wellington "V.W." Peters (1902–2012), a Methodist missionary to Korea, wrote a five-chapter biographical study of Kim that was published in *The Korea Mission Field* (January–May 1933). He concludes his fifth chapter with these insightful comments:

> Kim Ik Doo is still Korea's great evangelist. The glamor and stir of the past decade have changed,

---

296 For much of evangelical historiography and religious typology, putting "evangelical" next to "mystic" presents some challenges. When many consider the term *mystic*, they look at Catholics or Orthodox believers, not Protestants, and especially not evangelicals. I do not think the two terms are anything like an oxymoron, but that they have a relationship with one another similar to "Pentecostal" and "mystic." This is an area in great need of further research, but there is a start. See Daniel Castelo, *Pentecostalism as a Christian Mystical Tradition* (Grand Rapids: Wm. B. Eerdmans, 2017).

297 Kim In Soo, "Kim Ik Doo," in *A Dictionary of Asian Christianity*, ed. Scott W. Sunquist (Grand Rapids: Wm. B. Eerdmans, 2001), 443.

it is true, but we are not to think the glory is departed. He keeps traveling the length and breadth of the land and preaches to thousands. His messages are so simple that every old grandfather can understand and so enlivened with humor and homely illustrations from the lives of the people that young people also feel at home. It is a rare gift to be able to bridge the gulf between the young and the old, the educated and the uneducated in Korean congregations. . . . But the chief secret is that he preaches not with man's wisdom, but in demonstration of the Spirit and of power. [298]

Kim Ikdu has been called the "Billy Sunday of Korea," but I am waiting for the day when we can hear someone in the US called the "Kim Ikdu of America." Now, we will turn to Billy Graham, who has several solid Korea connections.

Billy Graham first entered the national spotlight when he held a major crusade in Los Angeles (1949), and he would enter the international spotlight when he preached to one million people on Yoido in Seoul (1973).

William Franklin "Billy" Graham Jr. was born in Charlotte, North Carolina, in 1918. His father was a dairy farmer, on a small farm with only a few cows. Raised as a Presbyterian, Graham would later become a Baptist pastor.

Graham was born again after hearing the gospel and responding at revival meetings held by Mordecai Ham in 1934. His academic preparation for global evangelism was limited theologically, but he did study at Bob Jones College (1936), Trinity College of Florida (1937–1940), and graduated from Wheaton College in 1943 with a major in anthropology.

---

298 Victor Wellington Peters, "Gold, Good Measure Running Over: Chapter Five, The Finest of the Gold," *The Korea Mission Field*, Vol. 29, No. 5 (May 1933): 110.

Bob Jones Sr. (1883–1968) would later, along with his son and grandson, distance themselves from Graham, viewing him as an apostate. What was Graham's crime? Graham had a heart for the lost, and he saw the fields as ripe for harvest. This only served to enhance his ministry to the multitudes, his commitment to the Bible, and his compassion for lost souls. What did the fundamentalists see wrong with this?

For the new generation of fundamentalists, there was a doctrine called "second-degree separation." It involves distancing yourself from people who do not believe the same way you do, those who do not share your scruples. When Graham began to preach, fundamentalists began noticing the guest speakers on the platform. There were Roman Catholic priests and Orthodox priests, all ready to receive grace, while others sat on the platform to minister to sinners turned saints.

Nonetheless, fundamentalist leaders criticized Graham and eventually distanced themselves from his ministry. All this because of second-degree separation, a mindset of "I will not fellowship with you because of those with whom you fellowship." Graham cooperated with Catholics and Orthodox Church leaders; fundamentalists saw this as a compromise of the true gospel.

Later in life, in an interview by Larry King on CNN, Graham was asked, "Do you have any regrets?" His answer was that he should have studied more, beyond a bachelor's to a master's and a doctorate. While Graham studied at Wheaton College, he would meet and date the love of his life, Ruth Bell (1920–2007); they were married in 1943. Ruth grew up in China and attended high school in Pyeongyang; her father was a Presbyterian medical missionary (Dr. L. Nelson Bell). The Grahams have five children, two sons and three daughters.

After a brief time serving as pastor of the Village Church in Western Springs, Illinois, and a time preaching for Youth for

Christ, Graham would also serve as president of Northwestern College in Minneapolis. He was the youngest college president in America, at the age of twenty-nine. Northwestern was the fundamentalist college founded by William Bell Riley who, near his own death, wanted Graham to carry on the tradition as president. Graham would preach at Riley's funeral in 1947.

Billy Graham entered the national spotlight when he held a major crusade in Los Angeles (1949). He was featured in the major newspapers of the time. Graham has prayed with and counseled US presidents ranging from Truman to Obama. Graham and his ministry were responsible for the launch and early publication years of *Christianity Today* (1956), and the beginning of worldwide meetings to plan and pray for evangelism. Initially, among evangelicals, was the 1966 World Congress on Evangelism (Berlin, Germany). Meeting in a then-divided city, marching in the streets of Berlin, the members of the Congress united on world evangelism, communicating the message of Christianity versus communism loudly and clearly. One of the speakers from Korea was "Helen Kim, president of the Upper Room Evangelistic Association and former ambassador of Korea to the United Nations, [she] dedicated her entire remarks to the discussion of the problem between the totalitarian threat to Christian life in the Soviet Union, China, and Korea."[299]

A lot happened in both American and European society between 1966 and 1974. The Civil Rights movement, the anti-war demonstrations, and the May 1968 civil unrest in France are of special note. Thus, the First International Congress on World Evangelization (ICOWE), also known as the Lausanne Congress or simply Lausanne '74 (July 16–25, 1974, in Lausanne, Switzerland), had much to discern and discuss on a global scale in order to breach the subject of evangelism. *The Lausanne*

---

299 Uta A. Balbier, "The World Congress on Evangelism 1966 in Berlin: US Evangelicalism, Cultural Dominance, and Global Challenges," *Journal of American Studies*, Vol. 51, No. 4 (2017): 1186.

Covenant, with a large collection of addresses and discussions, was edited and later published.[300] Part of the character of the covenant was seen through the identity of its author, John Robert Walmsley Stott (1921–2011).[301] Stott was an Anglican and a graduate of Cambridge. His view of evangelicalism was not the American version, which later caused some tensions over the balance (as Stott viewed it) or dominance (as others saw it) of social ministry over evangelism perceived by some American evangelicals.[302]

Fifteen years later (1989), a second Lausanne was held in Manila, the Philippines, producing *The Manila Manifesto*.[303] Most recently, a third meeting was held in Cape Town, South Africa (2010).[304] The Lausanne meetings and movement continue, as well as trainings and gatherings for evangelists, both at global and local levels. Amsterdam 2000 included more than ten thousand itinerant evangelists from 190 nations of the world. This nine-day event expressed the global shift which was already occurring from north to south and from west to east.[305] But for men who look back at the twentieth century

---

300 For a complete collection of all the papers presented and their responses at Lausanne (1974), see J. D. Douglas, ed. *Let the Earth Hear His Voice: International Congress on World Evangelization; Lausanne, Switzerland* (Minneapolis, MN: World Wide Publications, 1975).

301 For a scholarly biography of Stott, see Alister Chapman, *Godly Ambition: John Stott and the Evangelical Movement* (New York: Oxford University Press, 2012).

302 A full study of evangelism within global evangelicalism is Arthur Johnston, *The Battle for World Evangelism* (Wheaton, IL: Tyndale House, 1978). Arthur Johnston at the time was professor of mission at Trinity Evangelical Divinity School (Deerfield, IL) and began a debate with Stott that grew into a consultation in Grand Rapids, MI (June 1982) with a report: *Evangelism and Social Responsibility: An Evangelical Commitment*. The debate continues with some evangelicals uncomfortable with all three Lausannes.

303 *The Manila Manifesto* is available online. See https://www.lausanne.org/content/manila-1989-documents. Accessed 12 April 2019.

304 For an overview of all three Lausanne meetings, see Robert Hunt, "The History of the Lausanne Movement, 1974–2010," *International Bulletin of Missionary Research*, Vol. 35, No. 2 (April 2011): 81–84.

305 Gustav Niebuhr, "In Amsterdam, Billy Graham Torch will pass to Multitude," *New York Times* (July 30, 2000). https://archive.nytimes.com/www.nytimes.com/library/world/europe/073000amsterdam-graham.html. Accessed 15 May 2019.

and see Billy Graham, the real event remained the crusade, where mass evangelism was crafted by Graham himself, and where people knew him to be the preacher with a Bible and that powerful phrase, "The Bible says...."

We mentioned the Los Angeles crusade in 1949, but a few others preceded that, along with a multitude of hearers and throngs of people walking down the sawdust trail or, in most of his crusades, a number of stairs in a stadium that led to the field where you would pray the Sinner's Prayer. Some of the earlier crusades were in Grand Rapids, Michigan (1947); Charlotte, North Carolina (1947); London, England (1955); Melbourne, Australia (1959); Berlin, Germany (1966); Kohima and Nagaland, India (1972); Seoul, Korea (1973); Moscow, Russia (1984); Pyeongyang, Korea (1992); and Beijing, China (1994). That lists only the highlights of a long and fruitful ministry of preaching the gospel around the world.

In addition to being a faithful preacher, Graham was a prolific author of popular Christian books. Some titles (in alphabetical order) include: *America's Hour of Decision* (1951), *Angels: God's Secret Agents* (1985), *Billy Graham Answers Your Questions* (1960), *The Holy Spirit* (1978), *The Jesus Generation* (1971), *Just As I Am* (1997, his autobiography), *Peace with God* (1953), and *World Aflame* (1965).

The largest building on the Wheaton College campus in Wheaton, Illinois, is the Billy Graham Center, which houses the graduate school, the archives, a large auditorium, a museum, and a missions and evangelism library. But all of this never would have been if Graham had not settled this question in his heart long ago: Can I trust the Bible to be completely true?

Looking at his autobiography, we can read about the doubts that had been sown into Graham's mind through his conversations with Charles "Chuck" Templeton (1915–2001). Templeton was studying at Princeton Theological Seminary in 1948 and encouraged Graham to join him there for theological studies.[306] Here are words of the young Graham as he heard from the almighty God:

> The exact wording of my prayer is beyond recall, but it must have echoed my thoughts: "O God! There are many things in this book I do not understand. There are many problems with it for which I have no solution. There are many seeming contradictions. There are some areas in it that do not seem to correlate with modern science. I can't answer some of the philosophical and psychological questions Church and others are raising."
>
> I was trying to be on the level with God, but something remained unspoken. At last the Holy Spirit freed me to say it, "Father, I am going to accept this as Thy Word—by *faith*! I'm going to allow faith to go beyond my intellectual questions and doubts, and I will believe this to be Your inspired Word."
>
> When I got up from my knees at Forest Home that August night, my eyes stung with tears. I sensed the presence and power of God as I had not sensed it in months. Not all my questions were answered, but a major bridge had been crossed. In my heart

---

306 Charles "Chuck" Templeton was also an evangelist with Youth for Christ (founded in 1946). After Templeton's time at Princeton, he would leave the evangelistic ministry, enter politics for a while, and eventually turn to radio journalism and to writing books. He also became an agnostic. See Kevin Kee, *Revivalists: Marketing the Gospel in English Canada, 1884–1957* (Montreal and Kingston: McGill-Queen's University Press, 2006), 143–187. For his own story, see Charles Templeton, *Farewell to God: My Reasons for Rejecting the Christian Faith* (Toronto: McClelland and Stewart, 1996).

and mind, I knew a spiritual battle in my soul had been fought and won.[307]

We thank the Lord that Graham struggled over the question of the Scripture's full truthfulness, because it was his experience of going through the fight to reach the other side that brought grace to so many hearers at the Graham crusades. May we also share the commitment to the full inerrancy of Scripture and the full illumination of the Holy Spirit to make our reading possible, so that we can join with our brother Billy Graham and proclaim with confidence and power, "The Bible says!"

We move on to the third pillar of American evangelicalism (more accurately "neo-evangelicalism"). The Reverend Charles E. Fuller (1887–1968) was the son of an affluent rancher in southern California, a farmer, you could say in biblical terms, who had a vision for sowing seeds and planting a seminary. Today, the largest theological seminary in America bears his name, just as Bob Jones College carried its founder's name, and Oral Roberts University would herald Christ's name and minister God's healing to a broken world in Tulsa, Oklahoma, and to the nations of the world.

Fuller Theological Seminary (1947–) was built upon the foundation of a radio ministry by the name of *The Old Fashioned Revival Hour* (1937–1968). It "had audiences surpassing in size those of the most popular secular shows, including Bob Hope and Charlie McCarthy... estimated at twenty million worldwide."[308] At a banquet honoring Charles Fuller and Harold Ockenga, Billy Graham told the audience, "I've met people all over the world that say they were converted to Christ under the

---

307 Graham, *Just as I Am*, 139.
308 George Marsden, *Reforming Fundamentalism: Fuller Seminary and the New Evangelicalism* (Grand Rapids: Wm. B. Eerdmans, 1987), 14–15.

ministry of Charles Fuller—people he'll never know anything about until he gets to heaven."[309]

Fuller's first president was Harold John Ockenga (1905-1985), but that was only one of his firsts. Commuting between his pastoral ministry at Park Street Church in Boston to Pasadena, from the East Coast to the West Coast every week, Ockenga would also serve as the first president of the NAE and even later as the first president of Gordon-Conwell Theological Seminary in the Boston area. In his serving a triumvirate of presidencies, the first at every place, Ockenga was prepared by God. Ockenga would hear Fuller's specific vision for the new seminary in a letter:

> "The new institution would seek to provide the same caliber of training 'in the Gospel' as West Point makes available for students in Military Science or Caltech provides for those who wish to study engineering. Students who have been 'called of God' should have 'the very best of training in order to go out in His service as ministers, missionaries, evangelists [and] teachers.'"[310]

Fuller's early faculty included Everett Harrison, Carl F. H. Henry, Harold Lindsell, Wilbur Smith, and later Charles Woodbridge. These were the luminaries of neo-evangelical scholarship in the 1940s and beyond. Charles Woodbridge would later repudiate his association with neo-evangelicalism and retain ties with fundamentalism, especially Bob Jones University, until his death. Now we turn to the fourth pillar of American evangelicalism.

By the time *Christianity Today* was founded as a monthly magazine representing neo-evangelicalism, the other two branches

---

309 Daniel P. Fuller, *Give the Winds a Mighty Voice: The Story of Charles E. Fuller* (Waco, TX: Word Books, 1972), 175.
310 Rosell, *The Surprising Work of God*, 201-202.

of Protestantism had their own representative publications. The ecumenical Christians in America wrote *The Christian Century*, founded originally as a Disciples of Christ denominational publication in 1884, and later purchased by the liberal Disciples minister Charles Clayton Morrison (1874–1966) in 1908, and given its current name and media focus. The fundamentalists wrote *The Sword of the Lord*, founded and published by John Richard Rice (1895–1980) in 1934. Originally published as a local church newspaper in Texas where Rice was pastor, it moved to Wheaton in 1940, while Rice's children attended Wheaton College. But in 1963, as a protest statement against neo-evangelicalism at Wheaton (as well as a desire to find a less-expensive location), Rice moved the magazine's office to Murfreesboro, Tennessee. *The Sword of the Lord* surpassed *Moody Monthly* in number of subscriptions and remained the representative publication of American fundamentalism for decades.

Because fundamentalism, due to the second degree of separation, had no fellowship with other religious groups and even remained at a distance from all others, meaning non-fundamentalists, it was difficult to dialogue or even have a casual conversation with outsiders. Thus, the need became apparent, as evangelicals engaged in evangelism and mission, to study the world around them, but fundamentalists were not concerned with this. Therefore, the baton would need to be passed to a new generation of fundamentalists, or "new evangelicals."

"These scholarly fundamentalists, or 'new evangelicals,' as they came to be called, emphasized the need to meet the intellectual challenges of the age if the movement was to have a lasting impact."[311] Meeting "intellectual challenges" remained an important engagement that fundamentalists truly could not afford to bypass. After a decade of in-fighting, it appeared

---

311 Marsden, *Understanding Fundamentalism and Evangelicalism*, 150.

that the fundamentalists were losing the majority in their denominations (Presbyterian, Baptist, Methodist, Disciples of Christ), and with the loss of denominations came a diminishment in their respective colleges and seminaries. These were all missing, remaining the property of the modernists/liberals in each denomination. While Fuller became a representative neo-evangelical school of theology, it later would slip from its stellar position in the 1970s with the publication of Harold Lindsell's *The Battle for the Bible* (1976). Harold Lindsell (1913–1998) was one of Fuller's original faculty members, so his book spoke both prophetically concerning the shifting position of Fuller on Scripture and as an insider's voice, rather than a fundamentalist from another state or city. After neo-evangelicalism's birth in the 1940s, a dream of Wilbur Smith (on faculty at Fuller) was to start a flagship publication, an evangelical magazine that addressed both biblical subjects and contemporary culture. It was Smith's dream, but Billy Graham and his father-in-law, Dr. L. Nelson Bell, offered their oversight, and a Pew grant provided the financing. Wilbur Smith was asked to be the first editor, but he turned this request down, and Harold Lindsell had one name to recommend: Carl F. H. Henry (1913–2003), who was on faculty at Fuller and had published *The Uneasy Conscience of Modern Fundamentalism* in 1947. While some would see Henry as a moderate evangelical, others who wanted to steer *Christianity Today* viewed him as a fundamentalist. The desire to truly remain "in the middle" between liberal Protestantism and conservative fundamentalism was not easy. Thus, we can understand Graham's vision for the publication to "plant the evangelical flag in the middle of the road, taking a conservative theological position but a definite liberal approach to social problems. It would combine the best in liberalism and the best in fundamentalism without compromising theologically."[312]

---

312 Marsden, *Reforming Fundamentalism*, 158.

Christianity Today began in 1956, with its offices located in Washington, DC, the center of American political power. We have already looked at the NAE and the WEA. Now it's time to consider the ecumenical movement. Some would claim that the first Pentecost, around two thousand years ago, marked the birth of the ecumenical movement, just as Pentecostal churches mark their own birthday on Acts 2 and the day of Pentecost. In fact, most Christians, when asked for the date of the church's birth, would give Acts 2 and mention the day of Pentecost.

The real historical beginning of the ecumenical movement, however, was not in the first century but in the first decade of the twentieth century. The World Missionary Conference (Edinburgh 1910) marked the event.[313] At the time of Edinburgh, there was a unity of evangelicals which allowed them to remain within denominations not yet turned fully toward theological liberalism. As we looked briefly at the first two ministers who came to Korea as missionaries in 1885, we find that they viewed themselves as evangelicals as— if not more than—their own denominational identity of Methodist and Presbyterian.

You can say that the ecumenical movement began as a mission-minded thrust to the nations. John R. Mott chaired the Edinburgh Missionary Conference in 1910. After Edinburgh, there were more meetings of the International Missionary Council (to later merge with the World Council of Churches). They met in 1928 in Jerusalem, in 1938 in Tambaram, India, and in 1947 in Whitby, Ontario, Canada. While various parts of the ecumenical movement did merge to become the World Council of Churches (1948), other agencies or ministries remained independent. In 1937, a significant step was taken toward merger and unity when an agreement was made to combine the Faith

---

313 Brian Stanley, *The World Missionary Conference, Edinburgh 1910*, Studies in the History of Christian Missions (Grand Rapids: Wm. B. Eerdmans, 2009).

and Order movement and the Life and Work movement. It was made official on August 23, 1948, with the first assembly of the World Council of Churches in Amsterdam, the Netherlands. Later assemblies met at Evanston, Illinois (US)—1954; New Delhi, India—1961; Uppsala, Sweden—1968; Nairobi, Kenya—1975; Vancouver, British Columbia, Canada—1983; Canberra, Australia—1992; Harare, Zimbabwe—1998; Porto Alegre, Brazil—2006; and Busan, South Korea—2013. The current general secretary of the WCC is the Reverend Olav Fykse Tveit (a Norwegian Lutheran pastor). Prior to Tveit's term of service, the Reverend Samuel Kobia (a Kenyan Methodist minister) was the general secretary. The World Council of Churches has its offices in Geneva, Switzerland.

Only four Korean churches/denominations are members of the WCC. They are the Anglican Church of Korea, Korean Methodist Church, Presbyterian Church in the Republic of Korea, and Presbyterian Church of Korea. In Korea there is a national ecumenical body called the National Council of Churches in Korea (KNCC). Other members of the KNCC that are not WCC members include the Evangelical Church of Korea, Korean Assemblies of God, Korean Orthodox Church, and the Salvation Army in Korea.

The WCC encompasses 349 churches, denominations, and church fellowships in more than 110 countries and territories throughout the world, representing over 560 million Christians. While the WCC is considered *the* ecumenical movement, it might help to remember three distinctives between the NAE/WEA and the WCC, as listed by Jon R. Stone. First, evangelicals pursue spiritual unity rather than organizational or organic union. Second, the NAE's motto is "cooperation without compromise," meaning truth is not to be sacrificed in order to achieve unity. Third, evangelical unity allows for a continuation of denominational or church distinctives. In a sense, "evangelicals charged that liberal ecumenism forced ecclesiastical regimentation, thus usurping the authority of the local church and dampening individual initiative."[314] Now we look to the right—the far right—and see the fundamentalist version of an ecumenical movement.

The Reverend Carl T. McIntire organized both the American Council of Christian Churches (1941) and the International Council of Christian Churches (ICCC, 1948).[315] As noted already, the ACCC was formed prior to the NAE, and there was a desire on McIntire's part to have the two united as one conservative movement with hopes of maintaining biblical orthodoxy in the face of a church shifting toward liberalism.

McIntire studied at Princeton under Machen until the split that created Westminster Theological Seminary. After McIntire worked with Machen and was part of the Orthodox Presbyterian Church, he departed and made his own church/denomination called the Bible Presbyterian Church. He also founded his own seminary called Faith Theological Seminary (both in 1937). McIntire's departure from Machen's Orthodox Presbyterian Church was over one doctrine and one religious practice. McIntire believed in a premillennial view, adopting the dispensationalism of C. I. Scofield. He also was opposed to Christians drinking alcohol. As odd as it might sound to Korean Presbyterians today, some American Presbyterians not only drank alcohol but also smoked tobacco. Now that we have briefly surveyed the three ecumenical organizations and their views of and practices of church unity, we will transition to evangelicalism's conflict with communism.

In 2019, the world had been looking at North Korea and asking whether or not unification will ever come to the Korean

---

314 Stone, *On the Boundaries of American Evangelicalism*, 132.
315 For further reading on McIntire, see the insightful book by Markku Ruotsila, *Fighting Fundamentalist: Carl McIntire and the Politicization of American Fundamentalism* (New York: Oxford University Press, 2016).

peninsula and if it has ever been possible. Part of our answer will be in the narrative of introducing a body of literature covering the views of communism. While Korea remains divided between North and South, 2019 was also a year of summits and of seeing handshakes over the demilitarized zone, all with the desire to usher in unification.

In the late 1940s, the North Korean and Russian communist authorities had set up political organizations under Christian names, hoping to co-opt the Korean Christians to the communist cause. On November 3, 1946, a general election for establishing the government of the Democratic People's Republic of Korea (North Korea) was held on the Christian Sabbath (Lord's Day/Sunday). The church protested the election, and it became an issue that turned the communist government's attention against the church.[316] At the same time, the church also began to solidify their view of the separation of church and state. Considering that Korea had emerged from forty-five years of Japanese colonialism and the imposition of one denomination for all Christians (Kyodan), no doubt the hesitancy was a matter of caution.

The League of Christians in North Korea now had Kim Ikdu as a member, as well as Bak Sangsun, a famous missionary to Manchuria. The League of Christians also affirmed loyalty to Kim Ilseong, the first leader of the Democratic People's Republic of Korea (DPRK). Kim Ilseong forced the two Presbyterian seminaries in Pyeongyang to merge in March of 1950 and restricted the number of new students allowed. These actions indicated that communist North Korea was not going to cooperate with Christianity.

Then the martyrdoms began in North Korea. Pastor Kim Gwasik was arrested, tortured, and died in communist custody (1947). Kim Injun, president of the Pyeongyang Theological

---

316   Kim and Kim, *A History of Korean Christianity*, 164–166.

Seminary, and Pastor Lee Jungsim were arrested, detained by Russian Intelligence, and executed. Kim Cheolhun and Lee Yutaek were both executed in North Korea. The government forced union, just as the Japanese had done with the Kyodan.

Pastor Son Yangwon had been imprisoned for seven years during the Japanese colonial period. His two sons were unable to attend public school because, like their father, they refused to bow before the Shinto shrine. At the end of the war, they returned to ministry and to school. A group of Communists took over their village and executed Pastor Son's two boys. Even so, Pastor Son pleaded for mercy for the murderer of his sons.

Taking care of the many refugees was an ongoing concern of the Christian churches during the war. After the initial attack by North Korea, the front line shifted, which meant not only the deployment of military forces up and down the peninsula, but also the disbursement of refugees from the North being led up and down the peninsula, looking for a home on this side of heaven.

On July 3, 1950, the Korean Christian National Relief Association was started, with work in both Daegu and Busan, extending to thirty other centers. A total of nearly two thousand church workers and their families were given assistance during this time of turmoil.[317]

In the midst of ongoing investigations over who had committed apostasy, there were special outreach efforts on the part of Korean churches. The year 1952 was announced as a year of evangelism by the Presbyterian General Assembly. This is not only surprising, but also amazing, since the Korean War was still raging and would not end, but would cease hostilities on July 27, 1953. Even with the special ministries to assist families during the recovery, the Methodists gathered together to celebrate the 250th anniversary of John Wesley's birth (1703). In

---

317 Clark, *A History of the Church in Korea*, 247.

addition, a seventy-year anniversary of the arrival of Underwood and Appenzeller was celebrated in 1954 as a special time of evangelism and revival.

Rev. Bob Pierce, the founder of World Vision, first came to Korea in 1949, then returned in 1955 for a series of evangelistic meetings.[318] Rev. Billy Graham held a crusade, reaching out to the lost in Korea, especially the US military, in both 1952 and 1956. His book *I Saw Your Sons at War: The Korean Diary of Billy Graham* was a short book but one that returned the young faces of Americans, who were fighting in faraway Korea, home to America.[319]

While Graham was in Korea the first time, he viewed the dangers of communism and wrote about them in a pamphlet published by his ministry. The title was "Christianism vs. Communism." Graham wrote, "In Korea the blood of American soldiers is being shed every day to hold back this philosophy of Karl Marx." There is no doubt the rhetoric was "red hot" in response to communism. Graham, we can remember, visited North Korea in 1992 and 1994, and, at that time, preached at Kim Ilseong University to a large auditorium filled with North Korean students. Due to Graham's role in declaring first the dangers of communism, and then, forty years later, being willing to make peace, shake hands, and forget about what's evil and what's good, his ministry in Korea truly was significant.

It should be noted, however, that some authors view Graham's London crusade (1954) as the entrance to global evangelism for the North Carolinian. In contrast, I see the Seoul crusade (1973) as having more of an impact on both a nation and a region, since it turned the church in Korea toward global Christianity.[320]

---

318 Clark, *A History of the Church in Korea*, 250.
319 Billy Graham, *I Saw Your Sons at War: The Korean Diary of Billy Graham* (Minneapolis: Billy Graham Evangelistic Association, 1953).
320 For an example of the London view, see Thomas Paul Johnston, *Examining Billy Graham's Theology of Evangelism* (Eugene, OR: Wipf & Stock, 2003).

In the midst of the formation of the World Council of Churches came still additional church divisions in Korea, many related to the past views of either the church/denomination or pastor and the related conduct at Shinto shrines. The question for many evangelicals was not, "Did you fight during the Korean War (1950–1953)?" but became, rather, "How did you live during the Japanese occupation (1910–1945)?" To bow or not to bow before the Shinto shrine was the question.

The Methodist Church in Korea had united and held its first united conference in 1930, but it divided after 1945 between Jaegeonpa (Reconstruction) and Buheungpa (Revival) groups. Instead of permanent division among Methodists, union occurred again on April 10, 1949, at Jungdong Church.[321]

The Holiness Church held its general conference (Reconstruction) in November 1945, chaired by Cheon Sekwang (1904–1964). The denominational periodical *Hwalcheon* (*Living Stream*) was being published again. The Korea Evangelical Holiness Church reestablished ties with OMS in September 1951, and changed its name from Joscon Yesugyo Dongyangseongyohoi Seonggyeol Gyohoi (Jesus Holiness Church of the Oriental Mission of Korea) to Gidokgyo Daehanseonggyeol Gyohoi (Christian Korea Holiness Church).[322]

More significant changes in the Baptist Church (Fenwick) occurred after 1945. The church changed from Episcopal polity to Congregational polity. Leadership titles changed in order to follow the common evangelical usage in Korea: from Ansa to Moksa (pastor/teaching elder), from Kamro to Jangro (ruling elder), from pastoral assignment to pastoral election, and finally from Daehwahoi to Chonghoi (General Assembly). Additionally, the Baptists in Korea became the Daehan Gidokgyo Chimreho (Christian Korea Baptist Church) in 1949, and affiliated with

---

321 Clark, *A History of the Church in Korea*, 276–277.
322 Ibid., 252–255.

the Southern Baptist Convention that same year. The SBC sent Rev. J. Abernathy to begin the work in South Korea. Changes in titles and polity might seem minor, but they reflect a level of contextualization within Korean society and relationships within the larger evangelical family in Korea.

After the Korean War came reconstruction of many damaged and destroyed church buildings, as well as construction of many new buildings. Gemyeong Christian College was opened in Daegu, as was Daejeon Christian College. Many Bible schools, institutes, colleges, and seminaries were re-opened or newly founded after the war. In order to educate the large number of children who were unable to attend formal/regular elementary schools, churches organized Bible clubs.[323] The Bible club programs began during the Japanese colonial period when churches wanted to avoid government restrictions placed on schools. Many poor children learned how to read and write in Bible clubs, but, more importantly, became believers in Jesus Christ.

Korean military ministry included a government-sponsored (official) chaplain corps. President Rhee Syngman (1875–1965) issued the order to begin the organization of the chaplain corps on February 7, 1951. Foreign missionaries and Korean pastors ministered to the many North Korean and Chinese prisoners of war as well. Bible correspondence courses became an important ministry right after the war. The Korean churches began to send out missionaries themselves; in 1955, two missionary couples were sent to Thailand by the Korean Presbyterian Church.

As we see the ecclesiastical events happening during wartime Korea (1950–1953), it would be good to revisit the beginning of the Korean War on June 25, 1950, with the North Korean invasion of the South. The same war ended with a cease-fire signed on July 27, 1953. There is yet to be a permanent end to the war/conflict. No armistice has been signed.

---

323 Clark, *A History of the Church in Korea*, 282–285.

We should remember that during the Korean War, both the nation and the church suffered greatly. There are no verifiable figures for the total killed in the Korean War, but it is estimated that three million Koreans (roughly 10 percent of the population) were killed, wounded, or missing as a result of it. By 1953, 40 out of 144 Korean Catholic priests were held in the North, killed, or missing, along with many lay leaders. Of 153 foreign missionaries and religious workers, 57 were dead or unaccounted for. At least 202—and perhaps 400—Protestant ministers and seminarians were killed or imprisoned in the North. Presbyterians lost 619 church buildings, Methodists 239, and Holiness churches 106.[324]

Indeed, the list of martyrs is long. It includes Son Yangwon (1902–1950), Kim Ikdu (revival speaker), Noh Yeongsu (Salvation Army officer), and Jo Minhyeong (leader of the rural movement). Evangelical church leaders (Presbyterian) Bak Gyeonggu (1903–1950) and Jeong Ilseon (1883–1950) were also martyred by the Communists.

The Amputee Rehabilitation Project was started in 1953 by Dr. Reuben Torrey II, himself an amputee. This son of Reuben Archer Torrey (of Moody and Biola) was a Presbyterian missionary to China.[325] One of his sons, Reuben Archer Torrey III, came to Korea as an Episcopal missionary, first serving as rector of St. Michael's Seminary (1958–1965), until the time when he would establish Jesus Abbey in Gangwondo in 1965. Jesus Abbey is an intentional Christian community. So, ultimately, four generations of Torreys hold a Korea connection. Reuben Archer Torrey IV, son of the founders of Jesus Abbey, has returned to Korea and oversees a Christian school near Jesus Abbey. His mission focus is on North Korea, with

---

324 Kim and Kim, *A History of Korean Christianity*, 185.
325 Clark, *A History of the Church in Korea*, 272.

a ministry called The Fourth River Project.[326] Not only are four generations represented, all connected with Korea, but four denominations/church traditions are also present, somehow all generically evangelical. R. A. Torrey, disciple of D. L. Moody and later president of both Moody Bible Institute and Biola, was a Congregationalist. His son, who served as a missionary in China and ministered with amputees in Korea after the war, was a Presbyterian. Torrey III was Episcopal/Anglican, and Torrey IV is ordained with the Syro-Chaldean Church of North America, part of the Orthodox tradition. Some of evangelicalism's diversity manifests itself within the four Torrey generations.

On April 21, 1950, the General Assembly of the Korean Presbyterian Church (held in Daegu) began the division with two sides entrenched. The two sides, per usual, were: conservatives (Koryeo Theological Seminary) and liberals (Joseon Seminary). In May 1951, the General Assembly met again in Busan and condemned the Koryeo side. The Koryeo side left the General Assembly. In June 1953, the initial division was sealed but erupted again in 1954 with the division between Kijang and Yejang.

The split widened in 1959, when the 44th General Assembly witnessed the division of the Jesus Presbyterian Church into two sects: Hapdong and Tonghap, both sides equal in size. Hapdong became allied with the ICCC, and the Tonghap side continued its membership in the WCC, though many anticommunist South Koreans resisted the ecumenical movement, since the WCC had member churches from communist nations and did not support the South during the Korean War.[327]

Now, as we consider the 1950s and the second half of the twentieth century, we will visit the first of many megachurches

---

326 See Ben Torrey, "The Mission to North Korea," *International Bulletin of Missionary Research*, Vol. 32, No. 1 (January 2008): 20–22.
327 Kim and Kim, *A History of Korean Christianity*, 196–199.

in South Korea. The first had a North Korea connection. Donald N. Clark, retired professor of history at Trinity University (San Antonio, Texas) and third-generation historian and son and grandson of Presbyterian missionaries in Korea, pairs Han at Yeongnak and David Yonggi Cho at Yoido as representatives of Korean megachurches.[328] We will follow suit and look at the Yoido Full Gospel Church and Cho in chapter 9.

Yeongnak Presbyterian Church was founded by the Reverend Han Gyeongjik (1902–2000) on December 2, 1945, with a group of twenty-seven refugees from North Korea. Ground was broken for a new building on March 24, 1949, when the church outgrew the tent it was using as a sanctuary.

Han was born in North Korea to a Confucian family. At the age of fourteen, he became a Christian. In 1915, he began his studies at Osan Academy in Cheongju. Beginning in 1921, he attended college at Sungsil (Union Christian) College in Pyeongyang. He was often a guest at the home of an evangelical missionary from Kansas. Han would serve as secretary to Rev. William Newton Blair. Blair made arrangements for Han to study abroad. Han studied at Emporia College in Kansas (BA, 1926) and Princeton Theological Seminary (graduated in 1929). After his studies, he was hospitalized for two years in Albuquerque, New Mexico, due to tuberculosis. He would return to Korea in 1931. Han began his ministry as a teacher in a Christian high school for one year, then served as a pastor in northwest Korea. In three years, his church grew to fifteen hundred members. In 1941, Han was arrested by the Japanese for being pro-American, based upon his past studies in the US. He was released after a few weeks, but was forbidden to preach until Liberation. During this time of exile from the pulpit, Han ministered at an orphanage and a home for the elderly.

---

328 Donald N. Clark, *Christianity in Modern Korea*, Asian Agenda Report, 5 (Lanham, MD: University Press of America, 1986), 23–26.

After the Soviet occupation of the North (from 1945), Han escaped as a refugee to the South. During this time frame, he started the Yeongnak church. Han was the 1992 winner of the Templeton Prize. Previous winners include Mother Teresa, Billy Graham, and Alexandr Solzhenitsyn.

Now, let us review the church membership statistics at Yeongnak and begin to understand the exponential growth of a local church planted in Seoul, also a home for North Korean refugees. At the start there were 27 members (December 1945). By 1955, there were 3,000 members, and that number nearly doubled by 1961 (within six years), and again doubled by 1965, with 11,386 members. The increase was not exponential during the next fifteen years, but the church still experienced a significant amount of growth, having a total of 34,864 members in 1980.[329]

With the construction of the new building, the congregation had grown to more than four thousand. By 1992, membership had reached sixty thousand, making it the largest Presbyterian church in the world at that time. Currently, the church is pastored by Rev. Kim Woonseong (since 2018).[330] This megachurch was born in the womb of suffering from the refugee/pilgrim's experience of seeking a home beyond this world. It can serve as a model for anyone desiring to do mission/ministry to the millions of refugees on planet earth who remain seeking a heavenly home beyond these borders. We will move on to the next chapter where we look at the charismatic experience and the task of evangelism for all believers.

---

329 John N. Vaughan, *The World's 20 Largest Churches* (Grand Rapids: Baker, 1984), 63.
330 Youngnak's English-language web pages can be viewed from this site: http://en.youngnak.net/main/main.aspx. Accessed 11 May 2019.

8

Charisma and Evangelism

My hope remains that this textbook will not only make us aware of our evangelical identity and shared history, but will also cause us to embrace all our sisters and brothers within the evangelical family. We have not always been close, to say the least. Some of our family members have been disowned, and others, feeling the neglect from the rest of the family, have moved on to find a new family. Charismatics and Pentecostals are fully evangelical; there is no doubt when we look at our shared history, and again, remember we have the same grandfather, which would make us cousins. Yes, the Wesleyan-Holiness movement is cousins with the Pentecostals and charismatics. Let's welcome one another. Even better, let's love one another.

In case anyone remains unconvinced of our family relationships within evangelicalism, let me explain it from a different perspective. There seems to be, in my view, no argument that the majority of the Pentecostal movement was a product of the Wesleyan-Holiness movement, which shows the influence of John Wesley upon both global movements. Indeed, from the very core of the Wesleyan-Holiness movement was a prophetic call for a "new Pentecost" by leaders such as Solomon Benjamin

Shaw (1854–1941), George Hughes (1823–1904), and John Allen Wood (1828–1905).

To further clarify, Pentecostalism is the grandchild of John Wesley, with two parents from the radical Holiness movement of the late nineteenth century, one white and one black. Charles Fox Parham is the theological parent, and William Joseph Seymour is the missiological parent. Pentecostalism as an interracial religious movement was from the beginning egalitarian. Lines that had been drawn in society at large were erased in the Holiness/Pentecostal movement. Race, gender, and class all seemed to become non-issues among the Spirit-filled people of God. A specific verse from Galatians was used by Pentecostals to express this new freedom and egalitarianism in Christ. Galatians 3:28 (KJV) reads, "There is neither Jew nor Greek, there is neither bond nor free, there is neither male nor female: for ye are all one in Christ Jesus." I hope by the end of this section on Pentecostals and charismatics we can see again that we are all evangelicals. If the Wesleyan-Holiness saints are evangelicals, then so are the Pentecostals and charismatics.

We do not have the space to return to the first decades of the twentieth century and see again how Pentecostals were disowned and marginalized within evangelicalism. Indeed, the Pentecostal movement, which was rejected by many mainline denominations in the early twentieth century, was accepted in the 1960s. The charismatic movement brought the marginal tongues movement to mainline Protestantism, to the Roman Catholic Church, and in the "third wave" to evangelicalism. Interest in Pentecostalism was rising because the movement was growing phenomenally. Everyone took notice as Pentecostalism emerged from the back alleys to main street. Phenomenal growth outside of North America and in Brazil and other nations in South America caught the attention of missionaries and global Christians. Perhaps one of the more significant trends that made people aware of Pentecostals and charismatics was when the divine healing movement expanded and caught the world's attention during the 1940s.

The post-1945 rise of the divine healing movement in the US included William Branham, Jack Coe, and Oral Roberts. Later healing evangelists include T. L. Osborn, A. A. Allen, Kathryn Kuhlman, and Benny Hinn. Exodus 15:26 (KJV) reads, "I am the Lord that healeth thee." Healing was taught and believed to be part of atonement (Isaiah 53:5)—"with his stripes we are healed" (KJV). Anointing with oil was practiced literally by Pentecostals (James 5:15). Already, the Wesleyan-Holiness and evangelical movements had contributed much toward the Pentecostal view of divine healing.

One of the more prominent healing evangelists from the Pentecostal Holiness Church was Granville Oral Roberts (1918–2009). He was born in Oklahoma, Pontotoc County, son of a Pentecostal Holiness minister. At the age of seventeen, Oral was diagnosed with tuberculosis and was bedridden. In 1935, he was healed of tuberculosis and stuttering. He was ordained in 1936 in the Pentecostal Holiness Church (PHC). From 1941 to 1947, Oral served four pastorates in the PHC. He was "full of preach."

In 1947, Oral Roberts held his first citywide healing crusade in Enid, Oklahoma. That same year, he wrote and published *If You Need Healing Do These Things*. From 1947 to 1968, Oral Roberts ministered at more than three hundred major healing crusades. In 1955, he began a nationwide TV program, and the next year (1956) he would start a monthly magazine, *Abundant Life*.

Roberts became a bridge between Pentecostalism and the second wave (Protestant and Catholic charismatics). By 1968, Oral Roberts transferred his ministerial credentials from the

Pentecostal Holiness Church to the United Methodist Church (UMC), but by 1988, he would leave the UMC.[331]

From the beginning of Pentecostalism, there had always been times when non-Pentecostals experienced baptism in the Holy Spirit and speaking in tongues. Receiving baptism in the Holy Spirit and tongues meant you would convert from your church/denomination to Pentecostalism. Neo-Pentecostalism proved a different phenomenon. People would receive the baptism in the Holy Spirit and tongues but would remain in their own churches. Other mainline Protestants and evangelicals began to receive the baptism in the Holy Spirit and tongues. Among them were Howard Ervin (American Baptist), Harald Bredesen (Lutheran/Dutch Reformed), Howard Conatser (Southern Baptist), Ross Whetstone (United Methodist), Nelson Litwiler (Mennonite), Warren Black (Nazarene), and Larry Christenson (American Lutheran). Indeed, the new wine had come to the old wineskins.

Typologies are ways of making distinctions, classifying, and helping pieces fit inside a whole. In an article in *Life Magazine* (1955), Henry Van Dusen called Pentecostalism the "Third Force in Christendom." Lesslie Newbigin, in *The Household of God*, views three streams within Christianity: sacramental, evangelical, and Pentecostal.[332] In his *The American Pentecostal Movement: A Bibliographical Essay*, David W. Faupel organized classical Pentecostals as belonging to one of three groups: Keswick view of sanctification, Holiness view of entire sanctification (John Wesley's influence), and Jesus-only view of the Godhead.

By the 1980s, three waves emerged: first wave—Classical Pentecostalism, second wave—Pentecostal experience in mainline Protestantism and the Roman Catholic Church, and

---

331 David Edwin Harrell Jr., *Oral Roberts: An American Life* (Bloomington: Indiana University Press, 1985).

332 Vinson Synan, *The Holiness-Pentecostal Tradition: Charismatic Movements in the Twentieth Century*, 2nd ed. (Grand Rapids: Wm. B. Eerdmans, 1997), 280.

third wave—Pentecostal experience among evangelicals. In the late 1960s, the countercultural movement called "hippies" became attracted to Christianity, especially to Chuck Smith's Calvary Chapel. This was influenced by the ministry of David Wilkerson's Teen Challenge, especially in reaching out to the drug culture of America. Coffeehouses were the mainstay of the Jesus People movement.

Official church reports from the Presbyterians (1970), Episcopal Church (1971), American Lutheran Church (1973), and the Lutheran Church in America (1974) did not view the charismatic experience as being psychologically abnormal or theologically unorthodox. The United Methodists issued a report in 1976 that identified charismatic theology as not being related to Wesleyan thought.

What about the third wave? C. Peter Wagner coined this term in his *The Third Wave of the Holy Spirit*.[333] Third wavers do not see themselves as belonging to the first wave (Pentecostal) or to the second wave (charismatic). Leading up to the third wave were the healing evangelists, especially William Branham and Oral Roberts, and the Latter Rain (New Order of the Latter Rain).

One of the third-wave groups is Calvary Chapel. In December 1965, Chuck Smith, (1927–2013), ordained with the Foursquare Church, became the pastor of a small congregation in southern California (Costa Mesa). Three years later, the church became independent, leaving the Foursquare denomination. Calvary Chapel became part of the Jesus movement when Lonnie Frisbee, a hippie convert, moved in with the Smith family. Calvary Chapel held many mass baptisms in the Pacific Ocean. The mother church in Costa Mesa began giving birth to many daughter churches that are all over the globe.

A second group is the Vineyard churches. Vineyard churches

---

[333] C. Peter Wagner, *The Third Wave of the Holy Spirit* (Ann Arbor, MI: Vine Books, 1988).

existed from the mid-1970s, but the real impetus of the movement began when John Wimber (1934–1997) led his Yorba Linda congregation from Calvary Chapel to the Vineyard Association. Vineyard churches see themselves as the "radical middle" between evangelicals and Pentecostals.[334]

Wimber was raised in a non-Christian home and later became a successful executive in the music industry. He would experience a radical conversion in 1963, which was followed by a call to ministry. After graduating from Azusa Pacific University, he was recorded (ordained) in the California Yearly Meeting of Friends, serving as co-pastor of the Yorba Linda Friends Church for five years.

In 1975, Wimber joined C. Peter Wagner of the Fuller Evangelistic Association and began work as a church-growth consultant. Around this time, he co-taught a DMin seminar with C. Peter Wagner. By 1981, the seminar's title became "Signs, Wonders and Church Growth." From 1982 until 1985, Wimber taught "The Miraculous and Church Growth" at Fuller.

Wimber started the Anaheim Vineyard in 1977. Soon after, he and his congregation began to experience spiritual gifts, especially healing. Wimber began to minister internationally in signs and wonders. At this time, his church grew to five thousand attenders. An aggressive church-planting endeavor saw the birth and growth of the Association of Vineyard Churches. Wimber led this "denomination" until his death in 1997. Both the Kansas City Fellowship and the Toronto Airport Vineyard were part of Vineyard, but both later separated from the association. John Wimber wrote *Power Evangelism* (1986) and *Power Healing* (1987). These books were followed by those of other authors with similar themes: *Christianity with Power* by Charles

---

[334] See Bill Jackson, *The Quest for the Radical Middle, A History of the Vineyard* (Kenilworth, Cape Town, South Africa: Vineyard International Publishing, 1999).

Kraft (1989), *Spiritual Warfare* by Timothy Warner (1991), and *Surprised by the Power of the Spirit* by Jack Deere (1993).

The New Apostolic Reformation is a movement to restore the fivefold ministry gifts of Ephesians 4 to the modern church, with special emphasis on the gifts of apostle and prophet. Wagner calls this movement the most radical since the Reformation of the sixteenth century (Luther and Calvin).[335]

As part of the restoration of the prophetic and apostolic gifts to the church, a number of Christian leaders began ministering in the Kansas City area. Included among them are Rick Joyner, Paul Cain, Bob Jones, and Mike Bickle. Paul Cain had been part of the Voice of Healing Revival, started earlier by William Branham. Mike Bickle was pastor of the Kansas City Fellowship, now called Metro Christian Fellowship. In 1990, the Kansas City Fellowship became affiliated with the Vineyard Association for a few years. Beginning in 1985, Bickle began to focus on prayer and intercession. Kansas City Fellowship (KCF) became part of Vineyard (Metro Vineyard Fellowship) from 1990 until 1996. Currently, Bickle spends his time as director of the International House of Prayer (IHOP). IHOP, under Bickle's leadership, remains in the forefront of the 24/7 prayer and worship in the spirit of "the Tabernacle of David" (Acts 15:16 KJV).

Rodney Howard-Browne, a South African Pentecostal evangelist, is also known by the name "Holy Ghost Bartender." He ministered at the Carpenter's Home Church in Lakeland, Florida, for a while, before the "blessing" was taken from St. Louis to the Toronto Airport Vineyard Church by Randy Clark. The Toronto Airport Vineyard Church was under the pastoral leadership of John Arnott. In 1995, an amazing six hundred thousand visitors came to catch the blessing.[336] In December

---

335 See C. Peter Wagner, *Apostles and Prophets: The Foundation of the Church* (Ventura, CA: Regal, 2000).

336 John Arnott, *The Father's Blessing* (Orlando, FL: Creation House, 1995).

1994, John Wimber flew to Toronto to caution the Toronto staff. There were reports of "animal sounds" as extreme manifestations of revivalism. The Toronto congregation was disfellowshipped from Vineyard.

In June 1995, another revival broke out at the Brownsville Assembly of God in Pensacola, Florida. Stephen Hill was the evangelist, and John Kilpatrick was the pastor. A later revival would erupt in Lakeland, Florida. Prophecies are continually announced today, and, in the internet age, are sent out to thousands of Christians. An anticipation for a new revival began to grow in Florida. In the same city that Rodney Howard-Browne had hosted the holy laughter services, in fact, in the same church (Carpenter's Home Church), another revival began under the leadership of a tattoo-covered Canadian evangelist, Todd Bentley (1976–).

David Barrett's *World Christian Encyclopedia* gave figures that the Pentecostal/charismatic/third wave movements had passed up every traditional/confessional group of Protestantism, including evangelicalism, to be highest in numbers, second only to the Roman Catholic Church. If we count Pentecostals and charismatics and their megachurches, we can include Yoido Full Gospel Church, Jotabeche Methodist Pentecostal Church, Vision del Futuro, Deeper Life Bible Church, and Brazil para Cristo.

Predictions made as early as the 1970s by the World Council of Churches saw that the real growth of the church would take place primarily in those churches that were non-white, from the Southern Hemisphere, and Pentecostal or charismatic. This connects perfectly with Philip Jenkins's *The Next Christendom: The Coming of Global Christianity*.[337] Now that we have witnessed the revival side (charismatic movement and third wave), we will move on to evangelism, especially noting

---

337 Philip Jenkins, *The Next Christendom: The Coming of Global Christianity* (New York: Oxford University Press, 2011).

CHARISMA AND EVANGELISM

the Billy Graham crusade in Seoul (1973) and Campus Crusade for Christ's Explo '74.

From the first decades of the twentieth century, Korean evangelicalism has been noted for its zeal in evangelism. "No Korean is thought fit for Church membership unless he is vigorously engaged in propagating the gospel."[338] And again, "A marked feature of Korean Christianity is the recurrence of the life of the apostolic days when every Christian was a missionary to the people round about him."[339] That was the first of the century; by the second half, in the 1960s and beyond, there were ever-increasing new avenues of evangelism.

In 1960, 80 percent of the population in Korea was rural, hence came newfound fervor for rural/village evangelism. Efforts in contributing toward the building of churches in the countryside and the financial support of pastors there increased in the 1960s. Additional efforts in evangelism in the military and within the many schools in Korea came about. Some viewed these two contexts as ripe fields, since people serving in the military and students away from home were freed from an old context and open to a new one. This new context for life could be either a time of increased stress and waywardness in their Christian faith, or it could be a time of renewal and growth in Christ. The results depended upon whom they met first.

The diverse forms of evangelism and ministry and the many groups targeted have included police chaplains, hospital chaplains, street children, markets, industrial evangelism, and the working classes.

As we mention these in passing, we can turn our attention to the Billy Graham crusade in Korea, especially the meetings on Yoido (1973). Graham describes the services:

---

[338] Amos R. Wells, *Into all the World* (New York: Young People's Missionary Movement, 1903), 86.
[339] Alfred DeWitt Mason, *Outlines of Missionary History* (New York: George H. Doran, 1912), 131.

> I recall, for example, the closing service of our Crusade in Seoul, Korea, in 1973. Well over 1 million people crowded Yoido Plaza on an island in the Han River; that was the largest live audience we ever addressed at one time. (The number was not an estimate; the people were grouped in squares, and hence easily countable; and there was electronic tabulation too). My interpreter, Billy Kim, had just graduated from Bob Jones and had received a letter from Dr. Bob warning that if he interpreted for me, his support from America would be cut off. However, Billy Kim did interpret for me and said that he had never seen a Korean audience so still and so attentive.[340]

Billy Kim "was so good, in fact, that some Korean television viewers assumed he was the featured preacher, with Graham interpreting his message for American military personnel."[341]

It seems Americans know the name Billy Kim, but not Koreans. In Korea, Billy Kim is Rev. Kim Janghwan (1934–). Billy Kim began his ministry with Suwon Central Baptist Church in 1960, with only ten members. From that time, the church has grown to a current fifteen thousand. Kim served as president of the Baptist World Alliance (2000–2005). He retired as senior pastor on December 19, 2004. The current pastor is Rev. Ko Myeongjin. Billy Kim continues to serve as the chairman of the board of the Far East Broadcasting Company (FEBC) in Korea, after working at FEBC as its president for fifty years.

Billy Kim described "a great conflict" when he talked about the decision to be Billy Graham's interpreter during the 1973 Yoido crusade. He explained his conundrum as choosing between your

---

340 Graham, *Just As I Am*, 275.
341 William Martin, *A Prophet with Honor: The Billy Graham Story* (New York: William Morrow, 1991), 418.

"spiritual father" (Bob Jones) and your new "spiritual brother" (Billy Graham). As Kim made a shift from fundamentalism to evangelicalism, it was never easy. But Kim's attendance at the World Congress on Evangelism (Berlin 1966) was a first step toward evangelicalism, and a second was his invitation by Bill Bright in 1972 to address Explo '72 in Dallas. In the next two decades, Kim would have many more invitations; especially noted are his sermons at Promise Keepers events. Promise Keepers was a Christian men's movement where stadiums filled with men deciding to hear the gospel rather than watch a football game—truly amazing grace!

During Graham's earlier visit to Korea around Christmas of 1952, he had preached at Yeongnak church, with Pastor Hang Gyeongjik as interpreter. Graham describes the experience, saying:

> One highlight was preaching to 2,500 a night in the unheated but huge and beautiful Young Nak Presbyterian Church in Seoul, pastored by Han Kyung Chik. Many GIs got special leave to come from the front lines. I can never forget the sight of American soldiers alongside Koreans at the front of the church, responding to the Invitation. Korean pastors would grip my hand in their humble, gracious way and in tears thank us for coming to encourage them.[342]

Each visit that Graham made to Korea was a ministry experience of bringing people together. As an evangelical, the "invitation"—for Graham, that meant singing "Just As I Am"—was a means of gathering people to the cross. Another ministry of

---

342 Graham, *Just As I Am*, 197.

reconciliation, evangelism to college students, was founded by Bill Bright and extended to Korea by Kim Jun Gon (1925–2009).

William R. "Bill" Bright (1921–2003) was born in Oklahoma, educated there in a one-room schoolhouse, and graduated from Northeastern State College in Tahlequah, Oklahoma, with a bachelor's degree in education. John G. Turner rightly notes that other leaders among the postwar evangelicals were from small-town America, especially the Midwest and the South. Included in this list are Oral Roberts, Jimmy Swaggart, Rex Humbard, Jim Bakker, James Robison, and Billy Graham.[343]

Bill Bright would move west to California in 1944 for business opportunities, but through his attendance at the First Presbyterian Church of Hollywood (the largest Presbyterian church in the US at the time), he would become discipled by the Christian education ministry of Henrietta Mears (1890–1963). Mears was another Midwesterner turned Californian, born in North Dakota. She completed her bachelor's degree at the University of Minnesota and began a career as a high school chemistry teacher in Minnesota. During a trip to California, Mears was offered the position of director of religious education at the First Presbyterian Church of Hollywood. She already had significant ministry experience in teaching at the First Baptist Church pastored by William Bell Riley.[344] Her religious background was fundamentalist, but through her ministry at First Presbyterian (Hollywood), she would become a mentor to not only Bill Bright and his wife, Vonette Zachary Bright (Campus Crusade for Christ), but also to Jim Rayburn Jr. (Young Life), Billy Graham, and Louis Evans Jr., founding pastor of Bel Air Presbyterian Church, where President Ronald Reagan would attend.

---

343 John G. Turner, *Bill Bright & Campus Crusade for Christ: The Renewal of Evangelicalism in Postwar America* (Chapel Hill: University of North Carolina Press, 2008), 16.

344 Turner, *Bill Bright & Campus Crusade for Christ*, 18–25.

After beginning his religious education with Mears, Bill Bright traveled to the East Coast and studied at Princeton Theological Seminary. After only a short time, he returned to California to study at Fuller. While at Fuller, Bright became frustrated with the intellectual climate of neo-evangelicalism and could not understand why they were studying ancient languages and hard-to-understand theological concepts while the world around them, especially in America and war-torn Europe, was going to hell without having heard the gospel.

As a Fuller dropout, Bright moved to the campus of the University of California, Los Angeles, in 1951, and started what would become Campus Crusade for Christ (CCC) (now known as Cru). By 1959, "The Four Spiritual Laws" were being put together, first as a twenty-minute gospel presentation and later in a short tract (booklet). The Four Spiritual Laws were, with some later modifications: "(1) God loves you and has a wonderful plan for your life; (2) Man is sinful and separated from God, and thus he cannot know and explain God's plan for life; (3) Jesus Christ is God's provision for man's sin through whom man can know God's love and plan for his life; (4) We must receive Jesus Christ as Savior and Lord by personal invitation."[345] At a website sponsored by CCC you can see The Four Spiritual Laws in 166 languages.[346]

After meeting Bill Bright in 1958 on the Fuller Theological Seminary campus, Kim Jun Gon returned to Korea and founded the Korea Campus Crusade for Christ.

The real connection between the US and Korea would come in 1974, when Explo '74 was held in Seoul (at Yoido). It was a training program for three hundred thousand in evangelism and discipleship. The year before (1973), Billy Graham preached on Yoido and the press reported one million in attendance, and

---

345 Ibid., 99.
346 See www.4laws.com/laws/languages.html. Accessed 14 May 2019.

Bill Bright made the same claim.[347] In 1979, CCC would engage in global evangelism through the production and distribution of *The Jesus Film*.

Other parachurch ministries that began in America and spread to Korea include Navigators, founded in 1933 by Dawson E. Trotman (1906–1956), and the Billy Graham Evangelistic Association (BGEA), founded in 1950 by Billy Graham, with its headquarters in Minneapolis, Minnesota. At the personal request of Billy Graham, the BGEA would make extensive use of Dawson Trotman's materials in its follow-up ministry to people who made personal decisions at one of the crusades. One of the key texts was Trotman's "Born to Reproduce."

In addition to Campus Crusade for Christ was InterVarsity Christian Fellowship (IVCF). During the times of intense tension between mainline (ecumenical) Protestants and evangelicals, especially those more conservative, the established ministry of the Student Christian movement in Britain fell under suspicion, and a new ministry was founded to represent a more evangelical position within British Christianity, especially among Anglicans. IVCF was established in 1928 in Britain and spread globally, first to Canada, then to New Zealand and Australia, and next to the US.[348]

A key ministry that reached behind bars to help those incarcerated in the prisons of the world was Prison Fellowship, founded in 1976 by Charles "Chuck" Wendall Colson (1931–2012). Colson served as a special counsel (attorney) to President Richard Nixon. His loyalty to President Nixon was unmatched, and he remained ready to do anything for the administration, legal or illegal. Colson was arrested as one of the Watergate

---

347 Turner, *Bill Bright & Campus Crusade for Christ*, 151–152.
348 Geoffrey R. Treloar, *The Disruption of Evangelicalism: The Age of Torrey, Mott, McPherson and Hammond*, A History of Evangelicalism: People, Movements and Ideas in the English-Speaking World, Vol. 4 (Downers Grove, IL: IVP Academic, 2017), 238–242.

Seven, convicted, and sent to prison for obstruction of justice. This "hatchet man" was born again in 1973 while he was serving his time in prison. It was one of those dramatic conversions that we do not hear enough about today. Chuck Colson not only became an authentic Christian, but he also became a leader in prison ministry.

On the side of helping the poor are two prominent global ministries founded by Robert "Bob" Pierce (1914–1978). They are World Vision International (1950) and Samaritan's Purse (1970). We already noted that Bob Pierce had visited Korea in 1949 for the first time, and it was the following year in China that he committed to helping the "least of these" in Jesus's name. Young Life was founded by Jim Rayburn (1909–1970) in 1941, while he was being discipled by Henrietta Mears. David Wilkerson (1931–2011) founded Adult and Teen Challenge in 1960, which grew out of his ministry to street gangs in New York City. One parachurch ministry that Billy Graham was involved with in his early years is Youth for Christ International, founded in 1944 by Torrey Johnson (1909–2002). One final parachurch group, familiar to many young people with a desire to serve in missions as they are trained in discipleship, is YWAM (Youth with a Mission), founded by Loren Cunningham (1936–) and his wife, Darlene.

John Turner, in his book on Bright and CCC, identifies parachurch ministries as a major factor in the growth of postwar evangelicalism:

> The adaptability and marketing prowess of parachurch organizations like Campus Crusade for Christ are not the only reason for the post-1945 vitality of American evangelicalism. No amount of cultural adaptation and aggressive salesmanship would produce success if the basic evangelical

message had little appeal in the United States. The heritage of pre-1945 fundamentalism, the influx of Christian immigrants from Asia, Africa, and Latin America, the high birth rates of conservative Protestants, and the persistence of an American civil religion at least partly congruent with evangelicalism all helped evangelicals retain their hold on a substantial segment of the American population into the twenty-first century.[349]

Other parachurch ministries that either initially emerged in Korea or were transplants here include (dates are for the year when this ministry first emerged in Korea): JOY Mission (1958), Korea InterVarsity Christian Fellowship (1959), Youth for Christ (1961), University Bible Fellowship (1961), and Navigators (1966).

One ministry task that can be identified as being "parachurch" is the work of Bible translation. Some of the more recent Korean Bible translations in the second half of the twentieth century include The *Common Bible* (Roman Catholic), translated in 1971 (New Testament) and 1977 (Old Testament). The *Korean Living Bible* was published in 1985, with a second edition in 2002. The *New Korean Revised Version* (first edition 1998, second edition 2000, third edition 2003, fourth edition 2005) is the one Bible translation that, unlike versions in the US, has nearly universal usage by Protestant congregations (evangelicals) for both public and liturgical reading. The *New Korean Standard Version* was published in 2003, with the promise of being a more accurate translation in a contemporary idiom. Now, while we are looking at Bible translations, let us take a quick look at North Korea.

Pyeongyang, the current capital of the Democratic People's Republic of Korea, was the most Christian of all Korean cities

---

[349] Turner, *Bill Bright & Campus Crusade for Christ*, 11.

from 1910 to 1945, with 25 to 30 percent of its population identifying as Christian. It was called the "Jerusalem of the East." After the communist takeover, North Korea joined Albania as one of the two most repressive of atheist regimes in the communist world. While most watchers consider the church in North Korea as persecuted and underground, North Korea surprisingly published ten thousand copies of the New Testament and a hymnbook in 1983. The next year (1984), the government published the Old Testament. Upon close examination, the North Korean Bible was the same text as the *Gongdongbeonyeok* (published in South Korea in 1977).

In 1986, the WCC (at Gihon, Switzerland) sponsored talks between both South Korean and North Korean representatives. The talks were mainly about the political issues involved in reunification. In 1988, the government granted permission to build Bongsu Protestant Church. Another Protestant church was constructed in memory of Mrs. Deacon Gang Banseok, Kim Ilseong's mother. Her brother had been an ordained minister. Roman Catholics were also allowed to build Chang Chung Catholic Cathedral in Pyeongyang. Many foreigners view these churches in North Korea as merely propaganda constructions to present an image of religious freedom in one of the most spiritually oppressive atheistic nations in the world.

On one side, we might consider the invitation of Billy Graham to North Korea in both 1992 and 1994 as a sign that there is an openness to the gospel in the old Jerusalem of the East. There was not much news coverage of these gospel invitations in South Korea, since no South Korean citizen could accompany the Billy Graham team as they visited North Korea. The interpretation was done by Southern Baptist missionaries who had served in South Korea and were able to speak Korean fluently. Nelson "Ned" Graham, the Grahams' youngest child and second son, visited Pyeongyang with his father. During his visits, Billy Graham addressed groups of North Korean students at Kim Ilseong University as well as the congregations of both Protestant and Catholic churches in Pyeongyang, where he presented the gospel both simply and powerfully. He also, in 1992, personally handed a copy of the Bible to the North Korean leader Kim Ilseong.

But we have to admit there is oppression and persecution, as we remember the imprisonment of Kenneth Bae (Bae Junho). He was sentenced in April 2013 to fifteen years of hard labor. Kenneth Bae had emigrated with his family from South Korea to the US when he was eighteen years old and later obtained US citizenship. Bae's crime was that he was captured with an external hard drive that contained files and photos of missionary work in China and North Korea. The North Korean government saw this as a plot to overthrow the government. People who had watched other US citizens be arrested and held in prisons in North Korea expected one of the former US presidents, either Bill Clinton or Jimmy Carter, to fly to Pyeongyang and negotiate his release. It was not until November 2014 that Bae was finally released and able to return to the US. The publication of Kenneth Bae's story in both English and Korean helps Christians to understand his ordeal and to pray for North Korea. In English, the title reads, *Not Forgotten: The True Story of My Imprisonment in North Korea* (Thomas Nelson, 2016). We now turn our attention to two final topics that make up chapter 9: worship and megachurches.

9

Worshiping God and Making Megachurches

The twentieth century has significantly impacted how evangelicals worship God, with hymns and gospel songs, and the later rise of contemporary Christian music (CCM) as forms that have shaped the very breaths and words of divine worship. It has become almost trite to mention "worship wars" as a way of describing the changes, often drastic changes, that a congregation or denomination has faced through time, especially from the 1960s and beyond. First, we will look at Korea to highlight the history of evangelical hymnody, with the majority voice being holiness hymns. Second, we will go to the other side of the Pacific and briefly consider a history of gospel music and CCM.

If you do a quick hymn count by author in the latest *New Korean-English Hymnal* (2010), you will find the number-one position filled by Fanny J. Crosby (1820–1915, or Frances Jane Crosby), with twenty-two hymns. Second place goes to Charles Wesley (1707–1788), with thirteen hymns. Both Fanny J. Crosby and Charles Wesley have solid credentials in relation to being evangelical, and their hymns are expressive of evangelical spirituality, though written from different levels of liturgical arts. The journey which brought a *Union Hymnal* to evangelicalism in Korea was a long and, at times, arduous journey but was a fruitful one indeed.

In Korea, North American evangelical missionaries generally viewed revival as resulting from prayer and preaching; the preparation was prayer and the delivery was preaching. But there is also a third factor involved with revival: singing hymns and gospel songs. Sermons and hymns/gospel songs are part of the warp and woof of the North American evangelical landscape, but both have been overlooked in texts on religious history. Mark Noll and Ethan Sanders emphasize the need for further study of sermons and singing as components of worship that change over time and are themselves change agents.[350] The rich texture of evangelical hymnody is represented by "[l]ayers of Watts, Wesley, Sankey, and the Salvation Army mingled in different proportions throughout North America."[351] This newly formed tradition of evangelical hymnody was transported *in toto* from North America to Korea in the late nineteenth and early twentieth centuries. In its translation from English to Korean, evangelical hymnody became an active force in promoting revival and further was preserved through the Korea *Union Hymnal* to become the mainline hymnody in Korea to

---

350 As noted by Noll and Sanders, the corpus of studies on Christian hymnody is ever expanding. Recent studies include Edith L. Blumhofer and Mark A. Noll, eds. *Singing the Lord's Song in a Strange Land: Hymnody in the History of North American Protestantism* (Tuscaloosa: University of Alabama Press, 2004); Stephen A. Marini, *Sacred Song in America: Religion, Music, and Public Culture* (Urbana and Chicago: University of Illinois Press, 2003); Richard J. Mouw and Mark A. Noll, eds. *Wonderful Words of Life: Hymns in American Protestant History and Theology* (Grand Rapids: Wm. B. Eerdmans, 2004); Mark A. Noll and Edith L. Blumhofer, eds. *Sing Them Over Again to Me: Hymns and Hymnbooks in America* (Tuscaloosa: University of Alabama Press, 2006); and David W. Stowe, *How Sweet the Sound: Music in the Spiritual Lives of Americans* (Cambridge: Harvard University Press, 2004).

351 Mark A. Noll and Ethan R Sanders, "Evangelicalism in North America," in *Twentieth-Century Global Christianity*, ed. Mary Farrell Bednarowski (Minneapolis: Fortress Press, 2008), 172–173.

the present century. Revival hymns birthed by the British and North American Holiness movements of the late nineteenth century found a new home in mainstream Korean hymnody by 1949, the year many of them finally were included in the *Union Hymnal*. In the twentieth century, evangelical hymnody has moved from the margins of North American revivalism and fundamentalism into the mainstream of South Korean Protestantism, resulting in a unique mixture of both evangelical and ecumenical movements in the twenty-first century. One could say mainline Protestantism has been richly leavened by evangelicalism.

In 1915, William C. Kerr, a North American missionary in Korea, explained the importance of understanding the lyrics for "real worship":

> "It takes only a glimpse of the swaying of the bodies and the intent expression of the faces, not only of the children but of the adults as well, to show that the music, however foreign it may have been at the beginning, is one of the powerful inspirational features in a large gathering. How much of this is psychological and how much spiritual may be a question; but a brief explanation of the meaning of the words before the hymn is sung helps to elevate the singing to the level of real worship."[352]

Even beyond the level of understanding was that of translating. Translating hymns for evangelical missionaries involved three kinds of challenges. First, the contextualization of theology meant that some ideas foreign to Korean religious traditions would have to be communicated and understood by

---

352 William C. Kerr, "Music in Men's and Women's Bible Classes," *The Korea Mission Field* (April 1915): 105.

the Christians in Korea. Second, after translations were made literally from English to Korean, the more cumbersome task remained of making the new Korean lyrics fit within the meter. Third, there was an ongoing struggle over whether or not to use Western tunes among the Korean congregations, since traditional Korean music was so much different from the newly introduced Western forms of music.

In order to become more adept in their Korean literary skills, "some of the hymn writers took up the study of Korean poetry as a help, making note of figures of speech, and the parallelisms, alliterations and refrains that take the place of rhymes in Korean poetry, rhymes being impossible in this language."[353]

The product at the end of the long translation process was a book full of hymns that would comfort tens of thousands of souls. From an early stage in Christian publication that continues to this day, the New Testament (and later the entire Bible) and hymnal were bound together as one volume. The first hymnbooks were published before even the New Testament was first published in 1904, and the first *Union Hymnal* (1908) was published before the Old Testament had been completely translated in 1910 and published in 1911.[354] In a sense, the Korean hymnal was the Korean church's first "Bible," as it spoke powerfully of God's redemption and expressed so keenly the language of human emotions. Also, the Korean hymnal was a reading primer for many Korean women; they learned how to read by singing the hymns.

Part of the work of transitioning from denominational missions to a united evangelical church in Korea included the normal comity agreements, a standard Sunday school curriculum for all Koreans, a union Christian newspaper, and a

---

353 William C. Kerr, "Music in Men's and Women's Bible Classes," *The Korea Mission Field* (April 1915): 105.
354 George Thompson Brown, *Mission to Korea* (Seoul: Presbyterian Church of Korea, Department of Education, 1962), 75.

union hymnal. In the end, however, organic union never happened because of the resistance to such a merger from both the denominational offices in North America and the Korean church leaders themselves.

It is significant that far from North America and Europe, at the very ends of the earth, in Korea, there was a prophetic move toward evangelical unity. As George Thompson Brown aptly described it, "Five years before the great Edinburgh conference, which is usually considered to mark the threshold of the ecumenical movement, the missionary enterprise in Korea had achieved a workable, grass-roots ecumenicity based upon evangelical principles."[355] It should be noted that the word *evangelical* rather than *ecumenical* was used by Protestant missions in Korea to indicate their common identity and joint endeavors. Now, we will look at the other side of the Pacific, which stands in contrast not as a united evangelical church because of hymns, but rather as a divided church because of the "worship wars."

As early as the late nineteenth century, evangelicals were concerned about the addition of gospel songs to their already established (and mainstream) hymns, just as evangelicals in the eighteenth century were concerned about the addition of hymns to the Psalter (canonical 150 Psalms from the Bible). A Methodist from Kansas in 1898 clearly and concisely wrote his concerns over placing "gospel hymns" next to "stately hymns" in any hymnal: "It would put the hymnal on the level of chorus books" and "degrade worship."[356] What we call "worship wars" sits at the level of "disputes" that "divided churches and realigned denominational identities in relation to liberal and conservative evangelicalism."[357] This is not a minor doctrine

---

355 Ibid., 78.
356 C. R. Rice, "The Arena: Church Music," *Methodist Review* (November 1898): 971.
357 Tamara J. Van Dyken, "Worship Wars, Gospel Hymns, and Cultural Engagement in American Evangelicalism, 1890–1940," *Religion and American Culture*, Vol. 27, No. 2 (Summer 2017): 196.

when it possesses the power to divide the church. And divide the church it did, if not at a denominational level, at a practical level, resulting in some churches creating separate services, newly labeled either "traditional" or "contemporary."

Perhaps the first wave of contemporary music that entered the church sanctuaries of American evangelicalism was in the South, and it was called either "gospel music" or "Southern gospel music." Eventually, Southern gospel music became a more specific genre that denoted "white" evangelicalism rather than the black church's gospel music.

Southern gospel can be traced back to 1910 with the emergence of the first professional quartet (four male members generally with piano accompaniment).[358] Inexpensive printing processes allowed the mass distribution of songbooks and gospel hymnbooks. Two of the more popular gospel songs from that early period were "Old Time Religion" and "Life's Railway to Heaven." In this same time period were the rise and popularity of "singing schools" and "shape notes."

It is difficult to compare the levels of distrust of the earlier period at the beginning of the twentieth century over Southern gospel and the later period over CCM, especially so-called "Christian rock." With this transition, we can see the "world's music" entering the "holy sanctuary." Congregations became disturbed over not only the lyrics but also the musical style itself. The time when CCM emerged was the 1960s and 70s, and the context was the Jesus movement that started in California, with hippies becoming converted to "Jesus freaks."[359] Perhaps the most significant person in the rise of both CCM and

---

358 For a general history of Southern gospel, see James R. Goff Jr., *Close Harmony: A History of Southern Gospel* (Chapel Hill: University of North Carolina Press, 2002) and Don Cusic, *The Sound of Light: A History of Gospel Music* (Madison: University of Wisconsin Press, 1990).

359 For a full historical treatment of the Jesus People movement, see Larry Eskridge, *God's Forever Family: The Jesus People Movement in America* (New York: Oxford University Press, 2013).

Christian rock was Larry Norman (1947–2008). Norman was a member of a secular rock band named "People!" from 1966 to 1968. Norman would go on to gain popularity, although he disdained the attention and glamor that came with playing music all over the country and the world. One of those places was the Explo '72 in Dallas, Texas.

Since this was an ever-expanding movement, it would be difficult to make a list of prominent CCM musicians without leaving more than a dozen out. Of mention are Keith Green, Rich Mullins, Barry McGuire, The Imperials, dc Talk, Andraé Crouch, Michael W. Smith, Amy Grant, and Jars of Clay. This very short list will enable us to have a feel for the diversity in both musical styles and even compositions and lyrics that are part of this larger genre over the years.

Along with the names of individuals and groups who performed the music are the venues and the music labels that identified this larger music scene as CCM. Rather than being a studio type of music, CCM found its real location at the front of the sanctuary with worship leaders and musicians. Hillsong in Sydney, Australia, not yet at various international locations, was originally a part of the Australian Assemblies of God but became an independent charismatic church. With the first worship leaders Geoff Bullock and Darlene Zschech, the new style of music had both "hit songs" and greater influence beyond simply charismatic gatherings, to evangelical churches and finally to a global network of independent churches.

In addition to Hillsong and its own hit songs and performers was a list of music producers and industries that included Integrity, Hosanna, and Calvary Chapel's own Maranatha! Music. These growing businesses further introduced "praise and worship" music, beyond the newer categories of Christian rock and Christian folk genres. Not only was there a growing musical industry, but churches that were able to put together a band and worship leaders with enough sound/volume were also able to grow, meaning a musical style contributed to church growth. No doubt, this is not the first time that music became an attraction in the church. Now, we will look at Yoido and then other megachurches in both America and Korea.

In considering the construction of megachurches in South Korea and America, we can begin in Seoul with the spiritual formation of the two founders of the Yoido Full Gospel Church, Cho Yonggi and Choi Jashil.

The ministry of Cho Yonggi (1936–) and Choi Jashil (1915–1989) began very humbly with an army surplus tent pitched in a slum area of Seoul. The church grew beyond the walls of that canvas cathedral and was soon ready to construct a new temple. The new home was called the Seoul Evangelistic Center, and it fit well with the mission objective of the Global Conquest program, namely, to reach major urban centers with the gospel. Construction, after a halt due to the political turmoil of 1960, was well underway and nearly complete when a revival service was conducted by evangelist Sam Todd in September 1961.[360] The first service inside the new facility was held on October 15, 1961, and the place at that time was called the Full Gospel Revival Center.[361] In 1967, during an interview with J. Philip Hogan, Cho expressed "the burden of [his] heart" to begin giving, after having received for more than a decade from the American AG churches. The plan to return the fire was being birthed.[362] When the new building was completed on Yoido in 1973, it was funded by Koreans alone, without the financial assistance of American churches.[363] The year 1973 marked not

---

360 Raymond Brock, "Seoul Evangelistic Center Nears Completion," *Pentecostal Evangel* (November 26, 1961): 6.
361 Karen Hurston, *Growing the World's Largest Church* (Springfield, MO: Chrism, 1994), 26–27.
362 "An Interview with Cho Yonggi," *Pentecostal Evangel* (November 5, 1967): 8.
363 Gary B. McGee, *This Gospel Shall Be Preached*, Vol. 2, *A History and Theology of Assemblies of God Foreign Missions Since 1959* (Springfield, MO: Gospel Publishing House, 1989), 139.

only the completion of the new building construction, but also the staging of two major events that helped usher the Korean Church into the global age. First, Billy Graham preached a crusade at Yoido Plaza, not far from the church. With one million in attendance, it marked the largest gathering of Christians in Korean history. Second, Korea hosted the Tenth Pentecostal World Conference, the first time this triennial event was held in Asia. The small beginnings of a global movement, from the tent church started by Choi Jashil and Cho Yonggi in 1958 to the construction of the Yoido Full Gospel Church with a current membership of 800,000 (2018), and pastoral staff of 526, worked as a spiritual bridge over the Pacific, with traffic going in both directions.

Cho Yonggi expressed the Korean connection with the US in spiritual and diplomatic terms: "Korean Christians trace their spiritual roots to America. We are also a loyal people. America delivered us from the great oppression of the Japanese and saved us from an invasion out of the Communist North."[364] In a quest more for economic freedom rather than political liberty, Korean emigration to the US increased significantly by 1975. That same year, the Yoido church organized the World Mission Center and dispatched eleven missionaries to the US, both as means of providing pastoral support to the Korean diaspora. The foreign missions program of the Yoido church is only part of the overall Korean mission enterprise. As of December 2011, a total of 19,373 Korean missionaries have gone to 177 nations.[365] Part of that massive missionary enterprise was sent to the US.[366]

The spiritual biographies of Choi Jashil and Cho Yonggi

---

[364] This is one of many times that Yonggi Cho mentions the US in positive, nearly patriotic terms. Paul Y. Cho, *Prayer: Key to Revival* (Dallas: Word, 1984), 16.

[365] Steve Sang-Cheol Moon, "Missions from Korea 2012: Slowdown and Maturation," *International Bulletin of Missionary Research*, Vol. 36, No. 2 (April 2012): 85.

[366] It is interesting to note that Korean pastors in the US are many times referred to as "missionaries" (seongyosa) in both Yonggi Cho's writings as well as denominational directories.

contain the genesis of the Holy Spirit movement that later became transpacific revival fire. Further, we will identify some theological distinctives from their spiritual biographies, distinctives that add richly to the diversity of American evangelicalism.

Choi Jashil was born in what is now North Korea during the Japanese occupation. Her life was marked by hardships. However, due to her persistence, she was able to graduate from nursing school and succeed in various business ventures. A number of tragedies in her personal life brought about a time of emotional distress, marked by a suicide attempt in 1956. Already a Christian—her conversion came at the age of twelve through the preaching of the Korean Holiness evangelist Lee Seongbong—she returned to the Lord and entered the Full Gospel Bible College the same year.[367] It was there that she met Cho. Soon after graduation in May 1958, she had the financial means to purchase an army surplus tent and asked Cho to preach to the small congregation that was mostly children. From that small-tent congregation grew the world's largest church. Choi's daughter, Kim Seunghae, married Cho Yonggi in 1965. After entering the evangelistic ministry, with her first international crusade in Japan in 1964, Choi was ordained by the Japanese AG in 1972. In 1974 she spent eighty days in the US, preaching the necessity of prayer and fasting, the spiritual hallmarks of her ministry.[368] She also started new Korean AG congregations in Memphis, Tampa, and Orlando. The next year, Cho joined Choi for another missionary tour of the US.[369] In 1989, during

---

367 Julie C. Ma, "Korean Pentecostal Spirituality: A Case Study of Jashil Choi," *Asian Journal of Pentecostal Theology*, Vol. 5 (2002): 239–240.
368 Ig-Jin Kim, *History and Theology of Korean Pentecostalism: "Sunbogeum" (Pure Gospel) Pentecostalism* (Zoetermeer, the Netherlands: Uitgeverij Boekencentrum, 2003), 119–120.
369 *Siryeon kwa Yeongkwangui Baljachui Yeouido Sunbogeum Gyohoi 30 Nyeonsa* [Ordeal and Glory Through the 30-year History of Yoido Full Gospel Church] (Seoul: Yeouido Sunbogeum Gyohoi, 1989), 129.

what would be her final revival meeting in Los Angeles, Choi died of a heart attack.[370]

Cho Yonggi was born in southeast Korea in a small village in Kyeongnam Province in 1936. As a young man, Cho's middle-class family suffered financially from his father's failed attempt to run for a congressional seat in 1950, the year the Korean War began. During the war, Cho's health deteriorated due to a terminal case of tuberculosis. There was no hope for a cure, but an uninvited visitor to Cho's sickroom brought the message of the gospel. Having been weakened by tuberculosis, Cho turned his prayers from Buddha to Christ. After his initial prayer for help, "A Christian man came and told me about the Lord Jesus."[371] The visitor gave him a Bible, which began an unfolding relationship of understanding and trust in Jesus Christ. The healing of his lung condition soon followed. Cho Yonggi gave his testimony before the delegates of the Eighth World Pentecostal Conference in Rio de Janeiro, Brazil (1967). In line with the fourfold gospel of A. B. Simpson and the foursquare gospel of Aimee Semple McPherson, Cho affirmed in his testimony that "Jesus is living. He is not dead. Christ is living in us. He is mighty to save; He is mighty to heal; He is mighty to baptize in the Holy Ghost." Later, as his theology developed, the threefold gospel would become fivefold, by adding prosperity to the more traditional four of salvation, baptism with the

---

370 Y. H. Lee, "Choi, Ja-Shil," in *The New International Dictionary of Pentecostal and Charismatic Movements*, eds. Stanley M. Burges and Eduard M. Van der Maas (Grand Rapids: Zondervan, 2002), 522.

371 "Jesus Christ Gives Life," *Pentecostal Evangel* (November 5, 1967): 10. There are differing accounts of Cho's conversion; sometimes it was a young man, sometimes a young woman who witnessed to him. The authorized biography written by Nell L. Kennedy describes the visitor: "On a day when [Yonggi Cho] was coughing up blood and feverish, Yonggi was startled to see a girl come into his room and sit down. When he had heard her knock on the door, he would never have guessed he had a female visitor. In Korea the women were held in low esteem, the men being always superior. She carried a Bible in her hand, but she was only an eighteen-year-old girl. Bitterly, Yonggi ordered her to leave. The audacity of such a woman! Coming so boldly into the very presence of a man!" Kennedy, *Dream Your Way to Success* (1980), 79.

Holy Spirit, healing, and second coming. Cho presented his own theology of the fivefold gospel and the threefold blessing.[372]

There are strong connections between Cho's testimony of conversion and healing and his later theological development, making it undeniably Pentecostal. Cho shared the experience of healing from tuberculosis with Oral Roberts, the quintessential American Pentecostal.[373] Another common thread between Cho Yonggi and American healing evangelists is the use of Hebrews 13:8, which acts as an affirmation of the eternal experience of miracles. Cho's earliest contact with American evangelicals was when he met two American Assemblies of God missionaries, Kenneth Tice and Lou Richards, and acted as their interpreter.[374] Soon after his acquaintance with the AG missionaries, he decided to spend three days in fasting and prayer, during which he had a vision of Jesus. Kennedy's account of Cho's vision will help us to understand the intensity of Cho's call to minister.

> A neophyte at praying, he wondered why he had awakened at that exact moment. Suddenly a smell of smoke filled the air and to his left a cloud of gray smoke bellowed before him. In the same instant a fireman appeared in the room. Hadn't he locked the door after the delivery boy? He distinctly remembered locking it! All of this in a split second—the smoke, the fireman, his own flashbacks. But the fireman stood barefooted on the floor, a white robe draping his ankles. As quickly as it all happened, Cho glanced upward and his eyes fixed

---

372 See David Cho, *5 Jungbokeum kwa Sambakjachukbok* [Five-fold Gospel and Three-fold Blessing] (Seoul: Seoul Seojeok, 1983).

373 David Edwin Harrell Jr., *Oral Roberts: An American Life* (Bloomington: Indiana University Press, 1985), 33–35.

374 Young-hoon Lee, "The Life and Ministry of David Yonggi Cho and the Yoido Full Gospel Church," *Asian Journal of Pentecostal Studies* 7:1 (2004): 4.

on the face of a man who looked straight into his eyes. From a wound on His forehead there oozed a stain of blood and a wreath of thorns sat upon His head. "My Lord! My Lord!" The silence was broken by words from Cho's own lips.

Kneeling to Cho's level, the man pointed a finger at Cho and started talking clearly and distinctly: "Young man," he said, "you are ambitious. You are looking for fame and money. I tell you everything of this kingdom will crumble. But I have a kingdom that will not crumble. You are to go and preach about my kingdom that does not crumble.

Cho reached out as if to touch his visitor's garment. But he gently fell asleep and he did not awaken until morning.[375]

Based upon his radical experience of a call to ministry, Cho enrolled in the Full Gospel Bible College in Seoul and graduated in 1958, the same year he joined Choi Jashil in ministry at the tent church. His ordination followed in 1962.

Due to the stress of ministry and an admitted overdependence on his natural abilities, Cho experienced a nervous breakdown in 1964. Through this major crisis, he received the revelation concerning the cell-group system, a means to delegate ministry responsibilities to others and thus reduce his personal level of stress.

Cho, like many Pentecostals, was led by visions and dreams as the outflow of spiritual experience. Faith, or active faith, according to Cho Yonggi, has mystical qualities. One illustration of this should help convey the primacy and power of

---

375 Kennedy, *Dream Your Way to Success*, 120–21.

prayer at a crucial time in his ministry, when the Yoido church was moving from being an urban witness to a global witness.

> In 1969, when our church was considering the move to Yoido to build a new sanctuary accommodating 10,000 people, I was in doubt as to whether this was the Lord's will. At that time the cost of construction was estimated at two billion won, but our church could only finance two million won. Therefore, if it had not been in the Lord's will for us to move ahead with the building, my church might have gone bankrupt and would have pulled me down with it, hiding God's glory.
>
> At that critical hour, I knelt down before God and made an earnest supplication. I emptied my heart of all thoughts, plans and lust. Then I knelt in complete subjection. Suddenly, in the midst of my prayer the presence of the Holy Spirit, like liquid fire, rose up in my heart and a strong desire springing up to build a church that would accommodate 10,000 people, that would send missionaries beyond the five oceans and to the six continents. We started with empty hands and within five years we built the church that could accommodate 10,000 people. We have paid all the debts of that building program and we are preaching the gospel to the whole world through our missionaries.[376]

How can we describe what fuels the growth of Korean evangelicalism? Simply two things, as identified by T. Stanley Soltau,

---

[376] David Yonggi Cho, *Salvation, Health & Prosperity: Our Threefold Blessings in Christ* (Altamonte Springs, FL: Creation House, 1987), 100.

were responsible for "the phenomenal growth of the Korean Protestant Church [read evangelical here]." They were the Nevius principles (discussed at length in chapter 6) and revival, with prayer as the catalyst for revival. Thus, we can hear affirmed our two components of evangelicalism: revival and evangelism.[377]

As we move on to 1973, the peak year for Korean evangelicalism with the Billy Graham crusade at Yoido, we can hear the second-generation Korea missionary Samuel H. Moffett describe "what makes the Korean church grow." As he begins with a contrast between first Korea and Japan and then Korea and China, it is clear Korea has grown more, begging an explanation. Dr. Moffett turns to a statement made by his father in the early twentieth century: "For years, we have simply held up before these people the Word of God, and the Holy Spirit has done the rest." Moffett continues to describe the need for the correct and simple answer, saying, "Any analysis of Christian strength in Korea that does not begin, as [my father] did, with the power of the Spirit to cleanse and vitalize and the priority of Scripture in Christian faith and education will miss the mark. The mark of the Spirit was startlingly and indelibly imprinted on the Korean church in the very first generation."[378]

With a total membership of eight hundred thousand, Yoido Full Gospel Church ranks as the world's largest church and has held that position since the construction of the evangelical cathedral on Yoido in Seoul (1973). There are numerous megachurches around the world, especially since the definition of a megachurch includes any congregation with more than two thousand members. A more precise definition from the Hartford Institute for Religion Research reads: "The term

---

377 T. Stanley Soltau, *Korea: The Hermit Nation and Its Response to Christianity* (London: World Dominion Press, 1932), 24–25.
378 Samuel H. Moffett, "What Makes the Korean Church Grow?" *Christianity Today* (November 23, 1973). https://www.christianitytoday.com/ct/2007/januarywebonly/105-33.0.html. Accessed 20 May 2019.

megachurch generally refers to any Protestant congregation with a sustained average weekly attendance of 2000 persons or more in its worship services, counting all adults and children at all its worship locations." The same webpage from the Hartford Institute lists the largest majority of megachurches as being theologically evangelical (71 percent). This might come as a surprise to those who viewed megachurches as only being bastions of the prosperity gospel.[379] But when we again examine the megachurch concept of being evangelical, we see an enhanced stress on traditional and conservative Protestant beliefs or a more generic evangelicalism and a reduced or even hidden denominational identity and confession.[380] This manifests more clearly with the number of megachurches that switch from a Presbyterian or Baptist church name to become a "community church."

We will only name the largest megachurch in the US and give the most basic information for it. Each nation represented in the Wesleyan-Holiness Summer Study Program has numerous megachurches, and I would challenge each student to do research on his or her own nation. Since the advent of the internet, much up-to-date information is available online.

Let's begin to look at Lakewood, the largest megachurch in the US. Lakewood Church was founded in 1959 by John Osteen (1921–1999), and at that time it was a Baptist church, but as it grew, John Osteen, being a charismatic, changed the identity to nondenominational. Located now in Houston, Texas, Lakewood Church currently has a weekly average attendance of around fifty-two thousand. The sanctuary for the church is

---

379 See www.hirr.hartsem.edu/megachurch/definition.html. Accessed 10 April 2019.
380 For an academic study of megachurches, see Anne C. Loveland and Otis B. Wheeler, *From Meetinghouse to Megachurch: A Material and Cultural History* (Columbia: University of Missouri Press, 2003). Another resource, though dated, is John N. Vaughan, *The World's 20 Largest Churches* (Grand Rapids: Baker Book House, 1984). And one book, the result of mainline research, helped to direct academic and church attention to evangelicals: Dean Kelley, *Why Conservative Churches are Growing* (New York: Harper and Row, 1977).

a remodeled basketball arena (Compaq Center) that can seat sixteen thousand people. Because of the large size of the building itself, the church has four English-language services and two in Spanish. Joel (1963–) and Victoria (1961–) Osteen serve as pastor and co-pastor, Joel being the son of John and Dolores "Dodie" Osteen. For Korean readers, the issue of nepotism is a hot one, with an increasing number of Korean megachurches handing the pastoral leadership from father to son or to son-in-law. In America, this has not been uncommon, since readers will remember the first American megachurch in the twentieth century that we looked at was Angelus Temple (Los Angeles). Rolf McPherson (1913–2009) became the pastor after his mother's death, due to his older sister, Roberta Semple (1910–2007), having been removed from the church membership by Aimee Semple McPherson herself in 1937.

Joel Osteen is well known around the world due to his popular Christian motivational books. His first book, *Your Best Life Now: 7 Steps to Living at Your Full Potential* (2004), made it to the number-one place on the New York Times Best Seller List. A follow-up book, *Become a Better You: 7 Keys to Improving Your Life Every Day*, was published in 2007 and also hit the top of the New York Times Best Seller List. Lakewood is the largest evangelical church in America, but we need to add that it is within the Word of Faith movement, or even as some would term it, the Prosperity Gospel movement. While some would exclude the Word of Faith people from evangelicalism, especially the more "reformed" and more "conservative reformed," a view that holds the door open to Pentecostals and charismatics would also have to allow Prosperity Gospel folk into the "larger tent" of evangelicalism.[381]

---

[381] Two titles in this category are by John MacArthur. See *Charismatic Chaos* (Grand Rapids: Zondervan, 1993) and *Strange Fire: The Danger of Offending the Holy Spirit with Counterfeit Worship* (Nashville: Thomas Nelson, 2013). Another book in this group is Michael Horton, *Christless Christianity: The Alternative Gospel of the American Church* (Grand Rapids: Baker, 2008). An

If one would like to study megachurches, Korea would be the best place, since five out of ten of the world's largest churches today are in South Korea. But we should not leave the megachurch section without at least naming some others in the "largest" category in America.

One of the largest megachurches, what used to be largest in that category, is Willow Creek Community Church in South Barrington, Illinois, pastored for many years by Bill Hybels. What used to be ranked second is now number four—Saddleback Church in Lake Forest, California, still pastored by Rick Warren. It is a Southern Baptist Church but is not labeled with that denominational identity. Like Joel Osteen, Rick Warren is well known as an author, through his *Purpose Driven* books.

A newer megachurch that has received increased attention is LifeChurch.tv in Edmond, Oklahoma, pastored by Craig Groeschel. Within the Stone-Campbell movement, the largest church over the past twenty years has been the Southeast Christian Church (Louisville, Kentucky), pastored for many years by Bob Russell but currently led by Kyle Idleman, another evangelical best-selling author with his *Not a Fan* (2011), of which more than a million copies have sold.

Finally, another Baptist megachurch is North Point Church in Alpharetta, Georgia, pastored by Andy Stanley, son of the Southern Baptist megachurch pastor and also best-selling author Charles Stanley. Now, we turn toward the end; or is it revisiting the beginning again?

---

academic study is Kate Bowler, *Blessed: A History of the American Prosperity Gospel* (New York: Oxford University Press, 2018).

10

Conclusion: Being Evangelical, Doing Gospel, and Going Global

As global evangelicals, we have had a limited historical vision. We could only manage to see a few of our ancestors, perhaps Martin Luther and John Wesley, very clearly; the others, the multitudes of church leaders and members, were unseen, even forgotten, especially those from our own people. Those who should have been closest to us were the farthest away. When we look back through the two hundred pages of this textbook and through 120 years of transpacific evangelicalism, we can find a longer list (community) of names and a fair number of dates as well, but through the names and the dates, my prayer is that we will have more than a moment, that we will instead have a long season of communion together. This is what the Apostles' Creed calls the "communion of saints" (*communio sanctorum*), and this is what we confess. To believe in and confess the truth of the communion of saints means we are a true family: born again of water and the Spirit, breathing again his Spirit, and hearing words that cause our hearts to burn. Yes, we are family! And we are not a small, cozy family, but a growing family, in both revival and evangelism, with much more power and many more people.

But for our conclusion, we will need to leave history and turn to theology, a true sister in the faith. This is not an abstract or philosophical theology, but the kind that's connected with people and time. I want to address the need for historical theology and for living theologians in twenty-first-century global evangelicalism. By way of conclusion, after I share my one vision with you, I will address two "fours" and one "twos." No, this isn't mathematics or some type of gematria (numerical mysticism); it is only breathing the past in again so we can breathe out or speak to the future. Can you help me do that? Just try it slowly, breathe in the past and speak into the future. It's called inhaling and exhaling; we do it all the time even without thinking about it, always a physical movement in response to a brain signal. Breathing in and breathing out!

First, here's my one vision. It's on the front of my OMS prayer card. (You know, the card that people put on their refrigerator door and might look at when they open the fridge for a quick snack.) My card has my name, my picture, and my one vision. It says, "Forming evangelical theologians in Korea to transform the world with the gospel." My own ministry has been theological education, so you might expect to say the vision is to train pastors and missionaries (or others) so that they can reach the world. But as I read the last book of the New Testament, I see someone else in the middle, the middle between the Lamb of God and the multitude of people from all nations, peoples, tribes, and languages. What's there is a building, a house, the temple, built on twelve foundations. You see, between the Lamb (the Savior) and the multitude (the saved) were the apostles. Theology becomes the bridge that makes the transition possible for many to be converted, because theology (the gospel message itself) was contextualized. Just as on Pentecost, the

CONCLUSION: BEING EVANGELICAL, DOING GOSPEL, AND GOING GLOBAL

people heard in their own languages the wonderful news of what God was doing now. Yes, we can see the throne and the Lamb on the throne. Yes, we can see the people of every tribe, language, and people, and there's a temple. But can we see the apostles/theologians in the middle? While Pentecostals might like to think that speaking in tongues is the greatest gift and most important manifestation of the Spirit, Paul wrote to the Corinthians (1 Corinthians 12:28 NIV) in the section on the body of Christ and gifting, that "God has placed in the church first of all *apostles*" (italics mine). And also in Ephesians 4:11 (NIV) we read first on the list of ministries is "apostles." But after all the churches are gathered together to be with the Lord, we read in Revelation 21:14 (NIV), "The wall of the city had twelve foundations, and on them were the names of the twelve apostles of the Lamb."

I realize fully that my interpretation of these texts might be unique, but I can say there is an importance to forming evangelical theologians in Korea and in every culture and every nation of the world, the bridgemakers between the Lamb and the "great multitude that no one could count, from every nation, tribe, people and language, standing before the throne and before the Lamb. They were wearing white robes and were holding palm branches in their hands" (Revelation 7:9 NIV). Just as John the Baptist said, "Look, the Lamb of God, who takes away the sin of the world!" (John 1:29 NIV), prophets point to the Lamb of God for people to go in the right direction. Apostles have constructed a road, a theological method that makes it possible for people to not only go, but to also live and even to die as martyrs for the Lamb who himself was slain for my sins.

But with the rush to obtain theological degrees and ministry credentials, we are not growing in the Spirit and wisdom, not hearing and doing the Word enough to make conversion and sanctification possible for the multitudes. I was recently looking through one of three volumes that lists all the names of theologians and theologies in Asia (both Protestant and Catholic).[382] Among Protestants there were many theologians identified with a contextual and political theology called "minjung." Minjung theology is a theology of liberation developed in Korea in the 1970s, a political theology that acted as a protest to the Park presidency. Main representatives include Seo Namdong, Ahn Byeongmu, Hyeon Yeonghak, and Kim Yongbok. Kim Yongbok views the minjung as a messianic movement. It has connections with folk dance (mask dance), and it has an association of professors/theologians who meet and discuss political and cultural oppression in this nation and connect the prophetic message of the Scriptures with the "han" (pain, suffering) of the people. Other nations have similar "contextualized" theologies, for example, Latin American liberation theology, Black theology, Dalit theology, womanist and feminist theology, queer theology, and the list goes on. But in the middle of all those names and theologies, can you hear the gospel? Can you see the Lamb of God?

My question was, as I continued to look at all the names and read all the theologies, "Where are the evangelical theologians?" Just as John was looking and weeping for one who was "worthy to open the scroll or look inside" (Revelation 5:4 NIV), I have been looking for one who is fully consecrated to evangelicalism and fully trained as a theologian, just one. Yes, there are many theologians who might say they are an almost-evangelical, but not one name listed was an evangelical fully and a person doing evangelical theology only.[383]

---

382 John C. England et al., eds., *Asian Christian Theologies: A Research Guide to Authors, Movements, Sources*, Vol. 3, *Northeast Asia* (Maryknoll, NY: Orbis Books, 2004).

383 See an important work by Nazarene missionary and theologian Donald Leroy Stults, *Developing an Asian Evangelical Theology* (Manila: OMF Literature, 1989). See also Jeffrey P. Greenman and Gene L. Green, eds., *Global Theology in Evangelical Perspective: Exploring the Contextual Nature of Theology and Mission* (Downers Grove, IL: IVP Academic, 2012) and Craig Ott and Harold

CONCLUSION: BEING EVANGELICAL, DOING GOSPEL, AND GOING GLOBAL

Two prominent theological voices from the 1970s and beyond in America and within global evangelicalism were Carl F. H. Henry and Clark Pinnock. As we consider the vital and desperate need for evangelical theologians in the nations and cultures of the world, we can see two different representatives. Henry remained faithful to the inerrant Word and continued to write challenging and constructive evangelical theology. On the other side of evangelicalism was Clark Pinnock, who shifted toward the side of "open theism" in the last twenty years of his life.

Carl Ferdinand Howard Henry (1913–2003) was born in New York City and raised on Long Island. Henry was a newspaper journalist but later experienced a conversion to Christianity at the age of twenty. He studied at Wheaton College, Northern Baptist Theological Seminary, and Boston University, and was a faculty member at Fuller and later editor of *Christianity Today*. He wrote *God, Revelation and Authority* (1976–1983), six volumes.

Clark Pinnock (1937–2010) was born in Toronto, Canada. He studied at the University of Toronto and earned his PhD at Manchester University in England. He taught at New Orleans Baptist Seminary, Trinity Evangelical Divinity School, and McMaster Divinity College (Canada). He was a leading thinker in open theism and wrote *The Openness of God: A Biblical Challenge to the Traditional Understanding of God* (1994). Henry and Pinnock are only two examples; one remained steadfast, and one moved away.

We do not have time to deal with their theologies, but I would recommend Carl F. H. Henry to every aspiring evangelical theologian to know what evangelical theology looks like and what it sounds like, because Henry, from 1966 in Berlin

---

A. Netland, eds., *Globalizing Theology: Belief and Practice in an Era of World Christianity* (Grand Rapids: Baker Academic, 2006).

and on, called for not only evangelical theologies but also theologians/evangelists.

I offer a challenge to you personally: become evangelicals, do theology, and go global. But before you head out, please take the time to pack your theological "bags" with the right tools. Here are three tools essential for the doing of evangelical theology: the fourfold gospel, the Wesleyan Quadrilateral, and Luther's Word and Spirit.

First, the fourfold gospel has different contextual forms, although the text preached and later published by A. B. Simpson might be considered the "received text" or a standard form. One distinctive between the fourfold gospel by A. B. Simpson and the one taught by the Korea Evangelical Holiness Church is the emphasis. In Simpson's, the emphasis, I believe, is on Christology, while in the KEHC, it is upon soteriology or religious experience. Simpson gives the four points: Christ is Savior, Sanctifier, Healer, and Coming King. A similar form was used in Aimee Semple McPherson's foursquare gospel, with the emphasis on Christ and who he is. The KEHC's emphasis on soteriology or religious experience, then, gives these four points: regeneration, sanctification, healing, and second coming. We might consider the differences to be minor, but a fuller view of the fourfold gospel will see first of all who Christ is in his fourfold offices and how he is able to minister to people the grace sufficient for salvation/regeneration, sanctification, healing, and return. Simply put, if we place the emphasis primarily or solely on religious experience, we could lose our focus on Christ. Or, as the gospel song goes, "Once it was the giver, now it is the gift."

Second, you will need to pack the Wesleyan Quadrilateral in your theologian's toolbox. I do not need to explain this in detail, assuming you have heard it enough from your course in John Wesley's Theology, but I can remind you of the fullness of this theological approach that allows us to hear fully, understand fully, and experience fully the Word of God. Scripture is the foundation and not just one of the four sides of the quadrilateral. Let us quickly review the Wesleyan Quadrilateral.

The Wesleyan Quadrilateral is a useful theological tool coined by Albert Outler in the 1960s. Although the term itself was used first by Outler, the concept represents a fuller means of hermeneutics or theological method that was employed by Wesley himself. There are definite sources in Wesley's writings that support the interface of Scripture with tradition, experience, and reason.[384]

For Wesley, Scripture was the primary controlling agent in the defining of valid religious experience. Reason, as a secondary element, also had a voice in the judgment of religious experience. If an experience was non-rational or did not permit itself to be examined by reason, then, to Wesley, there was a danger of entering the arena of either enthusiasm or, as he termed it once, "madness."

One final theological tool to pack before your journey begins on the road to becoming an evangelical theologian is Luther's Word and Spirit.

What is the relationship between Scripture and the Holy Spirit? Some would argue for the priority and supremacy of the Word and have dismissed the working of the Holy Spirit beyond the first or second century AD. We could hear the voices of reason and restraint when people began to feel their bodies shake and were thrown to the ground. Easily dismissing these manifestations as being either psychological abnormalities or doctrinal heresies, the Scripture seemed to win and the Spirit

---

[384] For a discussion of the Wesleyan Quadrilateral, see W. Stephen Gunter et al., *Wesley and the Quadrilateral: Renewing the Conversation* (Nashville: Abingdon, 1997) and Donald A. D. Thorsen, *The Wesleyan Quadrilateral: Scripture, Tradition, Reason & Experience as a Model of Evangelical Theology* (Nappanee, IN: Francis Asbury Press, 1990).

lose. And many who were on the winning side called themselves cessationists.[385]

On the other side were those who experienced the Holy Spirit without restraint and challenged all standard modes of behavior. Whether they called themselves by the name "apostolic," "prophetic," or "revivalistic," they were seeing and feeling things that set them apart. They were criticized in the sixteenth century by Luther and by other high-ranking and highly educated church leaders through every century of the church's history. Names like "enthusiasts," "fanatics," and "Holy Rollers" made it appear that they truly belonged with the group of apostles in Acts 2 who were called drunks. And with the same experience as Peter on Pentecost, they would stand up and declare, "This is that," meaning we are now experiencing today what Joel prophesied about hundreds of years ago. The Spirit is being poured out repeatedly. Experiencing dreams and visions, we are prophesying, and as would happen in Acts, the lame would walk, the dead would rise, and demons would flee. Miracles, or signs and wonders, were still happening, and these people on the other side would call themselves Pentecostal, charismatic, or third wave. Theologians would call this position "continuationist." Indeed, it does appear that the evangelical world has been divided between these two sides for the past one hundred years, and even today there is limited fellowship between them and a certain level of mistrust and even disdain toward one another.

Now, let's look at Luther's view of Word and Spirit. Martin Luther held to a high view of Scripture and literally believed in the power of the words of Scripture, and this powerful word made Luther a prophet.

He believed that God's power actually rests in the gospel

---

[385] For further reading, see Richard B. Gaffin Jr. et al., *Are Miraculous Gifts for Today? 4 Views* (Grand Rapids: Zondervan, 1996) and Gregory A. Boyd and Paul R. Eddy, *Across the Spectrum: Understanding Issues in Evangelical Theology*, 2nd ed. (Grand Rapids: Baker Academic, 2009), 235–248.

(Romans 1:16), even as it is spoken or written by contemporaries. That belief permitted the ascription of authority to Luther's faithful repetition and application of the biblical Word. In addition, Luther's heroic confrontation of the Roman Catholic Church confirmed for his followers that he played a key role in God's directing the life of the church. They had no problems transferring authority to him and to his writings. Luther's prophetic office, his living voice, expressed the gospel for his followers.[386]

The independence—for the enthusiasts—of the Spirit from the Word made Luther more confident that "Word and Spirit... not only belong together but constitute an indissoluble unity."[387] The language he chose to express the relationship between Word and Spirit is reflective of the sacramental and homiletical Word within the community of faith, and it is powerful.

God's Word, according to Luther, is a Deed-Word. It creates new possibilities where no possibilities existed before. The Word of God is a Word which enriches the poor, releases the captives, gives sight to the blind, and sets at liberty those who are oppressed. The Word which the church proclaims is a Deed-Word. It is a Word which meets men and women at the point of their greatest need and sets them free. A church which has become modest about the proclamation of the gospel is not a church which has become more relevant to the human situation, but less relevant.[388]

Not only do the enthusiasts separate the Spirit from the Word, but they also emphasize human works and their own strength to reach Christian perfection to the extent in which they are able to obtain and to fulfill the requirements of the

---

386 Robert Kolb, *Martin Luther as Prophet, Teacher, and Hero: Images of the Reformer, 1520-1620* (Grand Rapids: Baker Books, 1999), 33.
387 Paul Althaus, *The Theology of Martin Luther*, translated by Robert C. Schultz (Philadelphia: Fortress Press, 1966), 38.
388 David C. Steinmetz, *Luther in Context* (Bloomington: Indiana University Press, 1986), 115-116.

law. For Luther, this is no different from the Roman Catholic Church and their version of "works righteousness."[389]

To all the enthusiasts and those who believe in works righteousness rather than "only grace" and "only faith," Luther wants to say, "It's right here in this book." And it is in the bread and the wine. We can all learn more of how to have a spiritual understanding that relies upon the Scriptures and the sacraments as means of hearing from God. We need theologians like Luther to continue telling us how God breathes life into his Word as we hear it and pours grace into his body and blood as we receive them.

You already have received two essential tools: the Wesleyan Quadrilateral and the fourfold gospel. Now add Luther's Word and Spirit. This, plus the history given in this book, will empower your preaching; it will cause you to turn to God's grace and anointing beyond the hours you spend in study; it will begin to turn you, yes, even you, into an evangelical theologian. *Soli Deo Gloria*—Glory to God alone!

---

[389] Stanley M. Burgess, *The Holy Spirit: Medieval Roman Catholic and Reformation Traditions* (Peabody, MA: Hendrickson), 150.

About the Author

William "Will" T. Purinton (PhD, Trinity Evangelical Divinity School) is professor of church history at the Graduate School of Theology, Seoul Theological University, and a special-assignment missionary with One Mission Society.

Select Bibliography

Beale, David O. *In Pursuit of Purity: American Fundamentalism Since 1850.* Greenville, SC: Unusual Publications, 1986.

Bebbington, David W. *Evangelicalism in Modern Britain: A History from the 1730s to the 1980s.* London: Unwin Hyman, 1989.

Blumhofer, Edith L. *Aimee Semple McPherson: Everybody's Sister*, Library of Religious Biography. Grand Rapids: Wm. B. Eerdmans, 1993.

Bowler, Kate. *Blessed: A History of the American Prosperity Gospel.* New York: Oxford University Press, 2018.

Boyd, Gregory A., and Paul R. Eddy. *Across the Spectrum: Understanding Issues in Evangelical Theology.* 2nd ed. Grand Rapids: Baker Academic, 2009.

Carpenter, Joel. *Revive Us Again: The Reawakening of American Fundamentalism.* New York: Oxford University Press, 1997.

Carpenter, Joel A., and Wilbert R. Shenk, eds. *Earthen Vessels: American Evangelicals and Foreign Missions, 1880–1980.* Grand Rapids: Wm. B. Eerdmans, 1990.

Case, Jay Riley. *An Unpredictable Gospel: American Evangelicals and World Christianity, 1812–1920.* New York: Oxford University Press, 2012.

Chapman, Alister. *Godly Ambition: John Stott and the Evangelical Movement.* New York: Oxford University Press, 2012.

Collins, Kenneth J. *The Evangelical Moment: The Promise of an American Religion.* Grand Rapids: Baker Academic, 2005.

_____. *Power, Politics and the Fragmentation of Evangelicalism: From the Scopes Trial to the Obama Administration.* Downers Grove, IL: IVP Academic, 2012.

Dayton, Donald W., and Donald M. Strong. *Rediscovering an Evangelical Heritage: A Tradition and Trajectory of Integrating Piety and Justice*, 2nd ed. Grand Rapids: Baker Academic, 2014.

Emerson, Michael O., and Christian Smith. *Divided by Faith: Evangelical Religion and the Problem of Race in America*. Oxford: Oxford University Press, 2001.

Eskridge, Larry. *God's Forever Family: The Jesus People Movement in America*. New York: Oxford University Press, 2013.

Frank, Douglas W. *Less than Conquerors: How Evangelicals Entered the Twentieth Century*. Grand Rapids: Wm. B. Eerdmans, 1986.

Greenman, Jeffrey P., and Gene L. Green, eds. *Global Theology in Evangelical Perspective: Exploring the Contextual Nature of Theology and Mission*. Downers Grove, IL: IVP Academic, 2012.

Hankins, Barry. *Francis Schaeffer and the Shaping of Evangelical America*. Library of Religious Biography. Grand Rapids: Eerdmans, 2008.

_____. *God's Rascal: J. Frank Norris and the Beginnings of Southern Fundamentalism*. Lexington: University Press of Kentucky, 1996.

Harrell, David Edwin Jr. *Oral Roberts: An American Life*. Bloomington: Indiana University Press, 1985.

Hart, D. G. *Deconstructing Evangelicalism: Conservative Protestantism in the Age of Billy Graham*. Grand Rapids: Baker Academic, 2004.

_____. *Defending the Faith: J. Gresham Machen and the Crisis of Conservative Protestantism in Modern America*. Phillipsburg, NJ: P&R Publishing, 1994.

Haykin, Michael A. G., and Kenneth J. Stewart, eds. *The Advent of Evangelicalism: Exploring Historical Continuities*. Nashville: B&H Academic, 2008.

Hutchinson, Mark, and John Wolffe. *A Short History of Global Evangelicalism*. Cambridge: Cambridge University Press, 2012.

Larsen, Timothy, and Daniel J. Treier, eds. *The Cambridge Companion to Evangelical Theology*. Cambridge: Cambridge University Press, 2007.

Lee, Timothy S. *Born Again: Evangelicalism in Korea*. Honolulu: University of Hawaii Press, 2010.

SELECT BIBLIOGRAPHY

Lewis, Donald M., ed. *Christianity Reborn: The Global Expansion of Evangelicalism in the Twentieth Century*, Studies in the History of Christian Missions. Grand Rapids: Wm. B. Eerdmans, 2004.

Loveland, Anne C., and Otis B. Wheeler, eds. *From Meetinghouse to Megachurch: A Material and Cultural History*. Columbia: University of Missouri Press, 2003.

Marsden, George M. *Fundamentalism and American Culture: The Shaping of Twentieth-Century Evangelicalism, 1870–1925*. New York: Oxford University Press, 1980.

_____. *Reforming Fundamentalism: Fuller Seminary and the New Evangelicalism*. Grand Rapids: Wm. B. Eerdmans, 1987.

Miller, Steven P. *The Age of Evangelicalism: America's Born-Again Years*. New York: Oxford University Press, 2014.

_____. *Billy Graham and the Rise of the Republican South*. Philadelphia: University of Pennsylvania Press, 2009.

Mouw, Richard J., and Mark A. Noll, eds. *Wonderful Words of Life: Hymns in American Protestant History and Theology*. Grand Rapids: Wm. B. Eerdmans, 2004.

Noll, Mark A., and Edith L. Blumhofer, eds. *Sing Them Over Again to Me: Hymns and Hymnbooks in America*. Tuscaloosa: University of Alabama Press, 2006.

Ott, Craig, and Harold A. Netland, eds. *Globalizing Theology: Belief and Practice in an Era of World Christianity*. Grand Rapids: Baker Academic, 2006.

Ramm, Bernard. *The Evangelical Heritage: A Study in Historical Theology*. Grand Rapids: Baker Books, 2000.

Rosell, Garth M. *The Surprising Work of God: Harold John Ockenga, Billy Graham, and the Rebirth of Evangelicalism*. Grand Rapids: Baker Academic, 2008.

Stiller, Brian C., Todd M. Johnson, Karen Stiller, and Mark Hutchinson, eds. *Evangelicals Around the World: A Global Handbook for the 21st Century*. Nashville: Thomas Nelson, 2015.

Strachan, Owen. *Awakening the Evangelical Mind: An Intellectual History of the Neo-Evangelical Movement*. Grand Rapids: Zondervan, 2015.

Stults, Donald Leroy. *Developing an Asian Evangelical Theology.* Manila: OMF Literature, 1989.

Sutton, Matthew Avery. *American Apocalypse: A History of Modern Evangelicalism.* Cambridge, MA: Harvard University Press, 2014.

_____. *Aimee Semple McPherson and the Resurrection of Christian America.* Cambridge, MA: Harvard University Press, 2007.

Sweeney, Douglas A. *The American Evangelical Story: A History of the Movement.* Grand Rapids: Baker Academic, 2005.

Thomas, Joseph L. *Perfect Harmony: Interracial Churches in Early Holiness-Pentecostalism, 1880–1909.* Lexington, KY: Emeth Press, 2014.

Thorsen, Donald A. D. *The Wesleyan Quadrilateral: Scripture, Tradition, Reason & Experience as a Model of Evangelical Theology.* Nappanee, IN: Francis Asbury Press, 1990.

Treloar, Geoffrey R. *The Disruption of Evangelicalism: The Age of Torrey, Mott, McPherson and Hammond.* A History of Evangelicalism: People, Movements and Ideas in the English-Speaking World, Vol. 4. Downers Grove, IL: IVP Academic, 2017.

Turner, John G. *Bill Bright & Campus Crusade for Christ: The Renewal of Evangelicalism in Postwar America.* Chapel Hill: University of North Carolina Press, 2008.

Wacker, Grant. *America's Pastor: Billy Graham and the Shaping of a Nation.* Cambridge, MA: Harvard University Press, 2014.

Witherington, Ben III. *The Problem with Evangelical Theology: Testing the Exegetical Foundations of Calvinism, Dispensationalism and Wesleyanism.* Waco: Baylor University Press, 2005.

www.ingramcontent.com/pod-product-compliance
Lightning Source LLC
Chambersburg PA
CBHW070131080526
44586CB00015B/1649